## MY STORY

# PADDY THE COPE

### PATRICK GALLAGHER'S AUTOBIOGRAPHY

WITH FOREWORDS BY
PEADAR O'DONNELL AND E.P. MCDERMOTT, D.D.

DUNGLOE
TEMPLECRONE CO-OPERATIVE SOCIETY

First published in 1939 by Jonathan Cape of London.
Republished in 1942 by Devin Adair Company, New York.
Reprinted in 1946, 1971 and 1979 by *The Kerryman*, Tralee, Ireland.
Reprint 2006 by:

Templecrone Press
Templecrone Co-operative Society
Main Street
Dungloe
County Donegal
Ireland
Tel: 074 9521022
Email: jimmie@thecope.ie

Typesetting: Guildhall Press
Cover design: Nolka Design
Copyright © Patrick Gallagher / Templecrone Press
ISBN 0-9554177-0-8
ISBN 978-0-9554177-0-2

# CONTENTS

# INTRODUCTION

The Committee (Board of Management) of the Templecrone Co-Operative Society, ie the "Cope", felt that it would be appropriate to republish *My Story* by Paddy the Cope as part of the celebration of the Centenary of the foundation of the Society[1].

Paddy Pat Bawn would be glad to know that the institution he founded in January 1906 is still very much alive and well. It now employs well over one hundred people and has a total turnover in excess of €15m a year.

It now has 2000 shareholders spread throughout the Rosses and is run by a Committee of twelve representing staff and shareholders who meet once a month on the premises, with a large framed photograph of Paddy himself overlooking proceedings.

Cleendra and the Rosses today are a different world from what they were in the first half of the twentieth century. In a way that would be impossible to do now, Paddy Pat has vividly set down for us what it was like to live in the Rosses in a period that spans two generations. His account is as good as any similar autobiographies. One thinks immediately of Tomas O'Criomhthain, Peig Sayers, Muiris O'Suilleabhain and our own Mici MacGabhann. *My Story,*

1 *My Story* was first published in 1939 by Jonathan Cape of London. It was published in 1942 in an American edition by the Devin Adair Company, New York. Subsequent New York editions and the London editions had a foreword by Peadar O'Donnell. An Irish edition – the one reproduced here – was published by *The Kerryman* in 1946, 1971 and 1979, with a foreword by the Canon Eugene McDermott. There are substantial differences between the texts of the New York and London editions, and smaller differences between the London and Irish editions. The two forewords mentioned above are reproduced in this edition.

in its description of life in the Rosses, mirrors these works, except that it is written in English. Indeed, had Paddy written his story in Irish, it would possibly have received greater recognition here at home.

*My Story* is remarkable in two respects.

Firstly, in a humorous but no-holds-barred fashion we have the story of a people barely surviving on little patches of earth between the rocks, with as many again forced to emigrate. Here we have a live example of that familiar pattern of Rosses life at the time: the Lagan, followed by tattie-hoking, farm-work and "the guttin" in Scotland. The child slavery of the Lagan – it was nothing else – lasted into the middle of the last century, out of necessity and poverty. But there were also good times and simple pleasures – the airneal, the dancing to lilted music and the odd drop of whiskey. We must be grateful to Paddy for the vivid descriptions he has left us of his and Sally's experiences, which mirror how the rest of the people of the Rosses subsisted up until relatively recently.

Secondly, his story is a tribute to the energy and vision of the man himself and his closest associates. He was a business pioneer and a true entrepreneur. In the most adverse conditions, he created an institution that spawned a large retail business, a knitwear factory that once employed 150 people, a bakery, a mill, a turbine providing electricity, an exporting soapstone mine in Crohey, processing and smoking fish in the Cooperage in Burtonport, also for export, and a motorised fishing fleet of five boats during the 1940s. We must pay tribute to and marvel at the leadership, vision and strength of character it took to achieve what he did. It seems that to him nothing was impossible if one had the will and determination to succeed.

It is difficult for us today to realise conditions in the early twentieth century and the challenges Paddy faced. This is well illustrated in Paddy's evidence to the Departmental Committee on Agricultural Credit in 1914[2]:

"Once a farmer gets into debt with the gombeen man... he is no better than a slave to the man who gives him the credit. He very often has to leave his home and family and go to America or Scotland to pay the call of the gombeen man. As his family grow up they are sent to service at an early age of from eight years upwards to help get their father out of debt... I know of several evictions in my parish by the gombeen man, and I never knew of an eviction in the same parish by the landlord, so of the two evils – landlordism and gombeenism – I have no hesitation in saying the gombeen man is much worse than the landlord..."

His evidence to the Committee is mirrored by his own account in his book of the necessity for him to walk to Letterkenny and take the Derry Boat to Glasgow to clear off family debts[3].

To take on such vested and powerful interests required enormous courage and steely resolve; to have succeeded was a result of hard work and determination over decades. While Paddy provided leadership and vision, it must also be recognised that he could not have succeeded but for the support of his family and loyal colleagues (he mentions in particular John Gillespie, Johnny Brown, James Liam Durnion, Dennis O'Doimell and John Charlie O'Donnell) and the people of the Rosses.

The greatest tribute that can be paid to Paddy Pat Bawn is that while he was Chairman and General Manager of

2 Bolger, Patrick, The Irish Co-Operative Movement, Institute of Public Administration, 1977, pp152-3.

3 *The Kerryman* paperback edition, p50.

the Cope since it was registered, he never himself gained financially from what turned out to be a substantial business which he himself created. It is clear that many of his employees earned as much or even more than he did, and that, had he wished, his own earnings could have been substantially greater[4]. In this, he was true to even more than his co-operative ideals. There are several lessons here of relevance to society today. At a time in Ireland of great economic prosperity, we might note that material reward in itself is often not enough – great satisfaction and reward can be had from altruistic effort to better community or society. Also, his achievements, at a time of relative poverty and hardship in the society in which he lived, should point other societies less privileged than our own today to what can be achieved by a community through co-operation and participation.

Let us leave the last word to another great son of the Rosses, Peadar O'Donnell, in a letter he wrote to Paddy in January 1937 about a draft of a chapter or chapters of the book which Paddy had sent him[5]:

"Your story is... not merely good. It is tremendous. And its merit does not rest on the material alone. The style of writing is excellent; bare, hard, live."

There could not be a better tribute to Paddy Pat Bawn and his story.

We hope you enjoy it in this new edition.

Kevin Bonner
Cope Committee
1 March 2002

---

4 London edition, 1939, p255.

5 Scanlon, Lawrence, The Story He Left Behind Him: Paddy the Cope, University Press of America, 1994, pp184-5.

# FOREWORD

This is a new kind of book to come out of Ireland and it is written by a new kind of Irishman. It is a first book written when the author is sixty-five years of age. He would never have written a line of it only he got to know that AE once said it was one of his dearest wishes that Paddy the Cope should leave his story after him when he went. The book might have appeared many years earlier only that at the previous writing, the odd sheets of notepaper, penny pass-books and the like on which he wrote got so ravelled that in, in despair, he burned the whole lot. But every now and then there was something to remind him of AE and the wish that he had made.

The story is now told, and it is a brave story. Thirty-two years ago, AE made a speech at a village chapel in a mountainous corner of Donegal. Among the audience was a young man of the district home from Scotland. He was back to pick himself a farm among his people. To them he was Paddy Pat Bawn. It was a surprise when one who shared their common obscurity walked up at the close of the meeting and offered to 'list in a bank', for only the shopkeepers were expected to raise their voices at times like that. They will tell you of their surprise to this day, and how they edged nearer and how they sensed that it was towards them the stranger's thoughts were running.

The bank was the wrong shape for the ideas that AE's talk set ablaze in Paddy Pat Bawn. With the backing of fourteen half-crown members, he founded the Templecrone Co-operative Society, and within the week he was ticketed, as he was to be known far and wide among his people, Paddy the Cope. But he had done more than found a society, he had stated a war. That war is largely his story.

The theme of his tale could be made appear common-place enough – the penniless peasant lad from the back of beyond making a name for himself before his people, and now in the end of his days, looking back to remind himself and them how it all happened. There is a number of such people, remembering and telling, in the Ireland of these days, but they are mostly men swept to high ledges on the crest of the waves of The Troubles. Paddy the Cope stands apart from them all. Whoever tells the story of these others is hard pushed to relate them in an inevitable way to the environment which was their background. Their rise has to be explained rather than revealed. No speedy lines can etch their image on the face of a tier of the nation as Connolly can be invoked out of the sturdy world of Dublin workers. Given plenty of coincidences, endless men could have reached those other heights, for the inevitability was in the ends, not in the persons.

Paddy the Cope's fame owes little to The Troubles within which his name made no noise. It was not inevitable that his townland should break out into a crusade against Gombeenism – the despotism of traders in rural Ireland thirty years ago. But it was inevitable that any such impulse should realise itself through him. He was no enthusiast, brooding apart over the misfortune of a people, pursuing a lonely way to his own destruction while bewildering those he would serve, but a neighbour with a ready elbow to start this person and that awake to what it was in their common power to do.

AE, in wishing this book into being, desired to spread the infection of this form of struggle. That 'Cope' which rested on fourteen half-crowns is now a mighty organisation serving a countryside. It is a network of stores with a turnover of £100,000 per year. There is a co-operative bakery, a co-operative factory, a co-operative mill, and a co-operative electricity supply. And back along the track, the smashed power of innumerable little tyrants.

As to the method of telling, what is there for one to say except that this man has a story to tell which he must tell in his own way? He tells us he enjoyed writing every word whether he was chuckling or blubbering as he wrote. And that is the sort of book it is – a human document alive with an infectious gaiety and hope.

Peadar O'Donnell

# FOREWORD
## *to Revised Edition*
### *by*
### E.P. McDermott, D.D.

The theme of this book is to be filmed shortly. That in itself will indicate the story value of the book. But a film need not necessarily aim at anything more than a colourful and dramatic portrayal of incident, whereas this story is a lot more than that. Already it has found an acknowledged place in the world of literature.

It is a book by an unlettered man, a man who just knows how to read and write, but that man talks straight out from his heart, and he plumbs the depths of a simple people's life, and reveals their thoughts and feelings, their struggles and ambitions, their joys and sorrows as only the greatest writers in literature have done. With the possible exception of Mr. Peadar O'Donnell's *Islanders* no book has so vividly portrayed the drama of Irish peasant life.

Paddy's story is thrilling. It is the story of a hero who triumphs over every obstacle – so much so that if we did not know him, we would say it was too good to be true. But it is not for its adventure that I treasure it, but for its picture of the big-hearted loyalty of the Irish country people, of the deep family affection that so intimately entwines their lives, of their generous trusting friendships, of their lovable ingenuousness that still goes hand in hand with their deep penetrating insight. I shall remember Gillespie, who out of his modest means gave Paddy five golden sovereigns when he was going on his first travelling trip abroad, when I have forgotten some of the more adventurous characters of fiction. And Sally, quiet and unobtrusive, must rank among the brave and noble women of the world, even though at times she seems to yield to much provocation as when she tells Paddy: - 'Go and wreck the bloody town' (though do we not love her all the more for this very pardonable human outburst?).

Not only Paddy lives in the book, but the simple folk of Cleendra, the migrants and the emigrants, the workers in the Lagan and the miners in Scotland, and quiet, unhappy, docile Jane, with all the courage, all the poignancy of their honest simple lives.

And the irrepressible gaiety bursting through all the time – sometimes simple humour, sometimes side-splitting laughableness. I have read the book three times, and every time I laughed out loud when I read the account of Paddy going to jail and hurrying his policeman guards out of the public house (where they all went in to drink together), lest they would deliver him late and so get into trouble.

The new edition continues the story up to the present time. Although the Cope has been solidly established by the time that it takes in the narrative, its career is still not without its hazards and its setbacks. Even in his established respectability Paddy cannot help being romantic, and, at seventy-two, he makes a journey to Scotland in an open fishing boat without a chart or ship's papers; and that is not enough; a fog must come along to make things still more difficult. The Cope, too, is unaccountably burned down, and Paddy must start again. The lively dialogue of the airneal chapter adds still more to Paddy's reputation as a story-teller; and the touching comradeship of Paddy and his father, and his sincerity to have his child born on Irish soil, though included in the period of the first edition, are here told for the first time.

Paddy is a symbol of the age, of self reliance, and of co-operation. His story is the story of the Irish people taking their destiny into their own hands. It is a clarion-call to hope, to perseverance and to progress. To the very midst of the barren rocks and brown boglands, and to a poor and uneducated people, he has brought prosperity, and if we are fairly to measure his achievements with those of other successful men, we must consider the environment in which he worked and amidst which he has remained. On such a comparison, he outmeasures all the rest.

At times he hits out hard, and at times he does not mince his words. But even those who disagree with his opinions, will admire the honesty and the sincerity of his purpose. And in spite of all his direct speech, in spite of an odd 'bloody' and an odd 'damn', his book is a book of reverent and faithful piety.

E.P. McDermott.

# CHAPTER ONE

## *Early Days in Ireland*

The Rosses is on the west coast of County Donegal, Ireland. There are one hundred and nine townlands in the Rosses. Cleendra is one of them. Cleendra lies on sloping ground facing the Atlantic. I often heard that Neil Og's house is the highest house in Ireland, and many a pleasant evening I spent there listening to Neil Og and his sister, Maire, telling stories. They are both dead long ago. Whenever I visit Cleendra, and look up at the ruins of the grand old home, I feel sad.

Hardly a day passes that there are not some of the Cleendra people standing or kneeling on the brae, watching across the Atlantic. Some of the older ones wondering why they cannot see their sons, daughters, brothers or sisters in that land across the ocean, as there are no hills, mounds, forests or bushes between Cleendra and America. If the naked eye could travel three thousand miles wouldn't it be a grand sight!

If the wind is blowing strongly from the West, and you standing on Cleendra brae, the scenery is beautiful, the sea forming in rolls about two hundred yards from the land, the rolls getting bigger one after the other; on and on they come, as if driven by some mechanical power;

and as they come within twenty yards of the shore, those big coils of blue water suddenly throw up a milky top, and come dashing in against the rocks breaking into millions of little white bubbles. The cormorant, seagull, rising happily on the waves, the pigeons flying out of the caves searching for a bite to eat, returning with a full belly; sitting content on their little rock seats until next morning, quite indifferent, quite independent as to how the sea rolls or the wind blows.

Well, my father was born in Cleendra. He was christened Pat Gallagher, but no one in the Rosses is known by his surname outside the school. They are called after their father or mother or by some nickname. Well, my father was fair-haired and he was called Pat Bawn. I was born in the same house on Christmas night, 1871. My father was possibly born in the same bed. My mother belonged to the next townland, Falmore. She was born about a hundred yards in from the cliffs that are over three hundred feet high. Her father was Shane Boyle but was called Sean Og (Young Sean) on account of his father being Sean too, so my mother was called Nancy Sean Og.

After I was christened Patrick Gallagher, I was then called Paddy Pat Bawn. I was the second eldest. My sister Mary was the eldest. There were nine of us, seven girls and two boys. Within a radius of threequarters of a mile of our house, there were John Liam's, Michael Liam's, my uncle Tully's, Peggy Davy's and Charlie's. There were not less than seven of a family in any of the houses, and our parents must have been all married within a few years of each other, as we were all youngsters together, and it was an old handy woman, Betty Davis, who delivered every one of us. It was never known for a doctor or a nurse to attend a birth in Cleendra in my day, or my father's day. Neither was there a sucking bottle used, and all were fine healthy children, thank God. Up to this day, I have not seen a deformed Cleendra child. I hope and pray there never will be one.

There never was a dispute amongst the Cleendra people. Never did a Cleendra man, woman, boy, or girl summon another Cleendra person.

Our house was like the other Cleendra houses; one room, thatched with straw, a small window of one pane. Even if people could improve their cottages they had to be careful about doing it, for as like as not the landlord would raise the rent.

We owned one cow, an old muelen. She had a calf every year. If it was a heifer we reared it and sold it when it was two years. If it was a bull we killed it, kept one quarter for ourselves and divided the remainder among the neighbours. The cow went dry every year for three months, but I think we never drank black tea, for the neighbours brought in bottles of milk every morning. To be sure we did likewise when our cow was milking and some other family was short. There were a couple of families who owned two cows and they were scarcely ever done helping somebody. There never was a penny worth of milk sold in the townland of Cleendra and I hope there never will be.

We grew potatoes, oats and cabbage. We threshed the oats with flails, and the threshing was a great day. Two men keeping time with flails is a grand thing to hear. When the grain was cleaned we took it over to the local kiln to be dried. Then the miller took it and ground it into meal. We got back the husk of the grain, too, and put it to good use. What you do is put some of it in a clean tub or an old churn and steep it in hot water. After a time the water becomes a sort of whey, and when cow's milk is scarce you can use it instead with your porridge. If you wanted to ask for it in any house in Cleendra you just asked for 'Bull's milk'. We never used Bull's milk with potatoes.

The main seasoning with potatoes was 'dippity', a drop of milk in a saucer with a good pinch of salt in it. We dipped the potato for each bite. If there was no milk we used water. At very odd times we had red herring; there was no herring fishing around the coast when I was a child. We ate potatoes for breakfast as well as dinner and supper.

Tea was already popular in my young days although my mother remembered when it first came in. Flour bread was rare. We had oat bread and boxty instead. Boxty was looked on as a rare feast. There were no shop graters to grate the potatoes on then. Every house made its own grater by ripping a canister and punching holes in it. We had great feeds of boxty on turf-cutting days and on the days of scouring flannel.

My mother made all our clothes. She scoured the wool, carded and spun it herself and then took the thread to the weaver. After the weaving came the scouring. For this job Cleendra had bought itself a great pot, every family having a share in it. The pot was set on the fire and filled to the brim. Three pounds of black soap were then melted into the water. The hot suds were poured over the flannel, which was in a sort of casing made by taking our own door off the hinges and doing the same to a couple of neighbours' doors. Men took off their trousers and went into this casing to kick the flannel. Heavy work it was, too. The women folk often took their turn at it; the nice white clean skin you would have after a day scouring flannel.

I went to Roshine school when I was about seven years. I was not very good at school, although I never 'lay out' for a day; there were lots of others did. In the springtime I missed many a day, especially during the time of the kibbing of the potatoes, and again in the harvest, keeping the hens out of neighbours' corn. What I hated most was herding the cow on long evenings in the summer; the mountain was not good for milk so I used to have to let her feed on the soft grass along the edges of the crops. One way and the other I lost a good many days and that helped to keep me back, but school helped to make me handy, for Micky Neddy, our schoolmaster, was a grand man and he encouraged us all to handle ourselves and often showed us how men should really box. There never were men as handy with their fists in any part of the world as Micky Neddy's scholars.

I am sure we had hours of play every day and we had the best of fun. There was no playground round the school, but the master told us what field to take each day. We never were in the same man's land twice in the same week. The master was nearly always with us and there was more devilment in him than all the scholars. He was great at the high jump. Some of the owners of the land would be very angry with us for playing in their fields. The master used to enjoy to see some of them angered. Johnny Cunleen was very crabbit; his was the only field the master would not go into. It was a long way from the school and there was high ground between the school and the field. The day we went to Johnny's field the programme arranged by the master would be long jumps for the boys and girls all over the field, and as the ground was soft we would leave our heel tracks in it. We were all in the bare feet. As soon as Johnny found us in the field he would come up from the house roaring like a lion. The master would be behind the hill watching, and we thought the fun better because of the way he enjoyed it.

When we got back from play the first lesson was on the play. The master would describe the difference in the owners of the land, and how some of them were so stupid that they could not see that playing on the land, cutting it up, making holes in it, would be good for the soil. Then he would talk about us and say who was making most headway at the games and whoever was judged best for home early.

The Bonfire Night, St. John's Eve, 23 June, was a great night with us. All the Roshine scholars attended the big fire on Cleendra Brae. It was made of roots of fir trees – grags – taken from gaps. The master would tell us that such a man had a fine lot of grags fencing his field, drawing into the talk some row as a hint. Many a man damned Micky Neddy after a Bonfire Night, but there never was a place in the world to equal Cleendra Brae on St. John's Eve with him as master of ceremonies.

When I was ten years of age I was in the second book, but until I had passed into the third book I would not be looked upon as a scholar. But I could not wait. The year before had been a bad year in Scotland, and my father had not enough money home with him to pay the rent and the shop debts. It was the same with neighbours. A crowd of us boys were got ready for the hiring fair at Strabane. Boys, oh boys, but we were glad. The big people warned us we would not have such a rush in our feet when we had the thirty-seven miles' tramp to Ballybofey past us, but we only laughed at them.

I'll always mind the morning I first left home to go to the Lagan; that was what we called the countryside beyond the mountains where boys went on hire. I think I see my mother as she handed me my four shillings for the journey. She was crying. She kissed me again and again. I can't say whether I was crying or not, though it's likely I was, for to this day it's easy to make me cry. It was in Irish she spoke and this is the sense of what she said: 'Paddy, son, here is four shillings. Two shillings will take you to the fair. If you hire, keep the other two shillings till you come home; if you don't hire, it will take you back to me. Wherever you go and wherever you be, say your prayers night and morning and say three Hail Marys to the Blessed Virgin that God will keep you from the temptations of the devil.' Everywhere you looked some mother was saying something to her own boy or girl, and I think they were all crying too. But anyway we got started. We were all barefooted; we had our boots in our bundles. There was not much weight in our bundles. There was nothing in mine, only two shirts, some patches, thread, buttons and a couple of needles.

We made a lot of noise along the road but there was still plenty of walk in us when we had finished the thirty-seven miles to Ballybofey. We lodged in a sort of barn, twenty-six boys of us on shake-downs on the floor. The old-fashioned fellows who went over the roads before advised us to take off our shirts to save ourselves from vermin. In the hurry in the morning the shirts got mixed up, but the one I got was as good as the one I lost. We paid three-pence each for our night's lodging. We ate what we had left over of our pieces and started for the station. The train fare for the rest of our journey was one and twopence, so I still had one two-shilling piece, a sixpence and a penny.

When we reached Strabane we all cuddled together, and were scared at first, but the big fellows told us to scatter out so as the farmers would see us. They made us walk up and down to see how we were set up and judge what mettle was in us. Anybody who looked tired or faulty in any way was passed over. The strong boys were picked up quickly, and I was getting scared I would be left. In the end two men came to me.

'Well,' said one of them. 'Wee fellow, what wages do you want for the six months?'

I said, 'Three pounds ten.'

He said, 'Get out, you would be dear at your meat. Walk up there to the market clock until I see what you are like.'

I walked up, he followed me and made me walk back to where I started from. I heard him whispering to the other fellow, 'He is wee, but the neck is "good",' and he then offered me two pounds ten.

The other man caught both our hands in his, hit our hands a slap, and said, 'Bought and sold for three pounds.'

We both agreed. My master took my bundle from me and told me to meet him there at that spot in an hour.

I wandered off, wondering was my bundle all right, until I found that was how it was with all the boys. Then I went to a stall and bought myself a fine big cake for a halfpenny, broke it in two, and stuffed one half into the pocket of my jacket and fairly laid into the other. After a while I began to notice things, to enjoy all the noise and everything. I saw a man working three thimbles and a pea on a table. He was saying he would bet a shilling that nobody would tell him which thimble the pea was under. I saw him put the pea under one of the thimbles and I popped down my shilling. He lifted the thimble but there was no pea there. He did the same again and I was sure this time I was going to make no mistake, when I saw him put the pea under the middle thimble down goes my other shilling. He lifted the thimble but there was no pea. I could not believe it, and I began to cry about losing my money. Two of my neighbours came on the scene, Johnny Ban and Hughie Nancy. They were strong fellows, and had been hired early in the day for five pounds each. Johnny Ban caught the thimble man by the neck, and told him that if he would not give the youngster his money back he would kill him. Hughie Nancy put his hand in the gambler's pocket, took out a handful of silver, and handed me my fine two-shilling piece. He put the rest of the money back into the man's pocket, separated the gambler and Johnny, and said, 'You can go to hell now, you bloody trick-o'-the-loop.' Boys, but I was glad. I went back to the spot where I was hired and did not move an inch until my master came riding up the street on his horse with my bundle in front of him. He trotted the horse out the Donemana road with me running after him. He slowed up about a mile from Strabane as he thought the horse was getting tired. I had my boots on, and my feet were getting sore. When the master slowed up I was not long slipping off the boots, and I slung them over my shoulder. It was a great relief to me. We did not stop until we came to the farmhouse, a short distance from Park, in County Derry, and about fourteen miles from Strabane. The mistress came to the door and spoke to the horse. 'Lizzie,' he said, 'what do you think of the caddy I brought you?' Well, they argued over me, and the wages I was getting and the size of me.

She gave me a bucket and said, 'Come along and milk the speckled cow.' She got another bucket and went into the byre. I followed her. She got hold of the stool, sat under the yellow cow, and began to milk with both hands. The rattle she took out of the bucket when she started – you would think it was some musical instrument that she started to play.

I began to try to milk, but I could only get a wee drop now and none again; my fingers began to get cramped. When she had her cow milked she got up, threw the stool among the hay, and came with a big bucket of milk to where I was trying to milk and said, 'Are you finished yet?' She looked into the bucket. There was not a half pint of milk in it. She let an unearthly yell out of her saying, 'Get up you – or I'll stick you in the cow's arse. Under God, was he drunk or mad when he took a useless – like you to me?'

I got up, left the bucket under the cow. The cow moved and tossed the bucket and spilled the wee drop that was in it. I got frightened and ran out. The master was rubbing the horse with a wisp of hay. I was crying and asked him to save me. I was sure she would beat me, and as she came out of the byre, the master said, 'Lizzie, what did the caddy do to you?' She did not speak but went into the kitchen with the bucket of milk. The master asked me what I did. I said, 'Master, I cannot milk.' He said, 'My God, no wonder she is angry.'

The mistress then came out swinging an empty bucket like mad. She nearly frightened the life out of me. I kept moving behind the master. Oh, she was in a hell of a rage. I thought that she was going to hit him with the bucket. I went inside and sat down near the fire, and fell asleep.

I do not know how long I was asleep, but Lizzie got hold of me by the jacket and she gave me a shake. 'Take you supper, wash those dirty feet, and go to bed,' she said. 'Be up early in the morning and dung out the byre.'

I got a bowl of tea and plenty of bread: I fairly laid into it, for I was terribly hungry. The bed was in a low attic over the kitchen. I could not stand up even in the centre of it. I slept and slept, and the first thing I heard was Lizzie at the foot of the steps calling.

I was not long in getting out. I got the barrow and cleaned out the byre. I let out the two cows and the two calves, drove them up the loaming, and put them into the field at the top, and came back immediately. She told me then to go to the stable and dung it out, give the horse some hay, rub him down well, and take him down to the river for a drink. I cleaned out the stable as well as I could. She next gave me a bag, and told me to go down to the planting, and gather a good bag of leaves for bedding, and if anybody came near me I was to say that as I had nothing to do I was gathering the leaves for fun; the planting belonged to the landlord and he did not want the leaves removed. It was a devil of a job to get a bagful of leaves in the month of June, as the grass had grown up through them. I managed it, however, but Lizzie said it was not half a bag.

After my breakfast I got the hens' meal ready. I was then sent up to the field for the cows, and I brought them in to be milked. I was greatly relieved that morning when Lizzie did not ask me to milk any of the cows. She made me wash the buckets and strain the milk. She said to me, 'I'll never let you pull a teat again. I did not get half the milk from the yellow cow last night, and I am sure you are unlucky. I may never have any butter again.'

The master was up and about by this time, and he asked Lizzie if she was finished with me. 'Take him out of my sight,' she said.

He took me into the stable and showed me how to harness old Charlie, the horse. When Charlie was harnessed and yoked in the cart, we backed him into the midden. He made me load the cart with dung, and follow himself and Charlie out to the turnip field. He then made me fork the dung in lumps, as he and Charlie walked along. We got our dinner about 12 noon, plenty of potatoes and buttermilk. The master and Lizzie sat at the table, while I sat on the floor at the basket. We got tea and baked flour and Indian-meal bread for supper.

I got plenty to eat. I was never hungry while I was with Jimmie and Lizzie, except at the turf-cutting on Minnie Hill. The master did the cutting, and I did the holing, one at a time, as I could not lift two. It was a tough job. My nose often bled, and every time it bled the master would say, 'That's good for you, you dog.' He never spoke roughly to me at any other time. We left for Minnie Hill at about 5 o'clock every morning with Charlie and the cart. I got a ride on the cart going out, and I always had to hoof it coming back, a distance of five miles. The master brought a bottle of milk, a scone of pure flour bread, with plenty of butter, and two slices of American bacon. I had a bottle of buttermilk, a small scone of flour and Indian bread, but not enough for a good feed. I was nearly always dead with hunger. When we got home, I had to bring in the cows and strain the milk before I got my supper.

There was no family, and boys! when Jimmie and Lizzie had their little tiffs there were some wild scenes. Lizzie often complained of a sore head, and it was easy

getting up her temper. One day after coming from Minnie Hill she was in a hell of a temper. As soon as we
emptied the load of turf and unyoked Charlie, she let
a roar at Jimmie: 'Jimmie! Give Charlie to that bloody
caddy, make him take off the harness and stable him.
Come on you, you useless fool, and milk the cows for
once in your life. You silly fool, paying three pounds for
that thing that cannot milk a cow. He is only ten years
ould, and I could get a twelve-year-ould for less money,
if I was in Strabane.'

Jimmie bared his teeth and said, 'Why the hell did you
not go, you crabbit ould witch?' Lizzie caught hold of a
tin can and flung it at Jimmie, but she had a bad shot and
missed him. This made her more angry, if that was possible, and then shouting at him, she said, 'You fatherless so
and so! How dare you talk like that to Lizzie McDonald!
I am very sorry I ever saw you.'

Jimmie ordered me to go into the house and to shut the
door. I went in, but I kept the door ajar.

He said, 'Lizzie, you insulted me in the presence of that
old-fashioned caddy, who will be telling again what you
called me. I wish I never saw you.'

'What are you talking about? Do you forget when you
were running down to Glenmornan after me, catching me,
and kissing me, saying that you loved me so much you
could eat me,' Lizzie replied.

Jimmie said, 'I wish to God I did eat you then: I would
be a happy man ever since.'

I must have shut the door then as I do not remember
any more, but I am sure Lizzie did not let him have the
last word, for she had a terrible tongue.

Johnny Doherty of the Lower Rosses was hired with

old Mrs. Houston, whose farm was about a mile from where I was. I met him for the first time the Sunday I was at Mass. He told me that he was on a very good house, that old Mrs. Houston was one of the best. She had one son, Robert, nearly as old as herself. He was over sixty years of age. Whenever I got a chance I slipped over to see Johnny. If the night was cold or rainy, Mrs. Houston would come toddling to the door, calling, 'Johnny, come in out of the cold, and bring the caddy with you.'

She had six cows giving milk. She milked two of them, and Robert and Johnny milked the other four.

One night when I was there Johnny was going to the milk-house after finishing milking his cows. As there was no one near he gave me a good drink of the milk. I had hardly my mouth cleaned when I saw poor old Mrs. Houston coming from the byre with her bucket of milk. She tripped on a stone, fell, and spilled the milk. Johnny and I lifted her, and armed her into the kitchen. Robert came along and saw the milk spilt on the street. When he came into the kitchen he said, 'Mammie, who spilt the milk?'

She said, 'It was I. I stumbled; it can't be helped now. Go you with the caddy and strain the milk, lock the door and keep out the cats.'

'I will, mammie,' said Robert. 'Jimmie's caddy will sit with you while we are out.' When they went out she asked me for a drink of water. I gave it to her in a bowl; it must have been too heavy as she let it fall out of her hand, and she slithered from the stool to the floor. I frightened, and ran out calling Robert and Johnny.

When we came in, the poor old soul was sitting at the fire. Robert began to cry saying, 'What is wrong with you, mammie?'

She said, 'Oh nothing, Robert, I'll be all right in a wheen of minutes.'

He lifted her and put her sitting on a chair and gave her a cup of water. She drank some of it and got better.

'Are you better now, mammie?' said Robert

'I am, Robert, but I am not going to milk any more, and the caddy can't milk six milkers, get a woman and marry her, get a good milker.'

Robert said, 'I will, mammie, who will I marry, mammie?'

She said, 'Please yourself.' Robert said, 'I think I'll marry Rebecca Smith. I know she can milk all right. I'll marry her in the morning.'

When I was leaving, Johnny came with me a bit of the way. Young as we were we nearly broke our sides laughing. Johnny said:-

'Paddy, my God! Rebecca will never take that old fool, he only washes himself on Sundays before going to church; he must be a big lot older than her father, she will never take him. But she might, the farm is good. I am sure they have plenty of money.'

The following Sunday when I met Johnny after Mass, he said, 'God, Paddy, Robert got married to Rebecca on Thursday, that was the day after you were there. He took her straight to the house. When he came in he said, "Mammie, Rebecca and I are married now. You will not have to milk any more."

'The mother said, "I am all right today, Robert, I can milk as well as ever."

"Are you, mammie?"

'Who do you think came in but Mrs. Hayes. She caught Mrs. Houston by the hand. I thought she was going to squeeze the life out of her before she let her hand go.

'She then said, "Well, Mrs. Houston, I came over to congratulate you on your boy's marriage." She then went up to the corner where Robert was standing and shook his hand and said, 'Robert, congratulations on your marriage. Rebecca is a good girl, she is indeed. There is not a better girl in the parish of Goscressin, only my own Lizzie. It will be good for the man that will get my Lizzie.'

'Robert said, "Mrs. Hayes, Rebecca is all right, but we have no great call for her now, as my mammie is better and can milk again."

'Mrs. Hayes never spoke to Rebecca. Sure as heaven, Paddy, I was afraid every minute that I would burst trying to keep in the laughing that was bursting on me.'

You would never get tired listening to Johnny Doherty telling a story. Another would tell the same story, but there would not be near as much fun in it.

My moleskin trousers began to go and I could not keep them patched. I was not very handy with the needle, so when many parts of my skin began to appear the master bought me a pair of corduroy trousers. He kept four and six out of my wages for the trousers. I will never forget those trousers. I could hardly get my legs into them, they were so tight and short. With all that, I was very happy the night before 12th November, when my hiring was up. I was up early next morning.

When I arrived in Strabane most of the Cleendra boys and girls were there. We were very glad to see one another, every one telling the other the kind of place he was in. They made fun of me about my trousers. Some called them 'Fiddler's trousers'. I did not mind what they said, I was so glad to be going home.

I went to a stall and bought a halfpenny clay pipe for my father, a pair of rosary beads for my mother, and three-pence worth of sweets for my sisters. All the others bought some things for their own people. We left Strabane about 12 o'clock by train for Stranorlar. As soon as the train moved off, all began to sing.

We got tea and cakes in Ballybofey, and each of us ate a big halfpenny cake. We then started for home in squads. There were nine of us – 'the Cleendra squad' – and we went by ourselves. We reached Cleendra about 2 o'clock next morning. John Liam's was the first house we came to, and to our great delight all our fathers and mothers were there waiting for us. I thought my mother would never let me go. She was crying with joy, and I cried too. Every other father and mother were just as glad to see their own. The flannel pot full of potatoes was on the fire at the gable of the house. My father and John Liam lifted it off, and teemed the water off the potatoes. I am sure there was at least six stones in it. They were not long scattering them around the house, on the table, baskets and plates. The small pot was full of trout; there was a flood in the river that morning, and John Charlie and my father rummelled it, and got a creel full of trout. I can tell you we fairly enjoyed ourselves. After that fine supper we all went home.

When we got into the house my mother lifted a coal out of the rakings, blew it and lit a rush candle. My brother and sisters got up immediately, and they were very glad to see me. Then they noticed my legs and they were frightened at first. When my mother saw it was the trousers she swore I wouldn't put a toe outside the door any more in them. Doney Gallagher the tailor, was sent for early next morning, and it was not long until he was sitting on the table making a pair of trousers for me. As soon as he had them finished I got out of bed and put them on. It was a great relief to all when they saw that my legs were not worn away after all.

After a few days' rest we all went to school. Boys! But Micky Neddy was glad to see us. The lesson that day was all about the Lagan. He got every one of us to tell about the places we were hired in. When any of us told a sad story you would see the tears rolling down his cheeks. When some funny story was told he would go into kinks laughing.

When playtime came he said as the day was cold we would have some boxing for the boys to see what the Lagan fellows could do. The girls were told to run along the road. He then made us march in twos under his rod. When he got us matched every pair of us had to box five rounds. The winners of the first three rounds got home immediately. He said the duds must remain till closing time, but it was long after closing time before the rounds were all over. Many such days we had at Micky Neddy's school. He was the grand master.

The Inspector only came once a year and none of the scholars passed except the few who studied at home. When the Inspector complained the master said, 'Sir, how could I make scholars of them and they in the Lagan? But look at them. There is not a finer lot of boys and girls in any school in all Ireland.'

But a new Inspector came. I'll never forget him. We were always scared of inspectors, but even Micky Neddy seemed nervous of this one. And he did not seem friendly to the master. After he looked over some books on the master's desk, he began to examine the first class. At playtime they got leave to go home. The Inspector looked angry and we saw clearly the master was upset. They talked together but we could not make out what they said. Next day he was back again and he came to my class, the second, and began to examine us. He took us one by one and puzzled us all. And next day again he was seen sweeping down on us on a car. As soon as Micky Neddy got the warning of his approach he buttoned his coat. The life left some of us with fright. Out with the master and out with us after him. The master met the Inspector at the gate and stretched him with a box. Then he flung the key of the school at him and went on. The Inspector was no coward either. We could see that. He ordered us back into the school and we went. But once we were inside we got our courage back. We wouldn't answer a question he put to us. He told us to go home. It was raining and we took shelter at a turf stack to watch him go. When he appeared some madness got into us all. We set up a yell and began showering turf on him. God save us, you would think we all went mad. He jumped on the car and only the jarvey drove away so quickly we might have murdered him for some of us got as far as throwing stones.

Next day we heard that Micky Neddy was going to America. All the Cleendra people, young and old, and all the Roshine scholars gathered to his house that night. His father and mother cried all the time. My father began to sing 'My barque leaves the harbour tomorrow, it's across the wide ocean I go.' We all began to cry. Brown made my father stop singing. It was a sad night on top of Cleendra Brae. That's where Micky Neddy's house was.

I never went another day to school, so I never became a scholar for I did not pass out of the second book.

The following year I went to the Lagan, and hired to another farmer for three pounds ten. He was a fairly good man. Later I was hired at Plumbridge. It got a bad name amongst the lads, but I could not say a word against my master. I was also hired near Donnyloop. The master I had there was a good man. The following years I spent in the Lagan until I reached the age of sixteen. I had some good places and some damned bad ones.

# CHAPTER TWO

## *Service in Scotland*

When I was sixteen years old I went to Scotland with a crowd including Charlie and Jimmie. They were about the same age as myself. We walked from Cleendra to Letterkenny, a distance of thirty-six miles, and trained from Letterkenny to Derry on the Londonderry and Lough Swilly Railway, built a few years previously. We arrived at Derry in good time for the Glasgow boat. I paid four shillings for my ticket. I suppose we were in the same steerage compartment in which my father often travelled. In any case the cattle and pigs were in the same flat. There was a bench or seat along the side of the ship, not enough sitting room for all the women and men in the compartment. There was no lavatory. (If it came hard on you, you had to go in among the cattle) It was a bit tough on the big women, as there was not much room. We landed at the Broomielaw at about twelve noon on the following day, and broke up into squads. The squad I was with (six of us in all) went to Queen's Street Station, and took our tickets for Jadeborough, Roxboroughshire, and as far as I can remember the ticket was six shillings and sixpence. We reached Jadeborough late that night, and got lodgings in Muldoon's Model, fourpence each for a bed. John Biddy and Hughdie Micky collected one shilling from each of us for the supper and breakfast. They were out to a small shop and got bread, bacon, tea, sugar and milk, the whole lot coming to four shillings and a halfpenny. I remember the price because we divided the change, fourpence each for five, threepence halfpenny for the sixth, and cast lots. John Biddy got the threepence halfpenny.

Next morning we went out amongst the farmers looking for work. We had no luck. All of us had a few shillings left, but there were no shops on our travels. When we began to get hungry, Frank Pat led the way to Stevenson's farm to cadge food. Frank and John knocked at the kitchen door. Mr. Stevenson asked them what they wanted. They said that they were looking for work. 'Come out in the morning if it is dry and I will start you two. Are you hungry?' They said that they were a little hungry. He went into the house and the girl came out with a big basket of pieces of bread and a fine can of skim milk with a big ladle stuck in it. She told us that we could go over the field and that when we were finished to bring back the basket, can and ladle. We went into the field, sat on our bundles and had a great feed. We brought back the dinner set. The steward came to us and asked what two did Mr. Stevenson engage. Frank and John made a fast rush to him, taking off their caps. Frank said, 'It is me and him, sir.'

'Well, come with me and I will show you your bothey,' said the steward.

We four that were left travelled on, calling on other farmers, but failed to get employment. As it was getting dark we went to a farmhouse. Hughdie knocked at the door. A middle-aged lady opened it and asked what did we want at that hour of the night. Hughdie said that we were looking for work. She said that the master was not at home but she did not think he wanted any Irishmen. 'Are you hungry?' she said.

Hughdie said, 'Middling.'

'Wait a minute,' she said. She and a girl came back again with a bucketful of scraps of bread, a large jug of milk, and a cup. We ate a bellyful and were well satisfied. Hughdie and I went back to the door with the bucket, the jug and the cup. Hughdie knocked again at the door and the same lady opened it. He handed her the utensils and said, 'Thank you, lady. May God bless you. Maybe you would let us sleep in the barn for the night. We are very tired and none of us smoke.' (That was a lie, as he smoked himself and so did Manus Johnny, but they did not smoke that night until all the lights in the farmhouse were out.) 'Well you can sleep in the barn if none of you smoke,' she said. We went into the barn, and made ourselves comfortable, and we were feeling happy. Charlie sang *The Banks of Clady*, Manus sang *The Bonnie Bonnie Banks of Loch Lomond*, and I told a story about Oisin and after that we said the Rosary. There was plenty of straw to put under and over us, and we had a good sleep.

Next morning we were off again. Hughdie and Manus got work at the first farm we came to. I think if Charlie and I were a bit stronger the farmer would have started us. Hughdie told the master that the two boys were hungry, and he went into the house. When he came out again he looked at us, and said, 'We have nothing to give you, but if you like to wait the porridge will soon be ready.' We were glad to wait and get a fine feed of porridge and milk. Hughdie and Manus were real sorry for us. They did not know what would happen to us, and they said if we did not get work to come back to them that night. Each of them gave us a shilling, and they had very few shillings left. We walked on over a big moor, but we could see no farmhouse, and one said to the other , 'We are astray,' and we got frightened. There was a mist rising on the moor and we decided to turn back to Manus and Hughdie, but no matter how far we travelled we could not get out of the moor. As it was getting dark, we came across a cart-track, we knew it would lead us somewhere. We happened to follow it in the right direction. We were very hungry tired, and downhearted. We lay down, and put our bundles under our heads; there was no cold and the heather was warm. Charlie said to me, 'We forgot to say our prayers.' We went on our knees, and when we had our prayers said a sharp breeze arose, and the night got colder. Charlie said, 'Paddy, look at the light!' I looked in the direction Charlie was pointing and I thought the light was coming towards us. I concluded that it was some of the fairies we left at home in the glen in Cleendra, and I felt delighted. I said, 'Charlie, the wee princes of Cleendra to our aid are advancing.'

'Ay, you bloody fool,' said Charlie, 'you know damn well no fairies would live in Scotland. Look again, the light is not moving; it is a house.' I did not think so. Charlie put his bundle on his shoulder and he said to me, 'If you do not come, you can stay. I am going to that house anyway,' and off he went. I was not long in following him. It was a house all right, and when we were within ten yards of it the light went out. Heavy drops of rain were falling. We decided that our best plan would be not to knock, but try and get into some of the outhouses until morning. After a while searching, we got into one of the byres where there were no animals, but there was plenty of hay. The wind was still increasing, and then came the lightning and thunder, and soon the rain was coming down in bucketfuls, but we were so fagged out we were soon fast asleep.

It must have been near one o'clock the next day when I awoke. It was still raining, and I shook up Charlie. I had a sore head, and was very hungry. Charlie was just as bad. Nobody about the farmhouse knew we had slept there all night, and we picked up courage and went to the door. I knocked, but no answer. We then went around to the back of the house, and met an old man with a long beard, and as many patches on his trousers as you would see on any old man at home. He looked at us, and we looked at him. 'What are you laddies doing here?' he said. Charlie answered, 'We are looking for the master to see if he would give us work.'

'I am Sam Douglas, master of the Crow's Farm; always was, and always will be,' he said. 'I have a field of turnips ready for singling. Can any of you lads single?'

We both said that we could. We had been practising with small rows of stones before we left home.

Hughdie spent a week training us to knock four stones off the top of a drill and leave the next in its bed without touching it. The day before we left for Scotland we were carefully examined by our fathers, Hughdie and the others. We satisfied the examiners, who told us it would be no shame for us to say we could single turnips. The other four in our squad were in Scotland often before. Charlie and I were the only new hands in the squad.

The master told us we could start in the morning. 'I will give each of you seven bob a week until the harvest if you are worth it; if not, off you go,' he said. 'I have no blankets until I get into Kelso next market day, and if you are worth the money I will get a new blanket for you. You can sleep over the horses, and I will give you plenty of bags to get into. It will not be always raining and blowing like this. Oh! Does either of you lads smoke?'

We said 'No,' which was the truth.

He then had another look at us, and said, 'It is wonderful how you Irishmen can always find Mr. Douglas' farm. How did you come? I did not see you coming up the road, and you are as dry as a pin-cushion.'

One waited for the other to answer. I thought Charlie should answer because he was older than I.

The old man spoke again. 'Did you no hear what I asked ye? What road did ye come, and how is it you are so dry? It is raining since Jane and I went to bed last night.'

I was still waiting for Charlie to answer, but he never spoke. Then I said, 'We got lost on the moor last night, and we saw your light and made for it. As we were coming to the door the light went out, and when we saw the lightning and heard the thunder and then the rain, we got frightened, and we went into the byre, where we were sleeping until a wee while ago.'

'Well, well, I dinna think I can blame ye: under the same circumstances I might hev done the same thing meself. One never kens what he will do when he hes tae dae it. Get into the barn yonder, or ye'll get wet. I am wet now standing talking to ye. When Jane has the dinner ready, Mary will gie ye a call, and one of ye will come doon for it.'

Off we went to the barn. Although we were wet we were quite happy knowing that we were going to work in the morning. We were not very long in the barn until we heard the shout: 'Paddies, let one of you come down to the kitchen for your dinners.'

Charlie insisted that I should go. He always bossed me. When I went to the kitchen door I heard somebody say, 'Come in,' and in I went. There were two women in the kitchen, one of them was as ugly as sin, about twenty-five years of age, with a bit of a moustache, and a tuft of long hairs growing out of her chin. Her eyes were as red as herrings that would be going sick.

Sam, in addition to being an old man, was no beauty. God knows, I immediately felt sorry for him. I thought it must be a bit tough to sleep with such an ugly-looking woman. The other was a very nice girl. She spoke first, and said, pointing to the table where there were two small loaves of bread and a jug of milk, 'This is your dinner, laddie; take it up to the barn, and when you are finished bring the jug back to Mary.' When I went up to Charlie I told him about the ugly woman, who I thought was Sam's wife, and the nice servant girl. Charlie said, 'I am glad I did not go down. I have a weak stomach, and an ugly sight like that would put me off my meat.'

We finished the dinner, and I went back to Mary with the jug. I came back to Charlie and told him I met Mary at the door and gave her the jug: I thought she was more ugly now than when I saw her at first. Then Charlie said, 'Mary is not Sam's wife; sure he said it was raining since Jane and himself went to bed last night, and Jane must be Sam's wife.'

'Well,' I said, 'my goodness, if that nice woman is Sam's wife I am damn sorry for her. Charlie! Wait until you see her. She is the most handsome girl I have ever seen. She has lovely golden hair, blue eyes, and her skin is as white as the lilies we used to get on the lough at home, and she has beautiful teeth. She is as good a figure as your sister Nellie. She is beautiful.'

It rained all that day. We stayed in the barn. We saw two other men and a lump of a boy going about the yard, feeding the horses and doing other things. We got to know afterwards that they were employed all the year round by Sam. They were called hinds, and the boy was the flunkey that did handy jobs about the house.

About seven o'clock we heard Mary again calling, 'Paddies, your porridge is ready.' Charlie ordered me to go for the porridge. I went to the kitchen door, and ugly Mary gave me a flat dish of porridge with a small well of skim milk right in the centre and two horn spoons stuck in the porridge. I carried the dish most carefully to the barn lest I should spill the milk. As soon as I entered the barn I said, 'She is worse-looking every time I see her.'

Charlie said, 'For God's sake do not talk of that woman again until I get my supper.'

I did not say another word about her that night. I lifted the dish and spoons and went back to the kitchen with them. There was no person to be seen. I left them on the table and turned to walk out when a door opened at the side and Jane stepped out. I looked at her. I think I must have watched her for about a minute or two. As I was going out she said to me, 'Did you get enough supper?' I do not remember what answer I made, as I know I got very excited, but I certainly must have told her that we had enough as there was some porridge left in the dish. She then said, 'Wait a minute.' She went through the same door from the kitchen and came back in a second or two, handed me a small parcel and said, 'Put that in your pocket; do not open it until you go to the barn; do not let Mary, the servant, see it; do not tell the hinds or anyone else I gave it to you.'

When I went back to the barn I opened the paper and in it were two nice cuts of bread and two slices of beef. We did not taste it until we thought it was bedtime. We then had a nice feed. Our clothes were dry and we were quite happy. We had plenty of straw to make a good bed. Each of us got two sacks, put one into the other, said our prayers and slipped into the sacks. Charlie sang, *Come Back to Erin*; I commenced to tell a story, but before I was halfway through we were both asleep, and slept as sound as two dogs until we were called by one of the hinds about half-past five in the morning.

When we came to the street, the hind whose name was Robert handed each of us a hoe and asked us to follow him. He took the first drill, Charlie the second and I the third. Charlie could easily single as much as Robert, but it was a hard struggle for me to keep up. At eight o'clock the flunky came to us with coffee and bread. The day was good and we sat at the top of the field while taking our breakfast. Then we singled again until twelve noon, when we got an hour for dinner, which consisted of a small loaf and a bottle of beer. Charlie and I tasted the beer. It was bitter. We spat it out. Robert was delighted. He was not long slugging our beer as well as his own. After dinner Robert slowed down. He did not go half as fast as in the morning. We stopped work about six o'clock, and got a fine dish of porridge and skim milk.

I always went to the kitchen for the supper, and if Mary was not about Jane would surely give me something nice in a parcel, it might be biscuit and cheese, or bread and butter. One market day when Sam and Mary were at the market in Kelso, I went for the supper. Jane was standing in the door and said, 'I have no porridge for you to-night.' I nearly collapsed when I heard this as I was very hungry. She told me to bring the other lad with me into the kitchen.

I went, and was soon back with Charlie. She asked us to sit at the table, and we did. She took a small 'skillet' from the fire and ladled out two fine plates of soup. Then she put down a big plate of bread and as much beef as would do four men, and also two big cups of tea. She told us that if she said 'Go', we were to go out immediately by the back door and come round the back side of the house, down to the wood, and then come back to the barn, and never tell anyone that we were in the house. 'You know that Mary, who is a friend of his, is not a good person,' she said.

For the first time Charlie spoke: 'Sure, mistress, she could not be good, God bless me, she is the ugliest beast I ever saw, she would put me off my meat.' Jane began to laugh. The sadness seemed to have left her eyes. Every minute she would look out of the window: you could see the Kelso road for over a quarter of a mile from it.

When we had finished the tea and eaten as much as we could, she said, 'When you go back to Ireland do you have any fun?'

We told her that during the winter months we would have the best of fun; we would have airneals every night:

'What is an airneal?' said Jane.

I said that it was a gathering of all the people of the townland into one house, for dancing, singing and story-telling.

She asked, 'How can you pay for dances and you so poor?'

I told her that we did not have to pay; that the dance would be in Charlie's house tonight, my father's house the next, and in different houses every other night.

'Oh yes,' she said, 'but who pays the fiddler?'

I told her there was no fiddler, that it was all lilting, that there was only one fiddler in the parish, 'Fiddler Nan', and he only plays at raffles. His charge was one and sixpence, and the stakes were threepence. The fiddler's money was the first that came out of the stakes. It was usually a goat that was raffled and we used to have the best of fun.

Jane laughed very much and said, 'I wish I could go with you to Ireland this winter. It is good for you, but I am here and will be here likely until I die.' She still kept watching out of the window. No one then spoke for a minute or so. Jane got up, went into the side room, came out with two bottles of beer and a cork-screw, and reached a bottle to each of us. Charlie said that we could not drink beer. 'You must take this from me; I know you can take it with your dinner. Now lads, take it quick as it is near time they were coming home.'

I said, 'We do not take it with our dinners; we are not able to.'

'What do you do with it?' she asked.

I said, 'We give it to Robert.'

'Oh, dear, we send his beer out along with yours every day,' she said. 'Why did he naw tell the master? He would give you something else – milk or something. You know Sam is not too hard, no matter how fond he is of money. He would not like to see anyone hungry. Now, I cannot tell that you are not drinking the beer. Mary would tell the master that I must have been speaking to you, and it would never do for the mistress (she did not speak for a minute) of Crow's Farm to be speaking to Irish lads. You must take this beer from me; you cannot work all summer and harvest without beer.' She got hold of the corkscrew, pulled the corks, and poured out the beer into two cups. Each of us began to sup the beer. We thought it was horrible. Just as we finished drinking she looked out of the window and said 'Go'. We went out quickly, down the road, sat there for some time, and then made our way back to the barn. Charlie said, 'My Goodness, such a good woman! Our own mothers would not be so good to us. She must have a fine big heart. Oh, Paddy, she is as nice looking as our Nellie. Do you know her skin has that nice pink like the inside of the shells in yon big oysters that Nancy John Jack used to get behind Innishane.'

I said to Charlie, 'She is a great woman indeed. We will go down again to see her. Come on.'

As I was going out of the door Charlie got hold of me. 'You bloody fool,' he said, 'you're getting soft. If the old buck got you about the door he would make you a damn sight softer.' Then I realized that I was going to make a mistake, but I was so extremely happy I did not think I had a poor friend in the world.

The bottle of beer did the trick. I was sobering up when Charlie began to get soft. If it had affected us both at the same time, I think we would have gone back to the kitchen.

We then made up our minds that we would drink our own beer the next day. The following morning when we discussed how we would go about the taking of our own bottles, we decided on a plan. Charlie was to say that he was very thirsty and take a sup of the beer. I was to follow suit. We were to drink a quarter of the bottle the first day, a little extra the next day, and by the end of five or six days we would be able to clear up our share. We wanted to keep in with Robert for fear he would make us work harder. When dinner-time arrived, we were handed our bottle and 'bap' of bread as usual. Charlie said that he was very thirsty and would take a sup of the beer. I said the same thing. Each of us had a sup. I think I can see the eye of Robert, under his bushy eyebrows, watching Charlie for fear he would take another sup. 'Dammit,' said I, 'I think the beer is not so bad after all,' lifting the bottle to my head and draining it dry. My goodness, the look Robert took at me! Charlie could not help laughing. He turned aside. As soon as he did so, Robert got hold of Charlie's bottle and emptied it. Charlie said nothing, but he did not laugh. I think I had a little 'giggle'.

When our hour was up we commenced again to single the turnips. I could knock them out like hell. I was in great form, but after an hour I was no better than the other two. The next day every man drank his own beer. We were not afraid of Robert. We were as good as he was at the singling.

After that night, Charlie never again asked me to go for the porridge. The sight of Mary never put Charlie off his meat. He did not get going for the porridge every night, as I was as anxious as he was; he never came back with an extra feed. I think he was unlucky, as Mary was always there; at least Charlie said so, but I pocketed many a good feed Jane gave me. She often came to our barn when there was no one about. The first time she came to the barn she asked me to get up for a dance. I was not able to dance and told her so, but I said that Charlie was a good dancer. Then she caught Charlie by the hand and said, 'Come on'. She asked me to lilt a tune and I was terribly embarrassed as I had not a tune in my head. Charlie saved the situation by lilting *The Flowers of Edinburgh*, and they jigged it through the barn. The one was as good as the other. I sat on a box like a wallflower. The first pang of jealousy went through me. I tried to keep pleasant-looking, which was no easy job.

Jane, I am sure, was one of the best women in the world. It was such a pity that she was not happy. Every chance she would get, she would slip into our barn and have a dance with Charlie. She could not lilt, but was a good singer. Her favourite was *The Bonnie, Bonnie Banks of Loch Lomond.*

One day there was a Show in Kelso. Sam kept Charlie and me washing four lambs for a week beforehand for the show. To our surprise, the two hinds, the flunkey, Sam and Mary, went to the Show. Charlie and I were sent out to clean weeds out of the turnips. As we were leaving the yard in the morning with our hoes on our shoulders, we heard Mary shouting 'Paddies!' We turned round and she came near us and said, 'Paddies, you will have to come to the kitchen door today for your meals. She will reach them to you. Be sure and leave the dishes back. Don't hang it on Mr. Douglas because the hinds will be away all day, but do a good day's work.'

Off she went. Charlie and I put some big ones on her. When he thought it was breakfast time, Charlie threw down the hoe, saying, 'Paddy, I'm going in for the breakfast.' After some time he came back and handed me a jug of tea, plenty of bread and butter and two eggs. He said, 'Paddy such a woman! Every time I look at her she does my heart good. She says we are to stop early as she wants us to tell her about Ireland. She told me the master and the others will not be home until late.'

When I had my breakfast taken, Charlie said, 'Now, Paddy, we will work very hard. When each of us will have forty drills done, we can stop; that is as much work as any of us did yesterday.' When we thought it was twelve o'clock, we went in for our dinner. Charlie knocked at the kitchen door and Jane said, 'Where is Paddy? Tell him to come in here. You will both have dinner here today.' Charlie called me in, and I can tell you we had a dinner.

We went back to the field, and I can tell you, Charlie and I did some slashing with the hoes; we were not long doing our forty drills. We did two extra and were at the kitchen door at four o'clock. Boys, but she was glad to see us. She had another feed ready but we were not able to touch it. She then said, 'Well, you will surely be able to eat something in an hour.' She drew the corks out of two bottles of beer and made each of us take one. She took none herself. When we had the beer drank, she caught Charlie by the hand and they began to dance.

When they sat down, she said, 'Now Paddy, tell us more about Ireland. Are they all as happy as your people and Charlie's?'

I said, 'I think they are all middling happy now, but in my father's time there were poor times and very little happiness. It was against the law for people to meet and have airneals.'

'But why?' asked Jane.

I told her that the English were ruling us and we could only do what they wanted us to do. When Jamsey Sweeney of the Corner House would not drive the police to the Gweedore evictions he was arrested and sent to Derry jail.

'Oh,' said Jane, 'that was not breaking the law; he must have done something else.'

I said, 'No, Jamsey was one of the quietest men in the world. He is now in London and is a great friend of everyone who knows him. Oh, Jane, if you saw his wife, another fine woman like yourself.' Charlie gave me a kick in the leg and I knew I had made a mistake. I said 'Excuse me, mistress, I think I did not speak right.' She looked at me and laughing heartily told us to always call her Jane if there was no other person near. We assured her that we would.

'Tell me now, Paddy, did they arrest any other person for not driving the police?'

'Yes, when they put Jamsey Sweeney in jail, the Rosses people, that is the people of the parishes of Upper and Lower Templecrone, boycotted the police,' said I.

'What is boycott, Paddy?' she asked.

'Oh, it is just a word that was made in Mayo.'

'Micky Neddy used to teach us that lesson every day,' said Charlie.

'Tell Jane the lesson, Charlie,' I said. 'You have a better memory than I have and you have nearly all Micky's lessons off by heart.'

Then Charlie told us all about Michael Davitt and the bitter hardship he endured in his early life in Ireland and England, and how as he grew older he became very determined to end the savage landlordism which had brought such sufferings to himself and the Irish people. During his campaign of resistance to evictions, a certain Captain Boycott, who was an agent for Lord Erene, became very prominent. The Captain dismissed some of his labourers and no others would take their places. The Captain got processes out to serve on tenants to evict them, but he could get no process servers to serve them. The blacksmiths would not shoe his horses, the postman would not deliver his letters and the bakers would not give him bread, because the people were shouting Boycott. Then he got fifty Orangemen from the north to do his work, and the government sent him two thousand soldiers, but instead of helping the poor devil, they ate him out of house and home. He had a big lot of turkey hens and cocks and a lot of sheep. The soldiers would have great feeds every night. When they had all the small things about the place eaten, they began to kill the bullocks. The Captain got fed up and asked the English to take their soldiers home. He hunted the Orangemen first: he said they were not worth their meat. So, you see, if there is a bad man you have only to say 'boycott' and he is boycotted. That was what made Gladstone pass an act in London, that the landlords could never evict a tenant if he paid his rent. Micky Neddy would finish up the lesson by saying that the Orangemen fought against Gladstone but were the first to take advantage of the Act.

'The Rosses people said "boycott" to the police,' I said, 'and no person would serve them with goods or do anything for them. Then the English made some kind of Law Court, it was called the "Star Chamber". They had a man named Hamilton at the head of it. He was a kind of magistrate. When Johnny Edward Boyle refused to supply them with goods, they arrested him. They arrested Paddy Roarty, his brother John, and Charlie Gallagher, the blacksmiths, because they would not shoe boycotted horses; and James Breslin, the tailor, because he refused to sew a button on Officer Markham's trousers; and Neilly Sharkey, the carpenter, because he would not put a lock on the Barrack door; and James Gallagher, because he would not make a table for Condy Nannie, the Bailiff; and Micky Hanlon, because he would not go down to Burtonport and bring up some fresh fish for them. They also arrested John Hamilton, Eddie Doogan and Jimmie O'Donnell and Owney Boyle.'

'And what did they do with them?' asked Jane.

'They took them to the "Star Chamber", that is the Court House, and the magistrate returned them all for trial for seven days. They were brought up at Dungloe but they could not get into the Court House as there was an inquest being held on Biddy Broadley. She was found drowned in the river the evening before. Hamilton called a lot of the fellows in and got them sworn to do their best according to law to find the cause of Biddy Broadley's death. He was the chairman. It was Johnny Diddy got the corpse in the river and he was the first witness called. It took nearly half an hour to swear him. Then Hamilton said, "Now, my man, tell us where you were when you saw the corpse?" – "I was nowhere, mister," said Johnny. "Don't address me as mister again," said Hamilton. "Address me as 'Your honour'." – "I'll do that," said Johnny. "All right," said Hamilton; "now tell the court where were you when you saw the corpse?" – "What am I to say now?" said Johnny; "is it, 'You're my honour' or am I 'your honour'?" Hamilton went raging mad, and said, "Your stupidity saves you, otherwise I would send you to jail for contempt of Court." I was often told that Johnny Diddy was a very clever man, a national schoolmaster. He was the teacher in Roshine School before Micky Neddy. They say he was as good a teacher as Micky, but I would not believe that. Every witness was as good as Johnny Diddy, so they kept Hamilton on the bench from eleven o'clock in the morning until nine o'clock that night. It was done on purpose. The jurymen would not agree to any verdict. When Hamilton would say, "Found drowned," some of the jury would say, "We have no evidence of her having been found by anybody." Then Hamilton would say, "Committed suicide while of unsound mind," and Mosey would say, "I wish my mind was as sound," and so on. At length, when the prisoners were taken before Hamilton, he must have been very hungry and he said he would let them off free for that time, but warned them that if they did not obey the police orders, the next time any of them came before him he would give them three months in Derry jail. The next day when the Rosses people heard of the prisoners being released they gathered into Dungloe in their thousands. The bands were out to celebrate the release and there was a big demonstration. When the police saw the procession coming they started to drill at the Barracks and came marching up the town with their batons in their fists. When they came within a few yards of the procession, the County Inspector drew a line across the street with his stick, and said, "If any of you cross that line, I'll arrest every man of you." The band struck up *Let Erin Remember*, and the lads rushed the police and drove them helter-skelter into the Barrack yard.

'At three o'clock next morning the police raided the houses and lifted all the prisoners. Seven days afterwards they were taken before Mr. Hamilton, who had an assistant this day, a Mr. Burke. John Redmond came all the way from Dublin to defend them, but in spite of his eloquence they got three months' imprisonment with hard labour.'

'Laddies,' said Jane, 'your people must have suffered much from the English, but my people in the Highlands suffered also. Many a night my father took tears to our eyes telling us of the persecution of the clans after the battle of Culloden. My father's name is Duncan Fraser, and he is still head of the Clan, but very poor. He is living now in a house in a street called Haymarket, in Edinburgh, but all the old Scottish patriots call on him. Sam's people came from the Highlands too. They lost their estates, and Sam called to see my father. That is where he saw me, and at my father's request I agreed to marry Sam. That is why I am here. My father would not let me go into service, and he would rather see me dead than a servant.'

Jane then stopped speaking. She stood between us and the window and we could see her sobbing. After about five minutes, she turned to us, the tears running down her handsome face. She said, 'Excuse me, but isn't this wicked world terrible? I must get you something to eat now, you are surely hungry.'

She was not long getting us another good feed. We kept watching the Kelso road while she was doing the cooking. When we had enough eaten, I said, 'You are tired, mistress. We will go to the barn and you can rest yourself.'

'No, no,' she said, 'you must stay until we see them coming up the road. You can slip round the back; they won't see you. If my eyes are a bit red they will not be noticed. I often cry, and a good cry does me good. Sam is good to me, but isn't he awful? – I mean Mary is very ugly.'

Again the tears rolled down her beautiful cheeks. I said, 'Mistress, would you like to hear a wee story?'

'I surely would,' she said. I then told her a story about Oisin, and Charlie sang *The Mountains of Mourne*, and to our great relief Jane started to sing *Loch Lomond*. I started to tell a story about Finn McCool, but Jane saw the lambs coming up the road and the hinds after them. Charlie and I slipped out the back and off to the barn.

We had a happy time at the Crow's Farm for the nine weeks we were there. Sam had no corn, and as the farmers who had corn were paying one pound a week, and Sam not having sufficient work for us, we had to leave. We were very sorry when it came to the last week. We had work to go to at the other side of Kelso. We used to meet the other lads every Sunday at Kelso and had always a feed on O'Donovans Hot Plate. Jane did not miss a night for the last week we were there without slipping into the barn, even if it was only for a few minutes.

The day before we left, I went for the porridge. When Jane got Mary's back turned, she slipped something into my pocket. When I went out I put my hand in my pocket and what do you think I found but a half-sovereign. I did a mean trick. I never told Charlie or anyone else until now. I felt very happy. I said to myself that it was as good as Charlie dancing *The Flowers of Edinburgh*.

I cannot put in writing how I felt when I heard of the unjust treatment that charming woman got, but if you were near me I would whisper it to you.

# CHAPTER THREE

## *Back to Cleendra*

When the harvest was over we came home. We were the first of the Cleendra lads to get back. It was the end of September, I do not remember the date. We went on the boat at the Broomielaw, Glasgow. It was a very stormy night. I am sure there was not a passenger in the steerage who was not sick. The storm was bad enough, and your own sickness was no joke, but when the others threw their sickness all over you it was terrible. Oh, such a sight when we crawled on deck as we were landing on Derry Quay. We were not able to eat anything in Derry that morning.

We got the train to Letterkenny. We went into an eating-house and got some bread and tea. We started for home, a distance of twenty-six miles. When coming over the mountains at Glendowan it commenced to rain. Charlie said, 'Thank goodness for that rain. Even if we get wet it will wash the bad smell of us.'

I think they were the only words spoken until we arrived in Doochary. We saw a light in Big Gracie's. We knocked at the door and Gracie opened it. We went in without being asked, went to the big turf fire and began to warm our hands.

'God bless me, boys,' said Gracie, 'where did you come from and where are you going such a night? You are drowned.'

We told her we were on the boat the night before and walked from Letterkenny, and that we were going to Cleendra.

The next question she asked us was, who did we belong to. When we told her she said, 'You must stay with me tonight, you could never travel to Cleendra. It was God saved you when you were not lost such a night as this.'

She got hold of a big pandy, put water in it and set it on top of the fire. She made us sit down. The water was running out of our clothes and the floor was getting all wet. Charlie said that we were sorry we were wetting the house.

Gracie was cutting the bread at the table. She said, 'Shut up your mouth or I'll hit you with this loaf. Aren't you nearly drowned. What about the floor, it will be dry before you are.' She then said, 'Give me a lift with this table.'

We both got up and helped her to bring the table over to the fire. She then poured out two big bowls of tea, and cut more bread than six men could eat. She took from the press a big lump of butter – it was freshly churned that day – and two eggs for each. She then went to the bar and brought up two glasses of whiskey for us.

'Take this wee drop first,' she said; 'it will warm you, and maybe it will save you from getting your death of cold.'

We told her that we never drank whiskey, but that we could take a drop of beer.

She said, 'I do not keep any beer. If I did I would not give it to you as it would starve you with the cold.'

She did her best on us to take the whiskey, but we would not take it. In any case, we had a great meal. Gracie thought we did not eat half enough. When we helped her to lift the table back in its place, she said, 'I have a bed for you. Go now to the room, take off all your clothes and when you are in bed I'll take them and put them on the backs of chairs around the fire, they will be dry for you in the morning.'

One of us looked at the other, waiting to see who would speak first. As there was no appearance of Charlie saying anything, I said, 'We must go home tonight. It is only twelve miles and we will be home before morning.'

Charlie said, 'We must go home. We would not like to pass through Dungloe in the morning. We would not satisfy them to let them see us in this state.'

Gracie did her best on us to remain, but we would not stay. Charlie said, 'How much have we to give you? You gave us a great supper and we had a good summer and harvest. We have over eight pounds each. Charge us plenty.'

'Get out,' said Gracie, 'I'll charge you nothing, boys. Whatever you earned you must have worked hard for it. Sure I'm a Rosses woman myself. I wish you would stay to morning. I hope you will make home safe. Put this wee drop in your pocket and if you get tired or weak on the road, take a drop of it, whether you like it or not. Many a life it saved.'

She put the bottle in my pocket. We bade her good night and thanked her the best we could. As we were going out on the door, she called us back, shook the holy water on us, and said, 'May God speed you, boys.'

When we went out it was not raining and our clothes began to dry. We were well refreshed and the travelling was no bother to us. Charlie was humming songs all the way. It did not rain a drop on us, and before we reached Dungloe our clothes were dry.

When we arrived in Cleendra at John Liam's house (Charlie's father) they were all in bed. It must have been near morning. Charlie lifted the latch and in we went.

'Who is there?' said John. Charlie said,

'It is Charlie and Paddy.'

Mary (Charlie's mother) got out of bed and began to kiss Charlie in the darkness. She then got the tongs, lifted a coal, blew it until it showed light, got a rush candle and lit it. Charlie went over to the bed where his father was. I tell you there was a welcome there for him. Then all the children got up. How glad they were for their brother. Mary was not long getting the fire on, and as soon as it was lit she put the pandy on top of the blaze. In a short time each of us had a bowl of tea and a lump of bread in our hands.

When we had the tea taken, I handed the whiskey to John, telling him how we got it. He turned the bottle over and upside down in his hands several times, stuck it under the pillow, got up, put on his clothes and boots.

'Paddy,' he said, 'I am not going to touch it until we go up to your father's. Mary, put on your boots. We will both go up with Paddy. Charlie can go to bed.'

Charlie said, 'I'll go up too.'

'No,' I said, 'you are tired, go to bed. As soon as I go home I'll go to bed.'

John got the tongs, caught two coals with them and as there was a nice breeze we had a splendid light. When we reached our house, Mary lifted the latch. She was the first to go in. When John went in with the coals the house was well lit up.

My father said, 'Blood an''ounds, is that you, Paddy?'

He, my mother, brother and sisters were all out of bed while you cough. There was some kissing and hugging there for a while. My mother lit two rush candles, had the fire going quickly and the pandy on top of it. I told her that we had tea in John's, and could not take any more.

Then the questions were beginning to come; where were we working, had we any trouble, where were the rest of the boys, when will they be at home?

After some time, John said, 'Pat, look what they brought us. Aren't they good? Paddy gave it to me, but it would do me no good to drink the half of it and send you the other half. We will drink it together as it should be drunk. Nancy, get me something to pull the cork.'

After some trouble, they got a big nail and hooked it out, then got two egg-cups, and had one each. They began again to question me about my experiences. Funny, none of them ever were in the Crow's Farm, neither did they know of it.

John told how we got the whiskey.

'Dammit, that's Big Gracie, it is just what she would do,' said my father.

When they had the bottle drank, they were both well on. My father began to sing, *Come Back to Erin.*

The following night the airneal was in Charlie's and there was a great welcome for us. We began to go out with the bigger fellows. We considered ourselves too big to go to school. Charlie did not need to go as he passed out of the second book and was a few days in third. When we gave up our money to our parents, each of us kept one pound, as we had decided beforehand. I had my gold half-sovereign nicely out of the way in the lining of my waistcoat. We considered ourselves big fellows and we were able to drink more than one bottle of beer. On some occasions we took more than we should. On one occasion we were along with some other fellows in the New Shop in Maghery and on our way home parted company with them at the foot of Cleendra Brae, and took the fields for a near way across by the Glen. When we came near the fairies' home we heard a fiddle up in the spink playing the most beautiful music. Although I had no ear for music I knew there was something great in the music we heard, for no earthly person could play like it. Charlie and I sat on the grey stone. Then the music stopped for about a second and I had just time to say, 'That's not Fiddler Nan anyway,' than the fiddle started again to play a hornpipe. As soon as the first note was struck Charlie jumped to his feet and commenced to dance. Oh, such dancing, I was glad Jane was not watching him. Charlie danced and danced until I thought he would kill himself. 'Stop Charlie,' I called to him, 'you will kill yourself.'

'Can't,' he said. Every time I would ask him to stop he would say 'Can't'. I was frightened and made for Peggy Manus' house, which was the nearest. I told her in Gaelic that I thought it was the fairies who were playing and that Charlie would surely kill himself dancing. She asked me if it was near the fairies' castle.

'Yes, just at the grey stone,' I told her.

'Run,' said Peggy, 'tell Charlie to thank the fiddler. If he does not do so before the sun rises the wee people will bring him into the spink and he will never again be seen.'

I went back to Charlie as fast as I could. He was still dancing like mad. Oh such music! I said, 'Charlie, say "Thank you, fiddler".

Charlie said, "Thank you, fiddler,' As soon as he said it, the music stopped and we walked home. He was not the least tired and did not seem to know he was dancing.

It took me a long time to convince him what happened. The next day Charlie and I went down to the grey stone where Charlie was dancing. There was not a track on the ground where Charlie was dancing for hours. We then went up to Peggy and asked her what did she know about the fairies. She gave each of us two turfs and told us to sit on them and she would tell us what to do whenever we met them.

Then she told us the story of the old ruins on top of the spinks and the misfortunes that followed the farmer and his family who failed on Hallow Eve night to leave a pot of praties and a can of milk full to overflowing for the good people to eat and drink their fill.

It was a long story and when we saw that Peggy was getting tired we got up to go home. But she made us sit down again while she got up and lifted a pot of praties off the fire, teemed the water off them outside the door, took in the pot, left it sitting at the fire and when they quit steaming she lifted a big plate full of the praties, put the tongs across the pot, and left the plate sitting on the tongs. The three of us went to them and had a good feed.

When we came to the grey stone where I sat while Charlie was dancing, Charlie sat on it, but we heard no music. He was crying more than I was because Peggy's story was very sad. He rose after a few minutes, but neither of us spoke to the other until we reached our own homes.

Charlie and I decided to spend another night with Peggy to hear more of her stories. Off we went. When we came to the door we heard talking inside and decided we would not go in. We went to Peggy Davey's where the airneal was. When we went in my father was telling a story. Its name was 'Speed Heavy and Light Foot'. It was a very good story. When he finished, Johnny Brown sang *Patrick Sheehan is my Name, I came from the Glens of Arklow*. Before he finished some of the women were crying. Then Mary Paddy began to lilt a 'satish'. All the young people were on the floor dancing, except myself. When we were going home, I said to Charlie, 'It is good for you that can dance. I am sorry I did not go into Peggy's. I would rather her stories than my father's. Peggy's are true ones but that story that my father told could not be true. The man he called Speed could not have left Donegal in the morning for the far Indies and be back before night, that was not true.'

# CHAPTER FOUR

## *Coals at Newcastle*

After we got the turf cut, Charlie and I decided to go to Scotland again. We left Cleendra and travelled to Letterkenny, trained to Derry, got our tickets and went to the steerage to select the best corner we could. We were too late, as the plank was already taken up. We placed our bundles in the very centre of the floor and sat on them. It was Charlie's idea that if the ones on the plank got sick they would not be able to spit on us.

After the ship sailed, who do you think comes in, only Hughdie Micky. He left home the day before to see his sister who was in the Lagan. When he came aboard the ship he went to the bar. When he came into the steerage he had a good few drinks in him.

'Heavens,' he said, when he saw us, 'are you there? But I'm glad to see you both. Come on till we have a drink.'

Before we had time, he reached out both his hands and caught each of us by the wee collar of our jackets and had us landed in the bar before we knew where we were. We had a good many locks of whiskey and quite a lot of fellows came in and stood beside us. I stood another drink for all of them, and when paying for it I found I was fourpence short. I did not like to say so. I said to the barman that I would be back in a minute. I went into the cattle department for an excuse. I took Jane's half-sovereign out of the lining of my waistcoat and paid for the drinks. When we got full we went back to the steerage, Charlie and Hughdie singing. We were as happy as happy could be. We were soon asleep and did not waken until we reached Greenock. When I awoke, such a head, I thought it was split in two, and what was worse, I remembered that I did not say my three Hail Marys. Between everything I had a bad time until we arrived in Glasgow.

When we landed at the Broomielaw we went into an eating-house and had tea, bread, bacon, and onions. We were soon all right. Hughdie wanted us to take a drink for a cure. 'Just a glass and a pint each,' he said (the glass was fourpence and the pint twopence); but if he put a knife in Charlie or I neither of us could look at a drink. Hughdie had a gill and a pint. We went to Queen Street Station then. Charlie and I were going to get our tickets for Jadeborough. We were almost sure we would get work with Sam Douglas. The drink began to work Hughdie, and more of the friendship began to come out of him. He said, 'Damn the ticket you will buy for Jadert' (Jadeborough was called Jadert by our people). 'Come along with me to Uphall and I will get you work in the Oil Works. Sure Jack Mulhern is the contractor, and he is a Cleendra man. If he has a job, you are damn sure to get it, and if there is no work for you, you can go to Jadert tomorrow.'

Charlie made up his mind immediately and told Hughdie we would go. I never had the courage to go against Charlie, he always bossed me, although there was very little difference in our age; but he was much bigger.

I was very sorry that Charlie decided to go to Uphall. I

was anxious to go to the Crow's Farm. I longed to see Jane again. When we came to Uphall Station we went down to the Randy Rows, and into Dan Bonner's house. Dan was from a neighbouring townland at home, and when he and Mrs. Bonner heard who we were they were glad to see us and gave us a good feed of tea, bread and bacon.

At six o'clock the night shift was starting at Jack Mulhern's Oil Works. The three of us went up to look for work. The gas nearly smothered Charlie and I. Hughdie went over to Pat (Jack's brother) – he was the gaffer on the night shift – to ask a job for the three of us, but Pat told him he had only one job and that he could come out in the morning. Hughdie said that he would rather give the job to Charlie or me, that he would get a job somewhere else.

'All right' said Pat, 'which of you boys will come?'

I said 'Charlie.'

'No, Paddy will come,' said Charlie. 'I will go along with Hughdie.'

I said, 'No, I cannot work here, that gas would kill me. I'll go to Jadert.'

Charlie began to laugh at me. Pat asked him what he was laughing at, but all Charlie would say was, 'I think Paddy is getting foolish.'

I got much ashamed, and for the first time I made up my mind quickly and said, 'Suppose I am foolish.' I walked towards Dan Bonner's. Charlie and Hughdie followed me. We were as black as soot when we got to the house. It was a devil of a job to get the dirt off, our eyelashes were the worst.

We were not long in the house until a message came for Hughdie asking him to go out and work a shift as one of the men was off. Hughdie went out. Charlie and I went to bed along with the other lodgers, three on each bed. Next morning when Hughdie and the other lodgers came in about four o'clock, got washed and their porridge taken, it was time for us to get up. Mrs. Bonner had our breakfast ready in good time, and the night-shift men slipped into our beds as soon as we got out, as there was no room in the kitchen for all the lodgers at the same time. Charlie forced me to go out to the job, but I would not go. Charlie was angry and said, 'Paddy, why do you not do what you are told?'

I said, 'Charlie, I could not work in that gas.'

'Well,' said he, 'go around some of the buildings and see if you can get a job. If you do not, I will go with you to Jadert tomorrow. Be sure and come back here tonight,' Finally he went out himself.

I went out to look for work elsewhere. I made up my mind that come what may I would not go to the Crow's Farm. I travelled all morning to every place where I saw men working. It was getting late. About five o'clock I was in Neddrie, where there were new retorts being built. I went to the gaffer and asked him for a job. He told me to come out in the morning. Boys, but I felt happy. I then went to look for lodgings and got them with Mrs. Muldin.

I started in the morning to carry bricks in a hod for the bricklayers. I got a very handy hod, but at dinner-time a little fellow from Edinburgh took my hod and left his own heavy one in its place. Someone told me that the Edinburgh tramp had my hod. I went to him and said, 'Give me back my hod. Here is your own.'

He said, 'I have not your hod, and if you say it again I will flatten that soft face of yours.'

He was so small that I could only wonder at his cheek, and only for fear of getting the sack I would have taken the hod from him. Anyhow, I left the hod with him. We worked ten hours a day at threepence halfpenny an hour. It was very little better than working with Sam Douglas on the Crow's Farm. The lodgings were two and sixpence a week, and for that the landlady gave you bed, soap, and milk for your tea. She charged a quarter pound of tea and three-pennyworth of potatoes to each lodger weekly. If you wanted porridge and milk for your supper you paid ninepence weekly for it. You could buy the rest for your-self, or if you wished, the landlady would buy what you wanted for you. For each lodger she had a dish with a cover on it for the sugar, the same for the butter and a plate for the bread, which was kept in the press. There were only four lodgers in our lodge, all working daytime, and we slept two to a bed. Two of the lads were Irish, working on the same job as I; the other was a Scotchman working in Glendevin Shell Mine. His name was Donal McLeod. I was put to sleep with him. Mrs. Muldin was a good landlady and most fair. When she got the beef from the butcher, she made him cut it up in half-pounds and then tie a string round each half-pound so that when the beef was boiled she lifted out each lodger's share. If it was steak there was some trouble, as all the butchers were not able to slice the half-pound in one cut. If there was one extra piece required he stuck a pin in it, and often the pin did not hold in the frying-pan, and the wee pieces got mixed up. Donal watched the frying most carefully; he made sure to have his own. He was a very nice man and absolutely honest, but very near. He often suspected the landlady of taking his sugar and butter. If he could get hold of a fly – and there were plenty of them – he would put it on the sugar-dish under the cover. He would sometimes pull a hair out of his head and lay it across the cut end of the butter. One of the other lodgers was always watching him (his name was Dennis Logue). Whenever he got a chance he would lift the lid and let the fly out, or remove the hair from the butter. Oh, if you could have seen the face of Donal when he would lift the lid off the sugar and find the fly gone, or when he would see the hair gone from the butter. Sometimes the fly would be dead in the sugar-dish. Donal would not always complain. He told me one day that he knew his food was being stolen, but he said he had been in worse lodges where they would steal more than the food.

There was a big difference in what each of us had to pay on Saturday. Some would eat one pound of butter, fourteen eggs and four loaves, others would spare the butter and bread and only take one egg each day. If we saw the bread and butter getting short on Friday we would all try to do our best to stretch it out until after dinner-time on Saturday, when the week would be finished. There were no crusts thrown away. If the bread was too hard we would put it into the tea, and if the landlady was not watching we would add an extra drop of milk to it.

The first Sunday that came we went to Broxburn Chapel to Mass. All the Uphall boys who were not working were there (there were seven shifts a week in the Oil Works). The first person I saw was Charlie. Hughdie was working that Sunday. Boys, but Charlie and I were glad to meet each other. A number of us, all neighbours at home, arranged to meet the following Saturday night in Broxburn, in the Cardross publichouse. So we did. We had some drinks and got extra friendly to each. After a while who did I notice at the end of the bar but my bold Edinburgh lad who took my hod! I went right over to him and said, 'Are you as good a man now as the day you took my hod?'

'I am,' he said, and he immediately squared for me although he had not a soul with him, and I had seven or eight lads.

Charlie shouted, 'Go for him, Paddy!' There was a ring made for us. The wee lad hit me a box in the nose and bled me. I tried to hit him but missed every time. He gave me a hell of a leathering and left my two eyes as black as soot. My pals would not have let me fight so long only they thought I would have beaten him in the end. When they washed the blood off me and gave me some brandy to pull me through, Charlie said, 'Thank God Micky Neddy is not here. You brought shame on Roshine school.'

When I got to my lodge in Neddrie the landlady was very sorry for me and put a big plaster of tea-leaves on my eyes, and when I got up in the morning I could hardly open them. You bet the Edinburgh wee lad put manners on me.

After a time I got a job on the retorts. It was very warm work taking the burned shell from the retorts. The shell was dropped red hot into hutches. Every two men went with a hutch, one in front, the other behind, drawing and pushing them out of the gullets to the endless chain which took them up to the top. There were three spells for work, from six to nine, ten to one, and from two to five o'clock. We got four shillings a day and seven days in the week. It was a good wage, twenty-eight shillings a week, but the work was very warm. Each of us used to drink at least half a gallon of water each spell, but it ran out of us in sweat as fast as we drank it. We wore a light pair of trousers, a small navy-blue simit with no sleeves; we had a belt or cord round our waist and cords round our legs under our knees to help keep up our trousers. When we young fellows would be going to our lodgings, if we saw any women coming along the road we would face the hedge, as the sweat would be running out of our trousers and we feared that he women would think we had wet them. We soon got accustomed to it and did not care who saw us.

We bought all our clothes in the pawnshop, where they were cheap. The second pay I got in the Oil Works, on Donal's advice I decided to get a suit of clothes made to measure. Donal advised me to get it in the Broxburn Co-op. Store, and I agreed. He and I went to the store and selected the cloth, the cutter took my measure, and I got a first-class suit of blue beaver for two pounds five shillings. Donal told me to put it through Mrs. Muldin's account, and didn't she get a dividend of two and tenpence in the pound on it! You could not get a suit near as good from any private shop for less than two pounds ten.

The following year Donal said that he could get me a job in the Glendeven Shell Mine, drawing from Jack McKinney, at four shillings and sixpence a shift. I decided to go. At first I thought the work very hard, but it was not half as bad as the work at the retorts when you got used to it. It was all daytime. I could get to Mass every Sunday and see some of the boys from home at the Chapel. I would meet Charlie every other Sunday. I think he never again was as good to me since the Edinburgh wee lad beat me.

When I was working about two years in the Mines there came the big Broxburn strike, just about the harvest time. Everyone was idle. The strike lasted about fourteen weeks. Charlie went to America.

I went to Jadeborough. My first race was to Crow's Farm. I met Robert, the hind, in the yard. 'Well,' said he, 'are you back again?' I said that I was. 'Well, I am sure you will get work, the master told me yesterday that if I saw any Irishmen knocking about to send them to him. You know we have a new master and mistress now?' I said that I did not know that. 'Well,' said he, 'you know it now. The old man died and left everything to Mary, except fifty pounds which he left to the mistress. She went home to Edinburgh, and Mary got married to her cousin, Sammie Houston. They say that was in the will. He is the master now. Go round and see him.'

I went and knocked at the back door. Who came out only Mary. Heavens, such a sight! She did not let on she knew me. I asked her was the master in. She said, 'What do you want?'

'Work,' I said.

She replied, 'There is no work here. We have two hinds and they are idle half the time.

They can easily save the harvest if they want to.'

I was glad that I did not get work. I went back and told Robert what she said. 'Oh,' said he, 'the bloody ugly bitch, that is her. I will not be long here.'

I left the 'Crow's' farm a sorry man, Lord, but I was sorry when I heard how the old man treated her, and that I had no hopes of ever seeing her again. I often wonder what happened to such a grand lady. I hope where ever she is that she will be happy, God bless her.

My Uncle John was many years about Jadeborough. I heard he was working in a farm called the 'Toal'. I went to the farm and started to work next day. When the harvest was over, my uncle was kept on for the winter, but there was no job for me. I knew there were waterworks at Otterburn in Northumberland. I decided to go and look for work there. My uncle took a day off to see me away. We went to Jadeborough, had a few drinks, and my uncle got me a good parcel of bread and bully beef, and I faced for Otterburn, over the moor. My uncle came with me for about four miles. When he was parting with me, he pulled a half-bottle of whiskey out of his pocket and said; 'Put that in your pocket, Paddy: when you get tired take a slug. You have a long way to go.' We shook hands. I think we were both crying when we parted.

I travelled on. It got dark before I reached the huts at Otterburn. The first hut I came to I asked for lodgings. I was told there was no room. It was the same story in every hut. Newcastle was about twenty miles away. There came on a light rain. I travelled on and as I was getting tired I met two men on the road. I asked them was there any place nearer than Newcastle where I could get lodgings. I was carrying a few shifting duds in a bundle. One of them said, 'Walk on for about three hundred yards and the first road you meet on your left-hand side will bring you to a farmhouse. The farmer, Mister Jones, was never known to turn a tramp from his door.'

I went up to the farmhouse and knocked. The maid came to the door, or it might be the daughter, for all I know. I asked her if I could get shelter for the night. 'Yes,' she said. 'Turn round that building at the corner and go up the first steps you meet. You will have plenty of room as I think there are only two others of your kind there to-night. If you are hungry I will get you something to eat.' I thanked her but said I was not. I went up the steps, it was very dark, and I had no matches.

Someone shouted at me, 'Shut the door, you bloody so-and-so.' I got a bit frightened, as I had seven or eight pounds on me. I only went in a few feet when I found myself right up against the hay. I sat down, took my brave bottle out of my pocket, and had a fine quiet slug. It was lucky my uncle left the cork on such a position that it was easy to pull. I began to get a bit cold, took another slug, began to get warm, slugged it all the third time. I rolled myself in the hay and fell fast asleep. I woke up early in the morning, and saw two tough-looking boys sleeping at the other end.

I was not long getting out, and hooked it for Newcastle. When I travelled about three miles I saw what I took to be a pit a distance from the road. I went to it. There were two carts there, one loading coal as it came up from the pit. I am sure it was at least one hour before the card was loaded. I went to the winchman and asked him did he think there would be any chance of getting a job if I waited until the men would loose at night. He said, 'You need not wait long. They will soon be up for their breakfast.' I had not time to say another word until I saw a man's head peeping out of a hole and coming to the surface. Others followed, nine in all. They went to a hut and had their breakfast.

When they came out, one of them, a middle-aged man, came to me and said, 'Are you looking for work?'

'Yes,' said I.

He then asked me did I ever work in a pit. I said that I did not, but that I worked in a shell mine. He then asked me if I had any tools. I said that I had not. 'Well,' he said, 'you do not want many tools, here, only a pick, shovel, candles and candle-holder. If I give you the tools I will take two shillings a week off your pay until they are paid for.' I agreed. He gave me a share of his breakfast, and I went down along with the rest. I took my bundle with me, and when he showed me my place I took off the clothes I had on and put on the old duds. We were only about forty feet under the surface. It was a funny pit, no ventilator, or no engine to lift the coal, just a winch, but there was plenty of air as there was a big fire in the bottom level and it caused a good draught. I think I sent up as much coal as any of them that day. Everyone had his own hutch with his own marks on.

When we stopped about five o'clock, I changed my clothes. Again the man who started me asked me what was I to do for lodgings. I said, 'I do not know'.

'Come with me,' he said, 'there is a cotter down the road; I am sure he will be glad to keep you.' Down he went to the house. I stood on the road. When he came back to me he said, 'Mrs Jones will keep you. You will earn good money and you can pay her well.'

'Come in,' she said.

'He is a good worker, Mrs. Jones,' said the man, 'and I will see that he gives you no trouble.'

'What is your name?' she asked.

I answered, 'Paddy.'

'That is a funny name,' said Mrs. Jones, 'I never heard of such a name before. Now, Mister Paddy, I will get you water and soap, and here is a brush. Wash yourself well, and I will have something ready for you to eat when you are cleaned.'

I gave myself a good scrubbing and I needed it. I got a good dinner and felt very happy. Two of the young men who were working in the pit came to see me and we went out for a walk. We did not travel far until we came to a wee inn. We went in. Each of them stood a drink of beer. I wanted to stand but they would not let me. We used to go regularly to the inn and had some good fun. The man who started me was the owner of the pit and he sold all the coal that we dug to the farmers. He was a very good man.

When I was there about a month, one morning at breakfast I heard a lot of whispering going on. I could not hear what they were saying, and I thought they did not want me to. I felt sorry, as up to that they treated me as one of their own. I was glad that night when the two young men asked me out for a walk. We walked by the inn but did not go in. One of them said, 'Paddy did you ever do any poaching?' I said that I did, that I often poached rabbits on the Maghery Banks. The other fellow said, 'He'll do, we'll go back and have our supper. Do not go to bed, Paddy; we will call for you about twelve o'clock.'

I asked no questions, went back to the lodge and at half-past twelve the two lads came to the door. I went out to the road. There were four others there, and each had a pick shaft in his fist and a bag over his shoulder. We went down a field. No one spoke. Then Jimmie Smith handed me his pick shaft and spoke very low:

'Not a word out of your mouths, and if the bailiffs come we will walk away, but it they try to interfere or make a prisoner of any of us, stand firm, use the pick shafts if necessary. Not another word.'

Each of us then tied a handkerchief over his face. This being done, Jimmie opened a bag he had in a parcel, made a screen of it, lit his lamp, put the lighted lamp in the bag until we reached the river. Then he took out the lamp and handed the bag to one of the lads. He went right into the river. Before I could see what he was doing, he had a salmon on the gaff, hanging across his shoulder. Watson had it in the bag while you would say 'Jack Robinson'. Jimmie did the same again, and in less than half an hour he lifted nine salmon. He would not let any other man hold the light, for fear he might not keep the light steadily shining on the salmon. No other man in the squad could do that. If any person tried to lift a salmon some other one would have to hold the light for him. In nine times out of ten Smith could take off the pair. He always gaffed the far-away one first. We did not see or hear of any bailiffs.

We did the same every week until about Christmas, when the salmon began to turn black and we stopped. Each got a salmon, and I think that the owner of the pit got one also, and some other friend of Smith's. I never saw a bailiff while I was there. It was a very nice place and the people were very kind.

About May I made up my mind to go back to Scotland. We had a big night in the inn before I left. They were all very sorry because I was leaving, and the landlady was shedding tears. That morning I got up on the bread van for Newcastle to get a train to Scotland. I landed in Edinburgh and got a train to Winsborough. When passing the beer-shop on my way to Neddrie I went in and bought a half-bottle of whiskey – I think the price was one shilling and fourpence. I put it in my pocket.

I landed in my old lodging-house. The strike was long since settled. All the lodgers were home from work, including Muldin himself. They were all glad to see me. I asked Mrs. Muldin for a cockscrew and a glass, and I shoved the whiskey round. They all got a share, and I gave Donal a good one. When you have only one glass you can make a wee lock of whiskey go a long way if you hold on to the bottle.

After we had a feed, Donal and I went out for a walk. He said that he had a rotten job now, and that the shell mines were no damn good since the strike. 'I am leaving on Saturday,' he said, 'for California, Paddy.' I asked him what was the passage. 'Only a bob to Polmont,' he said, 'and it is only a few miles from there. It is in Stirlingshire.' I was very surprised to hear that there was a California in Scotland. I said that I would go with him.

The following Monday we hooked it for California. Donal had his grath (mining tools) with him. We went to a pit there, failed to get work, and went to another at Crosscrows. Donal for a place in the pit, and I went to draw for him.

The first day we worked at the pit face, undermining the coal with our picks. We put in two shots and lit the squibs (there was no strum or fuse in those days) when we were leaving. We only heard one report. When we went back next morning we saw the squib was blown out of one of the holes. We had to hoke out the shot again. Donal was very annoyed and said, 'There must be a witch in this place.' The same happened a few days afterwards, and Donal said, 'Paddy, there is a witch here right enough. We must burn the bitch.'

I could not help laughing. I did not then believe in witches, if he said a fairy I would believe.

That night when we got home, Donal asked the landlady for an old blouse and skirt. He said he would pay her for them. She got him a blouse but no skirt, and would not take anything for it. He commenced in the room to make an effigy. The landlady had a washing out on the line. Donal asked me when darkness set in to pinch her knickers. I began to fear his mind was snapping. I went outside and said three Hail Marys for him. I told him there was no knickers on the line. He went out and came back with the knickers, stuffed them with paper and had a rough shape of a woman made up. He said he was not stealing the knickers, that there was an apron on the line, that he put a shilling in the pocket and that they were not worth half of it. He warned me not to mention it to anyone. He put all into a bag. We went off to the pit next morning. As soon as the fireman passed on his rounds, Donal took the effigy, set a match to it, and said, 'Now you bloody witch get out of our place. I hope you will get such a roasting that you will never come back.'

I did not know what to do. I was sure he had gone mad. As soon as the effigy was burned, he lay down and commenced holing under the coal. He said, 'Paddy, she is gone. The holding is not near so hard.' He had no trouble with the shots that day.

He came home that night and I never noticed a thing wrong with Donal. I did not want to mention the subject to Donal, neither did he mention it to me, but strange to say, we never had a misfire after, while I was with him.

We remained there for about two years. Donal decided to go to South America. I went searching for another job.

I met Spud Murphy at the Station, he was glad for me, he was on a bit of a spree, and he had a rotten week of it, and was going back to Denny in Stirlingshire, and he said that there was a vacant place on his road, and if I went with him he was sure he would get it for me. Off we went, I got the place, got Hugh McCauley to draw for me (Labour).

I worked for about two years, there in Denny Place coal pit. I lodged in Denny with a Mrs. MacAward. There were five lodgers of us, Dinger Doyle, James Doherty (a piper), Spud Murphy, Willie Laffy, and myself. They were a swanky crowd. When we came home from the pits, got washed and fed, the others put on white shirts and collars and hard hats, we only worked five days a week, attended all the dances, followed the Celtic football club every Saturday, everywhere they played. Willie Laffy and I became fast friends, he was a charming man and when he asked me to accompany him anywhere, I could not think of refusing. I had a place in the pit and was earning from £2 to £2 10s. per week.

The board and lodgings were twelve shillings; no lodgers were buying their own food. After a couple of months damn the penny I could save. I began to do the swank, dressed like the others, only I could never stick the hard hat. I got a new top-coat made to measure with a velvet collar on it.

When I could not save any money to send home I stopped writing. Then I began to get letters from my sister Annie, appealing to me to come home, saying my mother and father would go out of their wits if I did not write by return.

I would then make up my mind to write home on Saturday and send a £1 or perhaps £2. We were paid every Friday but when we got washed and dressed all the boys went to McCormick's if the evening was wet (we had no other place to go) and began to drink beer, it was cheap – then, only a shilling a half gallon. Next day, Saturday, instead of writing home I went with the lads to see Celtic play. On Monday I had no pound to send home. I had not the courage to send an empty letter, this went on for a long time.

On a Thursday when I came in from the pit I saw my father sitting in the kitchen. He did not know me. I was as black as soot. It was a dirty, dusty pit and all the colliers were as black as niggers, coming home. Well, God forgive me, I did not like to see my father. However, I went up to him and said, 'Father,' and caught his hand, he looked at me for a long time and held my hand tightly, and then said, 'It's you, Paddy,' the tears flowing from his eyes.

When I got washed and all the lodgers welcomed my father, I went out to Mrs. McCormick's, and got a bottle of whiskey on tick. I gave the first glass to my father and I shoved the rest around the house. After we had our dinner, Willy Laffy, said, 'Come boys, it is not every day that Paddy's father will be here, come with me.' We all followed Willy to Mrs. McCormick's, he ordered a half gallon of beer, a lot of other colliers gathered in and many a half gallon of beer was ordered. Spud Murphy got up and sang, *The Bonny, Bonny banks of Loch Lomond*. Heavens, he was no sooner sitting than my father for up and sang:- *Come back to Erin*. I think I hear the applause still, although I was crying. Oh! such a night!

He slept in my bed that night; although he had a good few in him he prayed for a long time. I said a few wee ones too. When we were in bed he said, 'Paddy, if we were at home, your mother would be angry with us for going to bed without saying the Rosary. We will go home tomorrow; your mother is waiting hard for us.' I said, 'Father, I can't go home now. I promise you sure I'll go at Christmas.' He said, 'Well Paddy, your mother told me not to come back without you, and I am not going to, I'll look for a job in the morning and will wait until Christmas, and then in God's name, we will go home together. God, but your mother and the children will be glad for us.' We soon fell asleep.

On Friday morning, I told the pit manager I was leaving

and would like to get my 'lying time', that my father came from Ireland for me and wanted me to go home. He said, 'All right,' so I picked up my 'greath' (tools) and called at the office. I had £2 12 6d. for the week and £2 15s. lying time. Before I went to the lodging I went into Mc-Cormick's and paid for the bottle of whiskey. Mrs. Mc-Cormick filled up a glass for me. I did not take it. I was fully determined to be away somewhere early on Saturday morning before my father would rise so that he could not trace me.

We are all in McCormick's on Friday night. No one, not even Willie Laffy could make me put anything to my lips. My father took a few but if you killed him he would not sing for them. We went home early as I wanted to be up early next morning.

My father said, 'Paddy, we will say the Rosary.' We popped on our knees and said the Rosary. When we finished I said my three Hail Mary's, and went to bed, none of us spoke for a long time. Suddenly, I said, 'Father, I have no money, but I am going home with you.' He lifted up his hand and said, 'Thank You God for hearing Nancy's (my mother) prayers.' He then put his arms around me and did not say another word. I am sure if I were offered the pit and all Scotland, aye, and Ireland, to hide on my father next morning, I could not do it.

When I went to pay Mrs. MacAward for my week's lodgings and my father's, damn but she wouldn't take a penny. When we reached Glasgow, I took my father into a publichouse, at the Broomielaw, got a glass of whiskey for him and a bottle of lemonade for myself, I told him to wait there until I returned. I had my topcoat which my father had never seen in a parcel – it had a velvet collar. I went to a pawn shop, slipped it in, got nineteen shillings on it and was soon back with my father. God bless my soul, I was the first of my race who had a topcoat, and I pawned it. My father knew I had a watch, otherwise, I would have pawned it instead of the coat.

When passing through Dungloe, we went into Brennan's. God but Anna was glad for us. Before I had time to order a drink for my father she had them up, she would take no money. My father said, 'Anna, give me a bottle.' She did.

When we got home my mother put her arms around me, kissed me like a baby and cried with joy. My brother and sisters were crying and laughing. All the Cleendra ones gathered in. Oh! such a night!

After I was at home for about three months, we got a letter from the shopkeeper demanding payment of his account. My father said, 'He will have to wait until Friday 'till I sell the heifer.' I remember well it was on a Saturday. Sunday night, I was late getting home, Annie was sitting at the fire, all the rest were in bed. I said, 'Annie, I am going to Scotland in the morning.' She began to cry, and said, 'Paddy dear, if you go to Scotland again you will break our mother's heart. God bless me if you saw her as we have seen the poor soul, night and day praying and crying for you, sure she has improved as well since you came home, she is herself again.'

I said, 'Annie, don't cry, I'll be a good boy anymore and I'll work until we are free from debt.' Annie said, 'I'll tell my father and mother.' I said, 'If you do, I'll run out now.' She went out to the henhouse, came in with a dead fowl, and was not long until she had it cooked, wrapped up in a cloth, she got half a scone of baked bread and buttered it well. She then said, 'Have you enough money?'

I said I had, although I had only 6/8d. She had a little purse and forced me to take all the silver that was in it, but I would not take it.

Off I went – walked to Letterkenny a distance of 36 miles. I was there at two o'clock next day, went into a public house, got a glass of whiskey, paid fourpence. for it, got the train to Derry, paid 1/4d. for train fare. I sailed from Derry to Glasgow, paid four shillings for the boat fare. I was out at the Great Western Road at one o'clock (dinner time) next day, where they were making a subway.

I went to the gaffer, asked for a job, he asked me if I could hold a jumper and strike a hammer. I said that I could, that I wrought in the pits and mines. The gaffer asked me to come out that night. I went to Maryhill, and got lodgings there and remained there for two months. Before I left Maryhill, I sent £5 to my father to compensate him for the animal he had sold on the fairday. After this, I continued sending a few pounds now and again, until we had the debt cleared. Thank God from that day on we were never in debt. I then went to Uphall, and got work in the Homes mine.

When I drank that glass of whiskey in Letterkenny, I took the pledge in my own mind for two years. I kept it, it is the only pledge I ever kept, but I never lost an hour's work through drink.

As I was finishing this chapter, a neighbour who has heaps of education came in, and said, 'Paddy what is this you are writing now?' I gave it to him, and after he had corrected the spelling and put in some punctuation, he said, 'Paddy, it is not a bad chapter, but if you want a free sale for your book, keep out religion; seventy-five per cent of the readers do not believe in religion.' I said, 'Mister' (I always address a man with education as 'Mister'. I can only remember one man protesting and that man was Micheal Powell the Film Producer, when I said, 'Mister Powell,' he said – 'Micheal please'). I am telling a true story, I do not wish to hurt anyone, but damn but I am not going to tell lies.' He said, 'That is for you to decide.'

A few days afterwards I was in Dublin, and I met a man with piles of education. He heard that I was writing a revised edition and was much interested, he said, 'Paddy, I hope you will not spoil it, as a rule the first edition is the best.' I said, 'Mister, that is funny. In my first edition I forget to tell of my father going to Scotland for me, and of me refusing to go home with him. Then he and I and all the lodgers went to a pub, and got fairly well fixed up, and when we were going to bed, he said, "Paddy, we must say the Rosary." We said it, and three Hail Marys. I shortly afterwards made up my mind to go home with my father.' He said, 'Splendid Paddy, that is good.' I told him then what my educated neighbour said. He said, 'Do not mind that. No people in the world has greater respect for tradition than the British people. It is not long since I was at a lecture in Cambridge. After the lecture we all sat down to dinner. Before we touched, tasted or handled, the President got up to say grace. He looked at a portrait of a not too handsome woman which was hanging on the wall facing him. He said, "For the happy repose of the soul of (looking at the portrait) of her Ladyship the Queen." Then we sat down to out feast. It was sumptuous, which means it was good.' He knew damn well that I would not know what 'sumptuous' was, so he added the tail for my benefit. I said, 'Mister, was that a Catholic party?' He said, 'No

I was the only Catholic present. The photograph was of King Henry VII's mother. She built the hall and gave it as a gift to the nation on one condition – that at every dinner the toast would be for the repose of her soul!' Now, aren't the British great for tradition? I do not think they will find fault with me, for telling how my father and I said our Rosary. In any case I think I was right to tell the whole story and leave nothing out.

Yes, look at the English pennies! In the inscription around the King's head on every English penny is found the following:- FID.DEF. which is an abbreviation for 'FIDEI DEFENSOR,' which when translated means – 'Defender of the Faith'! This title of honour was bestowed on King Henry VIII by Pope Clement VII and it has been retained ever since by the Kings of England.

# CHAPTER FIVE

## *Marriage*

I remained in Scotland for two years. I got a new suit of clothes for two pounds twelve shillings and sixpence. I also bought a silver watch, a hunting lever, and a thick silver chain with a badge attached to it. When I put on my new suit with my watch in my pocket and the silver chain across my breast I thought I was a great swell. Anyhow, I made for home at Christmas.

I decided when I landed in Derry to go to Strabane and see a good master with whom I was hired. When I arrived in the town I bought a bottle of whiskey for him. He did not know me when I called at his house until I told him I had been hired with him, and the year. He was delighted to see me and insisted on me staying the night with him. He came into Strabane with me next morning.

When I reached Dungloe, I went into Brennan's, got a wee lock of whiskey for my father and John Liam, a pair of boots for my mother and wee presents for the rest of the family. Boys, but they were glad to see me.

The following night all the neighbours gathered in, and there was no singing or dancing for a long time while I answered all their questions about my adventures in England and Scotland.

We heard on New Year's Day that there was a registered letter in Dungloe Post Office for my father. The office was four miles from Cleendra. My father threw his leg across the mare, went to Dungloe, and was back in a short time.

We were all sitting round the fire waiting on him, my mother, brother James and my seven sisters. My father had the letter opened. He handed it to James, saying, 'Read that. Damn, but I think whoever sent it to me sent me money too.'

My father never was a day at school in his life. James read the letter. It was from our cousin Peggie in Philadelphia. She told how kind the people were with whom she was working, and then went on to take the breath from us by saying she was sending Mary's passage and a bit of money to help dress her. She also said that she would send the passages of the rest of the girls when she was out a while longer, but she wanted James to stay with Nancy and Father.

When James finished reading the letter, my father rose from the chair and looked at James. He said 'Damn but'. He walked out of the house. My mother followed him. We got James to read the letter three times, we were so delighted to think of the prospects of going to America. After some time, I went out and as I went round the gable of the house I saw my mother on her knees with her beads in her hands, and she crying. I ran to her and said, 'Mother, what came on you?'

She did not speak for a long time. Then she said, 'Paddy, isn't this a poor New Year?'

I asked, 'Why?'

'Oh!' she said, 'did you not hear James reading that letter from Peggie. If Mary goes to America that will be the beginning of the breaking up of the family. Now when we are out of debt and all happy, it will break your father's heart. See how he had to leave the house. Dear, I wish it was another process we got the day instead of that letter.'

After some time I got my mother to come into the house. She was still crying. My father was a long time before he returned. When he did, we all cried our fill.

The airneal was that night in Charlie's. None of us intended leaving the house. When John Liam and Mary were passing our house they came in and wondered that none of us were going to the airneal. Mother told them about Peggie's letter and again began to cry. Mary and John began to blame my mother and father.

They said, 'You may thank God that the door is going to be opened for your children going to America. Look at our children that sent us twenty pounds at Christmas. Thank God, we were able to pay our debt and lift our heads. Come all of you up to Charlie's to the airneal.

'Come', said my father.

We all went to the airneal. As soon as we went in, my father sang, *My barque leaves the Harbour tomorrow*. My mother put her head in her lap. I am sure she was crying while he was singing.

Mary went to America on the first of March. The night before leaving, the house was packed with young and old. Johnny Brown and Wright went round all the men and collected from threepence to one shilling from each. No person was allowed to pay more than one shilling. When they counted the money they had seventeen shillings and sixpence. They called Manus McFadden out. The three of them went down to the Glen to Manus's still house and they were not long until they were back with a gallon of good poteen in a jar. Johnny took the jug and the glass from the dresser and began to shove round the poteen. Wright thought he was too slow. He went out to Tully's and got their jug and glass and began to go round the other way. It was the rule not to ask any woman or boy under twenty years to take poteen.

No one in Cleendra went to bed that night. It was singing and dancing, but no story-telling. Fiddler Nan was playing the fiddle. He never made any charge for playing the night before anyone was going to America.

We all walked with Mary to the town next morning. Such a convoy. When Mary went on the mailcar, Carbury, the driver, could not get the horse started with the number of people who were around it until the police opened the way.

My mother, father and all of us were very sorry. Our house was a sad one that night. That was the real break of the family. Annie, Maggie, Sarah, Bridget, and Madgie followed. James and Hannah remained at home. Maggie joined the Sisters of Charity and became a nun in Pittsburgh. My other six sisters got married. Sarah and Hannah are in Dungloe, Annie in Dublin, Mary, Bridget and Madgie in America. James is in the old home in Cleendra and two of his boys are working in the Cope.

The night of Mary's convoy I was sorry, but in addition, I was very much ashamed of myself staying at home and my sister going away to a foreign country. How I wished I had gone with Donal to South America, when we parted in Scotland. I would follow Mary that day, overtake her in Derry and be with her (there were no passports or restrictions in those days) only for I met Sally a short time before and I could not ask her to come to America as I had not sufficient money for both our passages. Scotland was our limit.

The following May Sally and I decided to get married, but we did not want our parents to know it; I especially, as I should not leave them for another few years as my earnings were badly wanted at home.

Anyhow, we got married on a Sunday evening in Dungloe. Sally had her sister Madgie for best maid and I had a cousin for best man. Sally went to her own home in the town with her sister, after the marriage. I went to my own home in Cleendra, and when I got a chance I packed up my clothes and slipped out after dark without telling any person. I stayed in the town with a friend of mine that night. He is now in the pits in Fife, Scotland.

I was up early next morning as Sally and I had arranged to go to Scotland. I waited at the corner until I saw her coming up the street with her shawl over her head. I was very happy, but when she came my length she was crying. I think I was crying too. When we got up on the side-car, who came round the corner only Sally's father. He reached his hand to Sally, and I am sure he gave her the last penny he had in the world. I know it could not have been much, but it was more for him than Lord Nuffield's gifts of millions. He shook hands with me and said, 'I wish Sally and you every luck. May God's blessing be on you. I hope you'll be good to Sally.' Carbury hit the old horse with the whip, off we went to Fintown Station and took the train for Derry.

We bought the usual steerage tickets but did not go to the steerage that night. Sally and I sat on the deck all night. When we landed in Glasgow we took the train for Uphall

Paddy and Sally going to Scotland the morning after their marriage.

and went to Mrs. McMachal's house in the Randy Rows. There was one bed in the kitchen, two in the room. There was no scullery. She had eight lodgers but she was glad for us. Before she went to Scotland she was a neighbour of Sally's, and she insisted on our staying with her until we got a house of our own. Sally and the landlady slept in the kitchen. Four of the lodgers were on the night-shift, and four on the day. We stayed there for a week.

The second day after arriving I got work in the Holmes Mines. The following week we got a furnished room at the station. There was much better accommodation at the station houses. There was a scullery and little outhouses for each house. In the Randy Rows there was no scullery; everyone had to wash in the kitchen. The oil workers were so dirty coming from their work that they had to take off their shirts while washing. There was no 'wee house', but one small yard in he centre of the Rows had to serve. This yard was for about twenty houses, every house packed with lodgers. There was a centre wall, one side for the women, the other for the men. It took you some time to know which was which, as there were no notices. There was a long stick for you to perch on and a big gullet underneath.

The first Saturday that I got my pay I went up to Pumperston Co-operative Store, a branch of West Calder Store, and asked to become a member. I was told the fee was five pounds, but I was taken in on the instalment plan by paying down one pound. It was as much as I could afford. We did all our dealings in the store. Some people did not deal in the store: they said the goods were too dear, and before the first quarter ended I was sorry for joining. However, when the quarter was ended we had over one pound dividend coming to us. Sally watched the book carefully and began to compare prices with others. She could not find a single instance of where she paid a halfpenny more in the store than what other women paid in other shops. If you bought butter you got margarine in other stores; it was down as Danish butter. If you bought butter in the Co-op. you got butter, and so on. Everything of the best was kept in the store. We soon learned that the people who were members of the store had money saved and were saving it. Take Mrs. Mullins of Neddrie. Her man was idle for fourteen weeks during the Broxburn strike, but if he was idle for twice that time she would have needed no help from outsiders. In any case, we stuck to the store and in a short time we rented a house and furnished it. We got the furniture in a second-hand shop in Edinburgh. We got the bed clothes in the Co-operative Store. Sally has some of the remains yet.

When we got the house fixed up we took in lodgers. They paid Sally twelve shillings per week. She had not the bother of stringing the half-pounds of beef, or pinning the steak, nor had the lodgers to put flies in the sugar, or hairs on the butter. She bought everything in the store. The store paid a dividend of three shillings in the pound on all goods purchased. The second quarter, our five-pound share was paid up by our dividend. The next quarter, Sally left the dividend on deposit and added a few other pounds she had saved to it. This happened every quarter. The Co-operative Store paid five per cent interest on deposits.

Our house was what was known in Scotland as a butt and ben. When you entered the hallway, the butt was to the left and the ben to the right. The same applied when you went upstairs. We were upstairs. We were in the butt, and there was a middle-aged couple in the ben. They did not agree. God save us, the language they used to each other was awful.

The first St. Patrick's night we were in the house, everyone from home came to see us, and the singing and dancing started, just the same as if we were back home in Cleendra. Johny Morroughou lilted, and my Uncle Jimmy danced a hornpipe, although he was sixty-eight years of age then. There were no girls in the house and Sally was the only woman. We all enjoyed ourselves, and Sally and I thought it was a great night.

The following evening when I came in from my work, the landlord was standing at the foot of the stairs, and he handed me a notice to leave the house within seven days.

'Mon,' he said, 'ye deceived me, I thought ye were a respectable mon, until Mr. – toul' me a while ago about the bad house ye were keeping.'

When I recovered from the shock, he was gone. The Mr. – whom he mentioned, was the man who lived next door. When I got upstairs and showed the notice to Sally she was terribly annoyed. The lodgers were as sorry as ourselves. Next day when I came home from my work, Sally was at the door waiting for me. She was smiling, and as I came towards her, she said: 'Paddy I have good news for you. I was in the Uphall village today, and I got a fine house on the ground floor for a shilling a week less than what we are paying here. It is not a butt and ben. The door is private. I know your walk will be a little longer, but, thank God, we will not be listening to the bad talk any longer.' I was glad, and so were the lodgers.

That night we decided to go into the new house as soon as possible, but then the question of flitting was a thorny one. We had so little furniture and all of it was second-

Paddy and Sally in Scotland.

hand. We knew our sticks would be on the cart that there would be plenty of gossip about our wretched furniture. We, therefore decided that our flitting should be a moon-light one. There was a carter at the Station Rows, I do not remember his name. He agreed to flit us at night for five shillings extra. He came to the foot of the stairs at twelve o'clock that night, and all the lodgers who were not on the night-shift gave willing hands to carry our bits of things down the stairs and put them on the cart. Little as we had, we were not able to take them all on the cart. All of us had to take as much as we could carry. Sally carried a few holy pictures. We met two men on the road, as they passed us one said to the other, 'Damn them gypsies, ye ne'er ken when ye'll meet them. None of us spoke for some time, as we thought they might be under the influence of drink. After a while my Uncle Jimmy said, 'If I was as young as I used to be, I would not let the likes o' them call us gipsies. I think we are more like the poor people that were put out on the roadside during the Gweedore evictions.'

When we got all the things into the new house we were very tired. We did not put up any beds, just spread the clothes on the floor, made one big shakedown, and all of us, including Sally, slept in our clothes that morning.

The following St. Patrick's Night, all the Cleendra boys who were in Uphall were with us. We had singing, but no dancing, and we never heard any complaints. We re-mained in that house while Sally and I were in Scotland.

I had a place in Portnuck Pit. I had four boys working for me and I was earning a good wage. Sally went to the Co-operative Store every Monday morning and lodged on deposit nearly every penny I gave her on the Saturday. She had six lodgers and they kept the house going. Although we had to be up each morning at 5 a.m. to be at our work at 6 a.m. we were very happy and had the best of fun. The lodgers were very good and used to help Sally with the housework. One day when I came in from the pit, Sally was at the door as usual waiting for me, and as soon as I looked at her, her eyes filled up and I asked, 'Sally, what is wrong with you?' She put her hand into her breast and pulled out two letters, and reached them to me. God, but she gave me a fright. I was sure some one was dead at home. I began to read the first as soon as I reached the kitchen, before I took off my lamp and cap.

Dungloe,
4th September 1898.

Dear Sally,

Heavens, but I was delighted when I got your letter, but I would like to see Paddy now. I went to the Chapel and prayed for you, and I say the rosary every night and offer up a prayer for you both. Mother wants you to come home Sally, do come, don't refuse your mother. Paddy should come too the poor fellow is killed working. My father will give him some of the land. Sure they say you have plenty of money. Come both of you home in God's name.

We are all well at home. The crop is very good this year, thank God.

Kindest regards, from sister Madgie.

The next letter was.

Dungloe,
4<sup>th</sup> Sept., 1898.

My dear Paddy,

I heard the good news, now you both must come
home, you know you never intended to live long in
Scotland, your child must be Irish not Scotch. We
will all be waiting. I am going out to Cleendra to-
night with the good news. I think I see your father
singing and dancing. Heaven ! but they will be glad.

I have no time to tell you any news, it is mail time.
Come home and don't disappoint us.

Sincerely yours, Madgie.


When I read the letters, I said, 'Sally, what are you crying for?' She said, 'Well, Paddy, sure we are very happy
here, and perhaps if we go home we will not be so happy.
Sure we are saving money every week, and if we go home,
we may have to spend it.' Then the lodgers began to come
in, and when we were at our dinner, you would think there
never was a tear in Sally's eyes, she was as jolly as ever.
But that night neither Sally nor I slept much, Madgie's
letter kept us awake.

Next day in the pit, I could not help talking to myself,
and every time I talked, this is what I said, 'Your child
must be Irish.' It was Saturday, after I got washed and
the lodgers and I had our dinner, I said, 'Come boys, we
will go out and have a drink.' As we were passing out,
Sally said, 'I hope you will not be long.' We went over to

Terrice's. I ordered a gallon of beer. During all the time I was afraid the boys would hear me saying, 'Your child must be Irish.' When the gallon was drunk. Johnie Murchu hit the table with the measure. When old Terrice came in, Johnie said, 'The same again,' flinging down his two shilling piece. I said, 'Boys, excuse me for a wee while.' Out I went for home.

When I went into the house Sally said, 'Paddy, you are back early, are the boys not coming with you?' 'No, Sally,' I said, 'You must go home, your child must be Irish.' 'Well Paddy, whatever you say,' said she, 'but won't it be a pity of the poor boys, that are working for you, do you think they would be able to get work with any other man?' I said, 'Oh Sally, I'll not go, I'll wait a wee while longer'; you go home and when you are better, look out for a wee farm; I'll be still earning good money and then when I go home, I'll never come back again.' Sally put her head down in her lap, and I am sure it was ten minutes before she lifted it. She was crying when she looked up at me, and said, 'I'll not go if you don't come.'

Well for the next few days, when we were by ourselves, we were crying. When the lodgers were in, you would think neither of us ever shed a tear. Anyhow, Sally in the end agreed to go home, and leave me behind. Patrick Mulhern, a neighbour of ours at home, was going home in a few days and it was arranged that Sally would travel with him. When I told the lodgers damn but every one of them was as sorry as myself.

The night before she left, the house was packed, everyone was jolly, but Sally and me, the boys saying 'It's good for you going home, I wish to God we were all going.' I did not go to work the following day. I saw Sally and Mulhern off at the station. I sold out the bits of sticks, beds and delph we had. Sally took all the clothes home with her. The lodgers and I separated here and there. I went to lodge with Dan Bonar.

Shortly after Sally left for home there was a fire in Portnuck Pit. We all escaped. My workers and I had the narrowest escape, as we were working in the high workings and did not hear the explosion. The first thing we found was the after damp. We made for the bottom as quickly as we could. When we reached the bottom we were nearly finished, but we were just in time for the last going up on the cage to see us. The cage-man came back and took us up. Some of us were ill for a few days. The pit was closed down and flooded to put out the fire. It belonged to Young's Company, the same company that owned Glendevin, the first mine that I went down. After a week or so we all got work in Glendevin on a night-shift. The places were hard and I could not make much of a wage. I left and went to Tarbrax, worked there for a while, could save no money, went with the boys to the pubs and football matches. Sally wrote to me every week to come home.

One day when I came in from the mine, there was a letter for me. I opened it. It read:-

Dungloe.

My dear Paddy,

Thanks be to God, Sally is better, she has a lovely child, born last night. Your mother and father are just after landing, they are delighted. The child is going to be christened this evening, and is to be called Annie for your mother. (My mother was called Nancy, Annie is the English for Nancy).

Lord ! Paddy, I wish you were with us tonight, we will have the best of fun on your father, they are getting jolly already. Now Paddy, surely you will come home, sure your child is Irish, God bless her. Come home.

Sincerely yours, Madgie.

A few days afterwards I had a letter from Sally, while reading it, damn but I was as bad as Sally, we both thought nobody had a child but ourselves. She finished up with: 'She is called for your mother, surely you will come home now.'

The following week I decided to go home. All the boys from home gathered into the lodging house in Tarbrax, the night before I left. I was sorry to part with them.

When I reached Dungloe, they were expecting me. My father and mother were in. Sally was at the door with the child in her arms. Damn but I do not think there was a happier man in the world than I was then. God bless my heart, if you saw Madgie, she was crying with joy. Oh ! such a night.

# CHAPTER SIX

## *The Cope Begins*

I was not long at home when one of the Cleendra farms was for sale. We sent to the Pumperstown Co-op. for some of our money and bought the farm. It was very small; part of it was in the Glen near the 'wee people's' home. The house was very small – twelve feet by thirteen. Sally did not like it; she would not let me build a room to it, she thought it was in a lonely place. The same year there was a bigger farm for sale with a big house on it, a fine big kitchen, a good sized room and a byre. We bought it and went to live in it. It was Micky Neddy's farm; his sister, Mary, sold it to us.

I'll never forget the first night we went there. All the Cleendra folk gathered in. All the women had a hen or two for Sally. My father bought us a nice cow, and my aunt, Saldy, brought us a sheep and lamb for wee Annie. (Annie was born before I came home). My mother brought us two holy pictures. The last to arrive was Sally's father, mother and her sister, Madgie. They had a fine young cow with them. I sent two of the boys for a wee jar of poteen. I can tell you we had a night of it, singing, lilting, dancing, and story-telling until daylight.

I was able to read some leaflets on tillage, which were

issued by the Department of Agriculture in Dublin. John Charlie and I discussed the leaflets. John was a scholar, as he was in the fifth book and he could pronounce all the big words. We decided that we should work our farms under modern conditions, and so we bought a plough in Glenties between us. It was the first plough that ever was in the district, and we were agreeably surprised at the amount of ploughing we could do among the rocks.

I was not long home when one Sunday the priest announced that our member, Mr. H.A. Law, would address the people after Mass. Nearly everyone in the congregation attended the meeting. After dealing with the political situation, he said that he wished to congratulate the people of the Rosses on their strong, active branch of the United Irish League. I was rather surprised at this statement as I had made several enquiries since I came home if there was a branch in the district. While I was in Scotland, I was a member of the United Irish League wherever I worked. I asked Mr. Law where was the active branch of the League. The chairman shouted at me, 'Order, order'. I said that I was only looking for information. Mr. Law then spoke to some of the men on the platform. I think he must have satisfied himself that he had wrong information. In any case, he said that he would like the man who asked the question to meet him in the hotel after the meeting.

When the speeches were finished a number of men urged me to go in and speak to the member when he had asked me. Big Johnny Brown said, 'You must go in and speak to the gentleman.' I went in. He was waiting in the door. We went into a room. Mr. Law said, 'I was surprised to hear you say that there was no branch of the United Irish League in the parish.' I assured him that as far as I knew there was not. Then he asked me many other questions, and, although the maid called for him several times saying his lunch would be cold, he did not seem to be in any hurry to get away from me. He took down my name and address.

When I came out from the hotel I was surrounded by a great number of people, everyone asking me what did the member say to me. Brown said, 'Come, Paddy, your father is over in Maurice's waiting on you. The horses are long enough fasting.' I was glad to follow Brown into Maurice's. My father and John were in the kitchen. When I went in my father questioned me to death about what the member wanted with me. We had a few half-ones before we took the horses out of the stables, and when we had gone a bit out of the town, I got on behind my father and John got up behind Brown. My father would not let me by the house until I told him the secrets the member confided to me, were we going to get Home Rule, or was the member going to do anything for Cleendra. We went into the house. Well, well, if you heard my father telling my mother about my having been speaking to the member. I did not stay for dinner as I knew Sally would be waiting. When I told her about my interview with Law, and the maid coming often to the room telling him his lunch was ready, she said, 'Paddy, I do not wonder. I suppose you are the first countryman that ever spoke to a Member of Parliament. God knows, if I had known, I would have killed a hen for your dinner.'

Not long after this there was another meeting in Dungloe after Mass. The priest had told us that there was a gentleman from Dublin who was going to start a bank. Everyone waited to hear what he had to say.

We saw a man getting up on the rising ground. He looked a strange kind of a man, with a great big beard and a very pleasant face. There was something about him that immediately you saw him you were interested. His name was George Russell (AE). He got up on the rising ground and commenced talking to the people and telling the farmers the benefit they would gain by having a Co-operative Agricultural Bank. If they decided to start one the Congested Districts Board would give them fifty pounds to begin with. He appealed to the audience to subscribe. He said the more they subscribed the more the Congested Board would give. The Parish Priest said he would give five pounds, and three or four merchants said they would give five pounds each. I said I would give five pounds. Mr. Russell said that, considering the wretched district we had, and the amount of poverty that existed, he was quite satisfied that there was as much support as could be expected, and that he would recommend the Irish Agricultural Organisation to get the Bank registered. He said that it was necessary to appoint a committee and a secretary. All the merchants appointed themselves on the Committee, the one proposing the other. Russell asked one of the merchants how many farmers were on the Committee. Someone said there were none. He said, 'You will need to appoint a Secretary.' The Dungloe teacher was appointed. He asked him to take down the names of the Committee and the names of all who had promised to pay five pounds. The Secretary did so. Russell then asked him to read out the names of the Committee and the names of the subscribers, which he did. Mr. Russell looked over the list, and noticed my name down as a subscriber, but not on the Committee. He said something to the Secretary which I did not hear. The Secretary spoke to one of the merchants. He proposed me on the Committee. There was no amendment and I became a member of the Committee.

We got the Agricultural Bank started. The Department of Agriculture used to send leaflets on agriculture to the Secretary. He would pass them on to me, and John and I would study them most carefully. We were reading up about artificial manures, and we decided that we would get the kind of manures which the Department recommended. We ordered such manures from the manure merchants. They refused to get them for us; we had to take what they stocked or leave it. It was about this time that the Secretary of the Bank got a letter from the Irish Agricultural Wholesale Society, Dublin, asking him to advise the Committee not to place their orders for manures until they would write to him again. The Secretary read the letter at the Committee meeting. I met him a few days before the next meeting and I asked him had he any further word about the manures. He said that he had some letters that day but had not time to read them yet. 'Come into the house, Paddy, until I see them,' he said. He turned up a price list for manures from the Irish Agricultural Wholesale Society. I asked him for it and he gave it to me. I took it home. John Charlie and I studied it most carefully, and needless to say we were dumbfounded at the difference in the price and what we were paying. I held tight to the price list. At the following meeting I proposed that we get the manures for the farmers through the Bank. The fat was in the fire immediately. I was told this would interfere with legitimate trade, and that that was not the purpose for which the Bank was started and would be against the rules. The rule book was studied carefully. The Secretary

"AE" (George Russell) in Dungloe, 1903.

examined the rules, and whispered to me to drop the question. I whispered back, 'To hell with the rules, we must get the manures.' I could not get a seconder; I was knocked out in the first round.

In Cleendra, the same as in the other townlands, most of the kitchens were big, eighteen to twenty feet long by fourteen feet wide. All the neighbours gathered into one of the houses each night for an airneal, old men and women, young boys and girls. After the youngsters would have some dancing, story-telling would commence, and Peggy Manus would sing a few songs every night. Her favourite – the only English song she had – was:

*If I was a blackbird and had wings to fly,*
*It is in my love's arms this night I would lie,*
*It is with my two black wings my love I would*
*surround.*

I forget the rest of it.

The night after the meeting of the Bank, the airneal was in my father's house. When we were all in, Mary Neil and Johnny began to lilt *Maggie Pickie*. I said 'Stop that lilting. I have something more important for you than dancing tonight.' (After spending so long in Scotland I was looked on by the Cleendra people as a man who knew much more than some of themselves). I then told them about the Agricultural Bank meeting, pulled the price list out of my pocket and showed them the difference in prices. There was not a murmur while I was speaking. There were some wonderful expressions after I finished. We decided then and there that, by hook or by crook, we would have to get the manures. We decided to meet in my wee house in the Glen the following night. Every man was to give his order for whatever artificial manures he would require for the season, and bring sufficient cash with him to pay according to the price list which I had, which set down seven shillings and fivepence for two hundred weights instead of twelve shillings and sixpence, which the merchants were charging. They all gathered in the wee house the following night, and quite a number from other districts. They gave me the money and the following day I came into the town, got a money order in the Post Office and sent it along with the order to the Irish Agricultural Wholesale Society in Dublin. To my surprise, in a week afterwards the money was returned (we had only one postal delivery each week in Cleendra), with a letter, stating that they regretted they could not supply individuals, that they supplied societies only. I then wrote to the Ulster Manure Company. I did not send them the money order, only told them to send me the bill and that I would pay. They wrote back asking me to call on one of their agents, one of the Dungloe merchants, who would supply me. You may guess I was then in a hell of a fix. There was a whisper in Dungloe that Paddy Pat Bawn tricked the people; he collected their money and he would be off to Scotland with it, that he knew damn well that he could not get manures for them; that manures could only be supplied by legitimate traders.

The story spread like hell. Sally's sister, Madgie, heard it, and immediately she did she put on her shawl and came out to Cleendra. I was working below the house. She ran across the field to me. She was a great favourite of mine and I was glad to see her coming. I stuck the spade in the ground and went to meet her. As I reached her my hand, the tears began to roll down her cheeks. I said, 'Good heavens, Madgie, what is wrong?'

She wiped away the tears and said, 'Do you know, Paddy, the town ones are saying that you are going to Scotland with the poor people's money, and I think they are trying to put the peelers after you. Kilmartin told me that he heard the ould Head say that he would soon have a good case. I heard Pat Bawn's name mentioned, and I am sure it was you they were talking about.'

We both went to the house. Madgie met our wee Annie at the door. She lifted her in her arms and forgot all about me for the time. Sally put on the pandy and had the tea ready very quickly. As we sat at the table, I told Madgie's story.

'Go, Paddy, and get your friends, the Wrights,' said Sally, 'and wreck the bloody town.'

My, but I felt proud of her.

'Oh,' said Madgie, 'for heaven's sake do nothing of the kind. It is we who will suffer, who have to live amongst them.'

I decided to go to the town with Madgie and get the money from the Post Office for the money order and give it back to the farmers. Off we went to the town, a distance of four miles. I went into the office. Madgie stood outside the door until I came out with the money. I wanted to go back as quickly as I could to Cleendra, but Madgie would not let me until I went over to the house and had a stawl of tea. The house was right beside the Barracks. One of the police was on sentry duty at the door. As Madgie and I approached, he went into the Barracks, and while you look round you every policeman was out. There were nineteen of them in Dungloe Barracks (there are only seven guards now), acting sergeant one stripe, another with two stripes and a sergeant with three stripes, and old Head with some braid strings across his chest. 'Heavens,' said Madgie, 'they are going to arrest you. What tempted me to go out for you? Paddy, you will never forgive me.' We walked by them. No one said a word to us.

When we went into the house, Madgie put on the kettle to make a stawl of tea. They did not use the pandy in the town, as it was not swanky enough for the town people. With all that, no man or woman ever got a bowl of tea as good as what came out of the pandy. If you doubt me, just try it. Put a pandy of water on a good fire; when it comes to the boil throw sufficient tea into it, and just leave it about one minute alongside the fire. I tell you you will have tea. I said, 'Madgie, take off the kettle, and put on the pandy as I am in a hurry to get home to give back the money.' Madgie took off the kettle and put some fresh water in the pandy. Her father came in and told us that it was the talk of the town that I had cashed the order. When the tea was ready I had a fine slug of it with baked flour, bread and butter. Off I went for Cleendra, past the police, but no one said anything. When I went to the corner to turn out home I decided to go into Brennan's. As I turned into the shop, I saw the Head and one of the two-stripes men coming after me. I asked for a glass of whiskey. Anna was in the bar and poured it out for me, she never stinted the measure. She asked me about Sally and wee Annie and nearly everyone in Cleendra. 'Paddy,' she said, 'are you not well? Is there anything wrong?' As I was going out on the door, she said, 'What hurry is on you? Wait a minute.' She reached me another glass. When I had half of it drank, I remembered that I read in the Irish *Homestead* that there was an Agricultural Co-operative Creamery in Donegal

Town. I finished the drink and went back to Madgie. As I was going down the street the town people began to come to their doors. I heard one say, 'He's drunk'; another said, 'He is going to give himself up.' When I went to the house, although I was not half an hour away, Madgie was as glad for me as if I came from another world. Madgie was a great girl. If I was a writer I would write a book about her. I told Madgie I was going to Donegal in the morning; that I was sure I would get the manures there. When night came we said the Rosary and Madgie continued praying for a long time after the Rosary was said. I am sure she was praying for me.

That night the airneal was in Tully's, Sally and wee Annie were there. The story reached Cleendra that I tricked them. Sally told John Charlie that I went into the town to get the money back for the people. He told the others and everyone was sorry that I failed to get the manures.

I got up early next morning, went round the back of the Barracks to get behind the houses to meet the mailcar going to Fintown. I did not want the Dungloe people to see me. Madgie was at the door. I turned round to shake her another goodbye, and to my surprise I saw two policemen standing behind the turf stack watching me. They stooped their heads. I walked along the ditch to wait the mailcar. While I was waiting I could see Smith, the acting, peeping round the corner of the Corner House, watching me. Madgie saw the Head going to the officer's private house. After threequarters of an hour he came back to the Barracks. Madgie never left the door. She saw the one-striped policeman and Constable Roberts leaving the Barracks, marching down the street with their helmets on their heads, batons and bayonets hanging by their sides. When they passed Brennan's they turned out the Cleendra road. Madgie went into the house. I heard her mother say that she threw herself on the bed and cried like a child. Her sister, Hannah, a little kid, came in. She said that as she was passing Kilmartin, the policeman told her to tell Madgie to follow him down the Meenmore road, that he had something to tell her. Madgie got up from the bed, wiped away the tears, put her shawl over her head and went out by the back door. She went down the Meenmore Road and when out of sight of the Barracks overtook Kilmartin.

'Madgie,' he said, 'I am sorry that your sister's husband is in trouble. That bloody Head will have him if he can before he gets away to Scotland. He took Smith into the office a while ago. I happened to be in my own quarters at the time. There is only a wooden partition between us, and I heard him tell Smith to take Roberts with him, go out to Cleendra, get some of the men whom Paddy got their money from to come into town and swear an information before Sammie Hanlon, and that Hanlon would then issue a warrant for his arrest; that Mr. Krueger, the JP., would only be too glad to sign it. He said that if he had his own way he would have Paddy arrested before he would reach Fintown, but that the old fool, the officer, went to his law books to see what section of an Act he would get him lifted under, and that the damn old fool could not get the necessary section. He said, "Now, Smith, if we can get this rascal six months by our action, you will be made a sergeant and likely I will be promoted to officer. If I do, I will see that His Majesty the King's law will be carried out without fear or favour. When you come within a quarter of a mile of Cleendra, slow down your steps, so as to give them plenty of time to clear away to the hill with their dogs. None of them has taken out a dog licence this year, or, as far as our books show, ever did. Then go into the first house you meet, by very friendly to them, and do not, for your life, ask any of them to swear any information before Mr. Hanlon, but tell them in every house that you go into that you saw that Paddy fellow going away on the mailcar this morning and that everyone is saying that he is away to Scotland. You are sure to come across some of the beggars who will squeal for their money. Then it is for you to act. Just tell them that to get their money back all they have to do is to go into town and tell Mr. Hanlon – they might not want to be seen walking with you but you can tell them that you will be in after them. Here is a halfcrown. Give it to the first man who comes to the town. Tell him to have a good drink for himself in Bonner's publichouse. Just say that you heard there was bad stuff in Brennan's, you know how that Anna one would be snooking for news, and if she thought anyone was going to do that Paddy fellow harm, she would fill them up and send them home again. On the peril of your life, do not tell that idiot Roberts what you are after. Do not let him into any of the houses. Tell him that you are searching for dogs, and if he finds any dog running out of the house to make sure and get a hold of him. Now, begone, and I will see that your promotion will be a quick one.'

'Now, Madgie, you go back home,' said Kilmartin. 'I will go round the Cruickamore Road; if I was seen talking to you it would be transfer, or dismissal immediately. If I hear anything else that I think you should know, I will put a long turf on the yard wall in front of your door, and when you lift it off I will go down the same road, and you can follow.'

Off Smith and Roberts went to Cleendra. Peggy Manus saw them coming. She gave the signal immediately, and in five minutes there was not a dog in Cleendra but was away to the hill. The signal was the same as was used during the Penal Laws when there was a price of five pounds on the head of every priest. During all that time there was Mass celebrated in Cleendra in a place called 'Ard-an-Affreann' (Height of the Mass). The people would not know what day Mass would be said until two hours before the time, for fear the priest-hunters would be near. There was and is a large white marble stone on the brae face, which can be seen for miles round. When the priest would arrive the Cleendra people would cover it with a black cloth and the people of Upper and Lower Templecrone would rush to Mass. Those who had far to come, came on horseback, with their wives sitting sideways behind them and a youngster in front. The islanders from Arranmore, Rutland, Innisfree, and Innishall came out in their boats, and it is said that at each Mass the side of the hill was covered with people. Whenever Peggy saw the police coming she covered the same stone with her black shawl. It was always successful.

The first house that Smith came to was my Uncle Tully's. When he came to the door, my uncle's wife, Maggie, was in and all the children, and some of the neighbours' children too. He took the bolt off the wee door and went right up to the fire, sat on the chair, and said, 'Isn't this a nice day, ma'am? You have a fine townland here. Do you know, I think this is the nicest Glen I have ever seen. There is no Glen in the south as nice as this. And haven't you a fine lot of children. God bless them.' Then pulling a fistful of halfpennies out of his pocket, he gave them one each.

'Go, now, children, and play yourselves,' he said, 'I

want to speak to your mammy.'

The children ran out immediately.

'Policeman,' said Maggie, 'you need not be coming here looking for dogs, for the devil a dog is there about the house, or in all Cleendra for that matter. All the dogs in the town died years ago with the disorder.'

Smith replied, 'Please do not speak to me about dogs. If you had twenty dogs I would not life an eye to one of them. Sergeant Murphy and I are great friends, and when I came to Dungloe about three months ago I made up my mind that I would never catch a dog or find a still.'

'Musha, God bless you, policeman,' said Maggie, 'you must be a good man.'

'I am,' said Smith, 'I am always looking after the poor. Do you know, Mrs. Gallagher, I just took a stroll out here today when I heard of the big loss the Cleendra people came to, to sympathize with them.'

'God bless you, what happened? Sure I didn't hear anything,' said Maggie.

'Did you not hear that Paddy Gallagher is away to Scotland today?' he said.

'Musha, the devil a word I heard. Poor fellow, and he has to go to Scotland for the manures. I knew he would get them somewhere. Good luck to him.'

Then Smith said that he heard in the town that he lifted the money in the Post Office the previous night, put it in his pocket and went on the mailcar that day.

'Poor fellow,' said Maggie, 'I hope he will soon be back with the manures. If they are not in time for the setting of the praties I am afraid he will have trouble. The people will begin to give up hopes, and the Wrights are so stubborn that if they don't get theirs, they will be angry.'

'Where is Wright's house? asked Smith. 'Just at the crossroads, the big long white –' and Maggie stopped speaking when she said 'white'. She was going to say 'white house' when she thought of herself. 'Wait a minute and I will get Jimmie to go up with you,' she said.

Maggie went out and in her hurry bumped up against Roberts who was standing at the gable. She ran over to the top of the Glen, called Mary and told her to run up the Glen quickly and tell Wright that the police were going up, and to send word to the boys on the hill not to come back with the dogs until Peggy Manus would lift the black shawl off the stone. She walked back slowly with Jimmie and told him to take the police up to Wright's house and make sure that he took them the long road, and not by the near-cut. When they went to the house, she said, 'Now, policemen, wee Jimmie will take you up to Wright's' and off they went. Roberts stood outside. Wright was putting a patch on the sole of his boot when in stepped Smith into the kitchen.

'Good day, Mr. Wright, and God bless all here,' said he. Wright looked at him and did not answer for some time. Then he turned round and said, 'Sit down. Children, go out and play yourselves.'

'Wait,' said Smith, 'God bless them, aren't they the fine children!' – reaching everyone of them a halfpenny.

'They are not mine,' said Wright, 'they are Peggy Ned's children. My boys are fine big boys, the best men in the parish. Have you any news from the town?'

'Not much,' said Smith, 'only what you all have, that Paddy Gallagher went to the Post Office last night, got the money order changed, stuck the notes in his pocket and went away on the mailcar to Scotland.'

'Did he?' said Wright.

'He did indeed,' replied Smith, 'I saw him with my own two eyes going on the mailcar.'

'Begob,' said Wright, 'if he is not back soon with the manures I will pull the neck out of him. What the hell capers is he at?'

'I am afraid he has tricked you, and the sooner you act, the better,' Smith replied. 'If you go into the town and make a wee statement in presence of Mr. Hanlon, you will have your money tomorrow, and we will allow you a good day's wages.'

'What would you be wanting with me in the town?' asked Wright.

'Oh, just to protect you and the other poor farmers and to see that you will not lose your money.'

Wright wound the hammer over his shoulder and hit the sprig such a clout that he put the head of the hammer through the sole. Smith was smiling from ear to ear – he could easily do that as he had a very big mouth. Wright threw the boot and hammer under the table and jumped to his feet with one boot on. He faced Smith and said, 'Do you mean to say that Paddy Pat Bawn is a thief and that he has stolen our money?'

'That is it,' said Smith.

'By my soul, you will pay for those words before you leave Cleendra,' replied Wright.

He rushed to the door calling 'Jimmie!'

Jimmie came running up to him and Wright said, 'Run up to the New Park, Jimmie, and tell the boys to hurry down. I want them to kick this dirty peeler out of the town.'

Smith made for the door, and Wright tried to shut it, but Smith was too smart for him. He shouted to Roberts,

'Come on quick. I promised to be back before now. We will have to run like hell or we will be dismissed.' Off they went and were halfway to Dungloe before the Wright boys got to the house.

Madgie was at the door and saw Smith and Roberts coming down the town. They had nobody with them, passed Sammie Hanlon's (clerk of the Petty Sessions) and went right into the Barracks. Madgie went right into the house and said, 'Mother, I am sure God has heard our prayers. None of the Cleendra people came in.' She went back to the door, and it was not long until she saw Kilmartin putting the turf on the barrack-yard wall. She lifted it off immediately and in a short time followed Kilmartin down the road. As soon as she was out of sight of the Barracks, she ran to Kilmartin and asked him what news he had. 'Oh, Madgie,' he said, 'I have the best. The Head is going mad through the office. When I saw Smith coming up the street I left the day-room and went to my own quarters. Smith went to the office and the Head asked him had he succeeded.

'"No, sir," said Smith, "I travelled every house in Cleendra and spent almost ten shillings of my own on the children. They were all very nice to me, but no matter what I said or did, I could not get one of them to come in to have a talk with Mr. Hanlon. I think if he took twice as much from them they would not complain." The Head said, "Go down and tell Murphy I want him." Smith went down to the day-room and up came Murphy. By God, Madgie, I wish you heard Murphy and the Head. It was the best bit of fun I had since I left Mayo. The Head, who hated the sight of Murphy, was so damn nice to him, that you would think he was his superior officer. I wish I could remember it all, but here's what I do remember. The Head said, "Well, Sergeant, the officer is much annoyed with me when I have not arrested that Cleendra Paddy fellow, who went away this morning with the poor men's money. I was reading up some of Her Majesty's Acts, and I did not come across the right one to act upon. Of course, I got promotion by hard work when I was a constable, and again a sergeant, as you are now. I had more cases before the Court than a dozen men and I never had any time to read through the Acts. You got your stripes easy. I never knew of you having a case, only one for simple drunkenness. Of course, you read all Her Majesty's laws, and that's how you got your stripes. Now, my good man, I will be ever so grateful if you can refresh your memory and tell me the Act which I can act on to get that fellow arrested. If I can do you a good turn you may depend on me."

I wished I could have seen Murphy then. This is some of what he said: "Sir, I remember reading some of the Acts that cover the very offence that you say Mr. Patrick Gallagher of Cleendra committed, but I am sure Mr. Gallagher has committed no offence. Any countryman whom I have been talking to says that he is amongst the most decent men in the two parishes. I heard Charlie Harley telling me the other day that he worked to Mr. Gallagher in Uphall in Scotland and he was one of the best men to work for."

"'Murphy,'" said the Head, "go and take Constable McCann with you on patrol to Meenatotan. Do not sit on the roadside, go right to the school; it is only five miles from here; and report to me when you come back. That will keep you out of the public-houses."

'Poor Murphy and McCann are getting ready now for

the devil of a walk. Go back now, and if you see the turf out again I will have more news for you.'

Madgie went home and Kilmartin went to the Barracks.

When I reached Donegal town I went straight to the Creamery Manager, told him my difficulty, asked him to order the manures through the Creamery, and that I would give him the money. He was very sympathetic but said, 'I dare not do it. We do nothing here outside the Creamery. The majority of the Committee are merchants, and I would get into trouble with them.'

I said, 'Sure they would not know if you sent the order and cash to the Co-operative Wholesale in Dublin and they sent the manures to Burtonport, and no one would know.' I promised him I would never tell how it was done. He agreed. I gave him a warm handshake when I was leaving. It was about two o'clock.

I went into an eating-house, had a good feed, and then as there was no train going back to Fintown, and a side-car would cost one pound ten, I decided to walk. Off I went. When I got as far as Frosses, I went into a pub and had a good glass of whiskey. I walked on. It got dark on me soon after leaving Frosses. When I arrived in Glenties the pubs were all closed except one. I went in and had another glass there.

My next stop was in Cleendra. The distance was thirty-five miles. I went into the house quietly, hoping that I would not awaken Sally or wee Annie, but Sally was not asleep. She knew I was in Donegal. Madgie sent her word, so she expected me home some time that night. She was glad for me, was up immediately and had a fire on while I was kissing wee Annie. It is easy to kindle a turf fire when raked properly, and Sally could rake a fire. She asked me no question until I drank a fine bowl of hen's soup with plenty of cabbage and oatmeal on it, ate the breast of a real hen and had a fine bowl of tea and a junk of flour bread and butter. I told her how I got on and she was delighted. She did not hear of Smith being out, as she was not at the airneal, which was at the foot of the town in John's house. We agreed, when I collected the money, to get the manures into Burtonport for this reason. Quite a lot of the people who gave an order were in debt and were afraid that if the shopkeepers saw them coming through the town with the manures, that they would immediately process them. The station was north of Dungloe, and Cleendra was south-west, but we could boat the manures from Burtonport and the town shop-keepers would not see us.

The day the manures arrived was a big day. The price was seven shillings and five pence a bag and the shop-keepers charged twelve shillings and sixpence. When I paid the freight at the station, it was twenty-five shillings less than we calculated. I told the men we had twenty-three shillings left and we spent it on tea and bread. We cleared all the manures. It was a bit of a sensation in the whole parish, and in the next parish, the lower Rosses.

A few days after the manures were landed, Sally went with her basket of eggs to the local shop. The boy behind the counter used to say when she would come in, 'Now how are you today, Mrs. Gallagher? How is wee Annie and Mr. Gallagher? I suppose he is killed working: tell him not to work so hard, there will be plenty of work after he is dead. Now, what can I do for you?' This day when she went in, he did not speak.

Sally put her basket of eggs on the counter and said, 'Are you going to take my eggs?'

After some time he lifted the basket and counted the eggs, and said, 'What do you want?'

Sally said, 'Half a pound of tea, quarter a stone of sugar, two pound of soap, pennyworth of thread, pennyworth of blue and the rest in cakes.' He gave her the goods. When she came home she made the tea and called me in for a drop and told me of the boy's attitude. Although he was no relation to the owner, I did not wonder much, as I always considered him a bit of a prig. Sally said, 'I am not going back to that shop, Paddy, should we starve.'

'All right,' said I, 'we'll go somewhere else.'

The airneal that night was in Dinnie's. Before the dancing started I made Sally tell exactly how she was treated and, in telling it, you would think Sally was making a speech. I never heard her speak so well before or since. Then we began to discuss the position. Before we left, we decided to start a Co-operative Society.

I wrote to Dublin to the Irish Agricultural Organisation Society to send an organizer to Cleendra to organize the farmers into a Co-operative Society. In due course I got a letter to say that a Mr. Shaw would arrive in Cleendra on Friday. John Charlie wrote notices that the Dublin organizers would hold a meeting in my kitchen on Friday night to start a Co-operative Society. When the Roshine teacher saw the notice, he wrote a note, and sent one of the scholars up to me with it, to say he would give the school for the meeting. I was delighted, and went immediately to John Charlie and got him to send out new notices. He wrote them, gave them to Moses Micky and he was not long plastering the new notices over the first ones.

Shaw arrived. I met him at the station and told him my story. I also told him how the prig of a shop-boy treated Sally, and that I would like a Society the same as they have in Scotland, where we could get everything we wanted. 'I am sorry,' said Mr. Shaw, 'we cannot organize a Society for that purpose; we can only organize a Society for agricultural purposes.'

'What purpose is that for?' I asked.

'Dealing in seed, manures and agricultural implements, also eggs and butter,' he said.

'Can you deal in spades and shovels?' I said.

'Yes, you can, that comes under agricultural work.'

'All right, Mr. Shaw,' said I, 'that is what we want, we want nothing else.'

That was the first deliberate lie I told in my life.

When we arrived at the school it was packed. We had a fine platform made with the seats, one on top of the other, and some chairs behind them. Mr. Shaw said that it would be necessary to have a chairman. Johnny Brown proposed me, John Gillespie seconded, and I sat in the chair while Mr. Shaw was speaking. I can tell you he was the boy could speak. He explained the benefit of joining together for the purpose of buying our agricultural requirements, that he need not tell them about manures as we had already seen the great advantage, 'thanks to Mr. Gallagher and Mr. O'Donnell'. 'Now,' he said, 'it is up to you all to become members. The share is one pound each, but you can join by paying two shillings and sixpence and the remainder when called upon.'

John Gillespie, who had spent a good while in Scotland, got up and asked, 'Can we buy our meal, flour, tea, and sugar?' If I was near Gillespie I would have shaken his hand.

'Oh, no,' said Mr. Shaw, 'that is against the rules.' I thought every face in the school looked longer than usual, with the exception of that prig of a shop-boy who stood at the door. He was all smiles.

Then Mr. Shaw said to me that if we were going to start an Agricultural Society, it would be necessary to appoint a secretary. I proposed John Charlie, and Johnny Brown seconded him. We did not ask for an amendment to anything that was proposed.

Then Mr. Shaw said, 'All now who wish to become members, come forward and give in your names to Mr. O'Donnell.'

I said, 'Put down my name.' To my painful surprise, the people began to walk out. Johnny Brown was the next to give his name, John Gillespie next, and so on until we got fourteen names and an equal number of half-crowns. The prig was still at the door with his neck stretched like a gander. He took down the members' names and early next morning all the town shopkeepers knew them.

When the meeting was over Mr. Shaw was very much disappointed. He said to John and I, 'It is no good. You could not start a Society here. You have not any members to talk of. You would at least require two hundred. You have no capital. Look at the wretched poor country you have here, nothing but rocks and bogs.'

We were very much disappointed. I took Mr. Shaw up to our house (John and I had previously arranged to do this), and Sally had a nice supper ready for us, a good plate of broth for each (bowls would not be nice for a Dublin gentleman), and a fine roast duck and potatoes. She had the kettle on the boil, got a nice teapot which she brought with her from Scotland, and gave us a cup of tea each. The cups were sitting on saucers. The tea looked muddy and tasted so. 'Sally,' I said, 'there is something wrong with the tea.'

She looked at me and said, 'I do not know what has happened.' I whispered to her that it was the kettle; and to make a drop in the pandy. Sally lifted the cup and threw the tea out of the door, put on a new pandy of water and had three more cupfuls for us in a few minutes. There was no improvement in the tea. 'The devil take him,' said Sally, 'sure I might have looked at that half-pound that he gave me. If anything bad was in the shop he would have given it to me. Thank God you did not taste it, for it may be full of poison. Get a bucket of water, Paddy; wash the doorstep for fear Jack (the dog) would lick it. Thank God I have a grain of good tea in the house.' I washed all the leaves from the door and Sally had three nice cups of tea on the table when I came in.

We enjoyed that tea. Mr. Shaw said it was the best he ever drank. Sally got hold of the remains of the half-pound and threw it on the fire. It blazed up and Sally said, 'It's a good job I didn't poison you. Look at the blaze. It is full of something bad.'

When going to meet Mr. Shaw at the station, I had gone into Brennan's, had a quick one, told Anna to give me a bottle of the best in the house, and so she did.

Before we started on the broth, I filled a big glass and gave it to Mr. Shaw, and another for myself. John never took any drink. Mr. Shaw said, 'That's very good whiskey, Mr. Gallagher.'

When we stopped eating, I filled out two more glasses and we drank them. I said to Mr. Shaw, 'When you go back to Dublin you will register our Society. Don't say no, you must register it.'

'I am afraid I cannot, Mr. Gallagher,' he said.

We finished our glasses. Again I spoke. 'You are promising me now in the presence of John and Sally that you will register our Society.'

'Damn me but I will, even if I lose my job. I cannot refuse that request,' said Mr. Shaw. Heavens, the smile that came on Sally's and John's faces! 'What name will you call it?' asked Mr. Shaw.

Sally suggested, 'Cleendra Society.'

John said, 'Cleendra and Roshine.'

'Cleendra, Roshine and Falmore,' I urged as Falmore was where my mother was born. We could not agree.

'Paddy,' said Sally, 'isn't it a pity we had not your father and Johnny Brown here?'

I got up, went right across to Cuinlleen's, and told John, who was in, 'Run, John, immediately, to my father's and Johnny Brown's, ask them to come to our house as quickly as they can, tell them the Dublin man wants to see them, that he has some fine stories about Finn McCool and Oisin they never heard.' (Another wee lie).

John had his boots off, he did not put them on but went off immediately. He was not long until he was back, and soon after him in stepped my father and Johnny Brown. Oh but Sally was glad; she was very fond of my father.

I filled out each of them a glass of whiskey and told them that the Society was started, all that was wanted was the name now. I told them of the names already mentioned. Both said, 'Damn the name or names: you want only Cleendra'. I said that Doney Tully and James Liam beyond Dungloe, John O'Donnell and Tom Glackin of Tubberkeen, my uncle Jimmie of Falmore, Johnny Given and the others of Roshine, bought manures, and that most of them became members, and we must get a name that will please all.

'Well, Paddy,' said my father, 'we will call it "Templecrone"; that is the name of the parish, and no one can grumble.'

'Damn but you are right,' said Johnny Brown.

That settled it. John gave Mr. Shaw the registration fee out of the money he collected. Then I gave my father and Johnny Brown a glass each out of the bottle. There was only a small drop left, which I gave to Mr. Shaw. He would not touch it unless there was an even divide for me. I agreed, although it was not worth dividing.

My father said, addressing Mr. Shaw, 'Now, sir, tell us some good stories. I heard you have ones that we never heard in Donegal. I'll tell you some of mine that you never heard after that.'

Mr. Shaw said that he never told a story in his life and that he could not tell any. My father and Brown were disappointed.

'Then,' said my father, 'if you do not care for stories, maybe you will sing us a song.'

'I can't sing,' said Mr. Shaw, 'but I can recite.'

'What is that?' asked my father. 'I never heard of it; I would rather have a song. Come on Johnny, give us *The Banks of Clady*.'

Johnny sang *The Banks of Clady* and my father sang *The Bonnie Bunch of Roses*. Mr. Shaw said to Johnny, 'It is a pity you were not trained in your young days, Mr. Brown, you would become a great singer. I never heard such a lovely voice.'

'He was well enough trained,' said my father. 'Who the hell could train him better than his own father, who was the best singer in Ireland? God have mercy on him.'

We kept Mr. Shaw in Cleendra that night. We did not want him to stop in Dungloe for fear anything bad would be put into his head. John left him to the station next morning.

In about a week's time we got notice that the Society was registered, and we got a copy of the rules. The Roshine schoolmaster, Mr. Sweeney, gave us the school for the meeting (we were lucky in always having a good, human schoolmaster in Roshine who could teach other things besides making patstick or folding wee bits of paper). We held the meeting on Friday night. No one attended only the members, fourteen of us, and the prig who stood by the door. I got up on the seat and shouted to Gillespie to shut the door and any person who was not a member to throw him out. Gillespie was a big, hefty man. He made for the door, but the boy was already gone.

I said, 'Now, men, our Society is registered. The first business is to appoint a Committee of twelve. According to the rules we must have twelve, not more or less.' We had not much trouble in selecting the Committee. Gillespie said that the twelve nearest should be elected. This was agreed to. Then the next business was to elect a President. Brown proposed me as President, Gillespie seconded, and I declared myself elected as President of the Templecrone Co-operative Society. The next business was the appointment of a Secretary. I proposed John Charlie, Brown seconded it and I declared him elected.

We decided that the next Committee meeting would be in my house on Sunday night before the airneal would commence, which was to be in my house that night. We had the meeting early, and the first business was to consider how much cash we had left after the affiliation fee and the rules were paid for. We had five shillings, as neither John nor I charged for any postage. The next business (we had no agenda) was to consider where we were to get grapes, spades and shovels. When we were discussing this, John Gillespie said, 'Damn spades and shovels. Get our tea, sugar, flour, meal and everything we want, same as they do in Scotland.' – 'Hear! Hear!' said Johnny Brown. John Charlie said that it was against the rules (John was a great man to stick to the rules) to go outside agricultural requirements. I was delighted with Brown and Gillespie, and suggested that we should order some tea and sugar.

'Sure,' said I, 'we cannot do much harm, and who knows anything about the rules only John? I'll take the blame.' After a long discussion, it was agreed that we order tea and sugar and a lot of wee things that the women would tell us. I warned every Committee man to keep a shut mouth and not to tell any person what we decided on. I was trying to impress this point, but before I was near finished the neighbours gathered in and the dancing started, but people would talk.

Wright asked me about all we had done. He found it hard to say Co-op and could only Co-co-co, until in the end he gave it a name he could say – 'The Cope'. That was the christening.

'Is it true what Gillespie was saying that you are going to get tea for us?' Wright asked me. I looked at Gillespie. He stooped his head. He had already told it to half a dozen.

The next day John Charlie sent an order to a wholesale house in Derry for half a chest of tea, a bag of sugar, two pounds of Gallagher's twist tobacco, four ounces of snuff, and a box of clay pipes. He got a reply back by the weekly post, thanking him for the order, and asking him to call on Mr. So-and-so in Dungloe, who stocked their goods, and they were sure he would supply him. We tried one or two others but with the same result. We then wrote to the Co-operative Wholesale Society in Glasgow (the Irish Agricultural Wholesale Society only handled agricultural goods in those days) for the goods. They sent us a pro-forma invoice. We took it for granted that they sent out the goods; we thought we had a real invoice. We had a messenger going every day to the station to see if the goods arrived. When we got sick of waiting, John wrote again, and he had a letter back in due course asking him to look at the proforma invoice and on receipt of his remittance the goods would be sent on.

As soon as John got the letter, he came over to our house. Both of us went to the Roshine schoolmaster, gave him the letters and invoice, and he was not long explaining the contents to us. I had some money in the house, John had the rest. Off he went to the town got a postal order and sent it to the Co-operative Society in Glasgow. In less than a week we got word that the goods were at the station. John yoked his horse in the cart and off he went, passing through the town.

The word went round that John was away to the station for a load of goods for the Cope. Sally's people heard it, and Madgie was waiting at the corner of the Barracks when John came up the road. She said, 'John, can you give me a pound of tea and a half-stone of sugar?'

'I am afraid I can't,' said John, 'I have no way of weighing it.' 'Sure I'll get you a pound bag for the tea and a half-stone sugar-bag,' said Madgie. 'You can guess it. Wait there,

I'll have a hammer in a minute for you to open the chest.'

She ran up to the house and was back in less than a minute and handed John the hammer. 'Now, my boy,' said she, 'open the tea-chest until we see what it is like.' John did so, and to his pleasant surprise wasn't the tea in nice yellow packets, put in half-pounds! He gave Madgie two of them, filled the half-stone sugar-bag to where the bend was in the top of it. The old Head, the sergeant, and most of the men were at the Barracks watching.

Madgie took one of the half-pounds out of her apron, pointed it to the Head and said, 'Head, get a half-pound of this good tea for the missus, it will make a new woman of her.' The Head made no answer. Murphy ran round the corner and nearly broke his sides laughing.

Before John reached Cleendra he had half the tea and sugar sold. The remainder of the goods were taken into my wee house. We had no weights or scales to weigh the sugar or tobacco. John was guessing away at it. I went over to Falmore to Kitty's; I knew she had a set of scales and weights when she had the wee shop, before she got married to the Whistler. She gave me them for two shillings.

At our next Committee meeting we decided that we would open our wee Cope on Tuesday and Friday in the evenings after six o'clock. Next day was Friday. After dinner-time, John and I went to the Cope to weigh up the sugar, tobacco and snuff. We were sure we had lost in the guessing. To our agreeable surprise we had a stone too much in the sugar, two ounces too much in the tobacco, but we were half an ounce short in the snuff. We did not tell the Committee. In two nights our goods were finished. We doubled the order the next time. I sent to West Calder Co-operative Society for all my deposit. I went to the

Bank and lodged it in the name of the Society, and I came home with a cheque-book.

The shopkeepers wrote to the Irish Agricultural Organization Society to say that if they did not stop John O'Donnell and me from causing so much disunion amongst the Rosses law-abiding people, they would wind up the Bank and withdraw their deposits. The Organization sent a Mr. Lyons to investigate. He stayed in Dungloe and had the investigation there. Neither John nor I heard of his coming or going. The following day I was in Maghery strand collecting seaweed when I met Frank Devenny, Johnny's father. He had a shop one time and had to give it up owing to opposition from Dungloe. He said to me, 'Paddy Pat Bawn, I thought after your experience in Scotland that you would have more sense than to try to start a shop in opposition to the Dungloe bucks. I knew when I heard it that you would not succeed. Damn my soul, if they would let me sell a cake. They had a man from Dublin in the town yesterday and he is away back to report against you.'

I said, 'What the hell do we care? We are started and I would like to see who will stop us.'

'Good luck to you,' said Frank, and he walked on.

When I went home with the load of seaweed, I told Sally what Frank said. I got a sheet of paper and I wrote a letter, a kind of letter (Micky Neddy never taught grammar or spelling until you went into the third book) to the Organization Society. I told them as well as I could what Frank told me, and asked them if it was true. I had a reply the following week. They did not mention Mr. Lyons, but said that Mr. Norman would call in Dungloe on a certain date, and told me to meet him.

I met him in the secretary's house. I think Mr. H.A. Law, MP., was present, but I am not sure of it to this day. Mr. Norman heard my point of view. The traders would not agree to have any discussion in my presence. Mr. Norman went back to Dublin. I understand his report was to the effect that after careful investigations he came to the conclusion that the efforts we were making to start a trading Society could only end in failure, and that he feared the Agricultural Bank would go smash, because if we did not stop our trading the businessmen would withdraw their deposits. It was the poorest part of Ireland he was ever in, and he knew that my supporters and I were making an honest effort to help the people, but all the odds were against us. I may not be quoting Mr. Norman's report correctly but I am quoting what I heard, and, as Mr. Norman is still alive, he can correct me.

We got in another small consignment of goods from the Scottish Co-Operative Wholesale Society. The next meeting of the Bank resulted in all the business men withdrawing their deposits. We had only left the Congested District Board's fifty pounds, the parish priest's five pounds and my five pounds, and the feeling got very bitter. I had a paid bill from one of the dealers and I sent it to the editor of the *Irish Homestead*, Mr. Russell (AE), and this is what appeared in the next issue of the *Homestead:*

*Irish Homestead*, 20th January 1906.

### Survivals of the Past

There are still enterprising and go-ahead people in Ireland, who view with dislike the modern apathy and stagnation. They reside in out-of-the-way places like the north-west of Donegal, and follow the avocation of manure dealers. An organizer of the IAOS was up there lately, and came back full of enthusiasm for the business methods of these new survivals, as from the gombeen age of Ireland – primeval giants of finance, scornful of the ethical weaknesses of a later age. They believe in the intensive cultivation of money in rapid growth. They wave a magical wand over accounts, and lo! in three months they have advanced twenty per cent; a bag of manure costing eight shillings for cash will in three months advance to ten shillings, and so the debtor hastens to pay up lest he be altogether devoured, and in his place know him no more.

Ere it is too late, ere these primitive survivals perish from the country they have ruled, would it not be in the interest of the country if some official of the National Museum went up to Donegal to photograph these men and their account books, and preserve some record of their work for future historians, biologists, and ethnologists in Ireland? We are sure the IAOS organizer will assist in guiding the persons appointed into this haunt of the surviving gombeen men.

# CHAPTER SEVEN

## *Eggs for Sale*

Meantime, we were making a little progress. We opened the Cope every other night. We started buying our member's eggs, and when we had a case, John and I packed the eggs. We never packed eggs before. We had the *Irish Homestead* in front of us with a photograph of a case of eggs packed in nice uniform rows, which got a first prize at some exhibition in London. We came to the conclusion that the eggs were all on end. We commenced to pack our case, and put them on end. Mind you, it was a devil of a job. Next day we railed the case to the order of the Irish Producers of Dublin, at Glasgow. When they arrived at Glasgow, they were all smashed, were refused by the Glasgow buyer and we were sent a debit note for the carriage by Mr. Adams. He advised us not to handle any more eggs until we got someone trained for packing, that there was a Poultry Society at Castle Rock, Co. Derry, and if we sent some person there, Mr. Barr, the manager, would train such person in grading, testing, and packing eggs.

We called a special Committee meeting, and it was decided that I should go to Castle Rock. Off I went, arrived at the store, met Mr. Barr, and started packing eggs. The second day I was there Mr. Barr closed an hour earlier than usual. He told me that he had to attend an Orange meeting. He gave me a fright. With an Orangeman training me, how could I have luck. I went to the boarding-house and spent a miserable night. Sometimes I thought he was only pulling my leg, as he seemed to me to be a very decent fellow. I could not imagine him riding a goat, and he could not possibly be an Orangeman unless he did. (We Rosses people always heard that to become an Orangeman you had to ride on a goat three times round the room). Next day when I went to the store, Mr. Barr was extremely kind to me and took the utmost pains in showing me how to handle the eggs.

The following Sunday after Mass, a man spoke to me outside the chapel door and asked me how I liked Castle Rock.

'Very well,' I answered.

'Are you going to be here long?' he said.

'Only a few weeks for training in the egg business.'

'Well,' he said, 'you could not be with a better man than Mr. Barr.'

I said that he was very nice indeed, but that he gave me a shock the second day I was there when he said he was going to an Orange Society meeting.

'That would be right,' he said. 'This is a great place for Orangemen, some good, some bad, just like ourselves; but Mr. Barr is one of the best you ever met.'

I said that this was a terrible surprise to me, as I thought they were all bad men.

After two weeks, Mr. Barr considered that I would be able to grade and pack eggs. Off to Cleendra I went. We had a quotation from the Irish Producers offering threepence per dozen above the local price, if the eggs were carefully packed and graded.

The night I came home the airneal was in my father's house, and there was a great welcome for me. There was no dancing or singing that night; it was all about Castle Rock and the packing of the eggs. I told them I had been with an Orangeman. My mother blessed herself and said, 'Paddy, why did you not come home at once? God help you. I was afraid something would happen to you. I think there is something unlucky about the Cope.'

The Committee were all present. I said, 'The Cope will be opened to-morrow night early and we will take all the eggs we can get and pay threepence per dozen more than the town traders are paying.' This announcement created a sensation.

Next day after dinner-time we saw the women coming to the Cope with their baskets of eggs. John and I left our work and opened the door. The place was so small that we could only let in three at a time. I took the eggs, while John gave the goods. We were sold out before bedtime. John went to the town next morning and wired for a good quantity of goods. The Co-operative people shipped the order the same day although we had not sent any cash. We were beginning to do a nice trade. We had to open the Cope every night.

The shopkeepers were not idle in the meantime. They started a little 'Co-operative' on their own. They joined together in a 'Trader's Association'. Their Committee sent out a circular to all traders to organize in order to crush illegitimate trading. There was a special appeal sent to the Derry Wholesale houses, pointing out that it was necessary for them to subscribe liberally to the Association's

Defence Fund; that it was in the wholesalers' interest to crush this unjust trading body. If not, that they would suffer; they had already lost some business, as the Cleendra fellows were getting their goods from some Trade Union Society in Scotland.

The next meeting of the traders was held the following Sunday in Dungloe. All the shopkeepers in the district were present. The subscription list was read out from the Derry wholesale houses. One or two Belfast houses had subscribed. The amounts varied from one pound to ten pounds. This was considered very satisfactory. Then it was proposed that all the traders in the Upper and Lower parishes should subscribe one pound each. This was seconded, but one member jumped to his feet, he was one of the Lower Rosses men, and said that it was not fair, that he had only a wee shop and did not sell one-tenth the amount of goods that Mr. A. sold. He was supported by another small merchant. A long discussion followed. Finally it was agreed that all should subscribe as near as possible in proportion to their dealings. The next item on the agenda was how were they to fight the present evil. It was proposed by Mr. A. that the shops nearest Cleendra pay one penny per dozen for eggs more than the Cope, no matter what price the Cope paid for eggs, and that these shops should be recouped out of the Defence Fund. This was unanimously agreed to, and the meeting terminated with B. proposing a hearty vote of thanks to the chairman for the able way he had conducted the meeting, which had been called in order to protect the public against this foreign evil that had raised its head amongst them. There was great applause. One of the traders, Mr. C., was a great friend of Sally's mother. He used to pass her door on his way home and always went in to light his pipe. After the meeting he took a couple of half ones, went to see Sally's mother as usual, got a bit soft and told her that he feared Sally would lose all the money she had saved in Scotland. He whispered to her all that had happened at the meeting. When he had finished his smoke he went off home.

Madgie came in not long afterwards. Her mother told her what the shopkeeper had said. Madgie immediately put on her shawl and landed in our house about two hours after the traders' meeting. She told me what the shopkeeper had told her mother. Sally made a stawl of tea for us. I went over to John Charlie's and told the story.

The airneal was in John's that night, so we decided to have a Committee meeting after the dancing was over, for fear the people might think there was something wrong. We gave the tip to the Committee to remain in the house when the airneal was over.

When I told them of the traders' programme, we planned our counterattack. It was to buy a horse and van, send our goods into Dungloe, down to Lower Rosses and round every shopkeeper's door who was in the Traders' Association.

John and I went out every other day with the horse and van. Any house we came to that was not in sight of the traders, gave us most of their eggs and bought goods from us. Most of the people were in debt and were afraid to be seen at the Cope van. We put up the price of eggs in the Lower Rosses the same as we did in Cleendra, that was threepence per dozen more than the Lower Rosses shopkeepers were paying.

At the next meeting of the Traders' Association the Cope neighbouring shopkeepers presented their bills for losses sustained on their week's purchase of eggs. As Mr. A. was going to pay them, all the Lower Rosses traders presented similar bills. The amount claimed for the first week threatened to absorb more than the entire fund. Mr. A. suggested to adjourn the meeting, and they would nominate a committee of three and himself to examine the bills, as he felt sure there did not leave as many eggs from the two parishes for the last twelve months as the bills represented. Then some of the traders wanted their bills back. Mr. A. said that he would not give them back until his Committee had seen them. He told them that the next meeting would be held on Sunday after Mass, and that all just claims would be met.

The traders went home. Mr. C. called in with Sally's mother, had a chat, lit his pipe, and said, 'I think we country shopkeepers are not going to get much of the money that was collected for us. We got none today. The town bucks are too smart for us. I did not pay my ten shillings yet, and if I do not get the three pounds fifteen shillings and sixpence that I lost in eggs last week, devil the penny they will get.'

The airneal was that night in Hughdie's. (We had our Committee meeting the same Sunday night. All meetings political or otherwise, were held on Sundays.) We had nothing serious to report only that the wee house was getting too small for the business, so we agreed to look out for bigger premises.

I wanted Gillespie to keep his mouth shut. He turned very angry and said, 'What the hell are you pointing to me as a story-teller? There is Brown, and he cannot keep quiet. You want a bigger house. How are you going to get one if we all keep our mouths shut?'

I had to admit I was wrong. As Gillespie was going out, he turned round and said, 'Paddy, I am not angry with you. I am at your back and will be until I die.'

Brown said, 'Paddy what about you giving us your house, the kitchen would make a grand shop, and the room would be a safe place for the Committee to meet. The wee house would do Sally, the child and yourself for a wee while; if you do that, I'll propose that we build a room to the end of the wee house for you.'

In the meantime I had been angling to get the store into the town, the enemies' stronghold, and I had Madgie on the look-out. She came to Cleendra one Saturday night. Wee Annie saw her first, and said, 'Oh Daddy, here is Aunt Madgie.'

My heart jumped when I heard she was coming. I met her before Sally at the door and asked, 'Have you any news?'

'I have,' said she, 'Con Doherty will give his house. He is going out again to Alaska for a few years. He does not want any rent for it only that you promise you will give it back to him whenever he wants it.' I was delighted.

Madgie stayed with us that night. She and I went in next morning to Mass.

I had met James Liam Durnion the previous Sunday. He was a great friend of mine. He was an American-born and was as straight as a rush, both morally and physically. He was very much concerned about the success of the Cope. He asked me how much it was to become a member. I told him that the fee was one pound but that he could enter for two shillings and sixpence. He pulled a letter out of his pocket, and handed me a five-dollar bill, saying, 'Take that for my membership fee. I got it yesterday

The wee house in Cleedra where the Cope was started.

from Hannah in Philadelphia. She is the best sister ever a man had.' I thanked him very much and said I had no change, but I would get it in Brennan's. 'No change for me,' he said, 'the God-damn thing isn't worth changing. Put it down for me. I'll have a good few of my neighbours joining next week.'

I said, 'It is a pity, James, we are so far apart. I have been thinking for some time that the town would be the best centre; it would be so near the station, and if we were in the town we would get members in the enemies' stronghold.'

'By Gad, you are right, Paddy,' said James, 'I guess you are a smarter guy than I figured.'

I bade James good-bye and went to Madgie's house. She had a fine dinner ready on the table.

'Good gracious, Paddy I have heaps of news for you. Mr. C. was in here half-shot and told us about the row they had at the meeting. Mr. A. and his Committee got a list of the dozens of eggs that each of the traders sold to the Derry egg buyers for the last two weeks, and it was only four hundred and seventy-six dozen altogether. They made it up and the loss was only seven pounds eighteen shillings and eightpence at fourpence per dozen, but the country traders were claiming thirty-six pounds seven shillings and threepence. Mr. A. went mad and told them that if that was the way they were going to do business he would not act as chairman any longer. He appealed to them to send him and his Committee the exact amount and they would all get paid at the next meeting.'

As soon as I had dinner taken and the news swallowed I made for Cleendra. We had the airneal that night in Tully's. Before the dancing started, I said that I wanted the

Committee outside. When I got them out I told them to come with me to my house. We gathered round the fire, John took his copy-book out of his pocket and said, 'Boys, this is the minutes of the last meeting, which I am going to read; the names of the Committee present at the last meeting …' Then he read, 'The following business was decided on, that the Committee look for a bigger house for the business.'

He asked us was that a true record of the meeting, and we all agreed. He asked me to sign the minutes. I asked him what would I sign them for? He took the rule book out of his pocket and read the rule governing Committee meetings. I signed my name on the copy, and we were all highly pleased with John and his minutes. It added a new tone to our meetings. Then John produced another sheet and said, 'Men this is the agenda. The first item is, did we get a new shop?' One looked at the other and all looked at me, expecting me to answer. I said nothing.

Then Brown said, 'Paddy, what about your house? It is a fine big kitchen and would hold plenty of stuff. You, Sally and the children could live in the wee house until we get time to build a room for you. All the members will gather when we get the praties shovelled, and damn the long we will be building a nice room.' I said that they could have the house and welcome as far as I was concerned, but as the wee house was beside the Glen I was afraid Sally would not live in it. (I had Sally already advised not to go to the wee house under any conditions). After a long discussion we decided to adjourn consideration of new premises until the next meeting. I then pulled out James Liam's five-dollar bill and handed it to John saying. 'He paid his share in full and he hopes he will soon have many more members from the Croveigh district.' I proposed that we add James Liam to the Committee. John pulled out the rules and said that we could not have more than twelve on the Committee, and if James Liam was added that we would have thirteen. Dennis said that thirteen was unlucky.

'Unlucky be damned,' said Gillespie, 'I second that James Liam become a Committee man. If one of you useless creatures do go it will not be much of a loss and then we will have only twelve.'

I said, 'It is proposed and seconded that James Liam be added to the Committee. There is no amendment. I declare the motion carried.' John shoved the rule book under my nose and his pencil pointed to the rule. I could not see it.

I said, 'Now, let everyone do his best to get a suitable house before we meet on next Sunday night, and it will not be my fault if the Cope does not be in our house.'

The next Sunday after Mass I met James Liam and told him that he had been elected a member of the Committee, and that we were going to have a very important meeting that night; that we could get Con Doherty's house if the Committee would agree to change the Cope into the town. I said, 'For your life, do not tell the Committee about Con Doherty's house. Let us work it in a quiet way and we might succeed. You must come out to Cleendra with me. When my father heard that you were on the Committee, man alive, but was he glad. He made me promise that you would come and have a good dinner with him and my mother. I had to promise that I would take you to his house first. When I was passing this morning, I heard the hens squealing, and I am sure my mother will have a good feed for us.'

'I guess it is up to me to go,' said James. 'Thank God I am not going empty-handed. I have a list of fourteen new members for you from the Croveigh district.'

I was delighted. Off to Cleendra we went, into my father's house. James was a distant relation. They were delighted to see him. My mother dished out a fine bowl of soup to each of us and a good plate of potatoes, and a whole hen divided evenly between us.

As soon as the dinner was over, my father said, 'James, I suppose you heard all about the Cope. Dammit, it is a great thing. Isn't it a pity you have not one in Croveigh? You would get everything you would want of the best. Look at the tea you are drinking, Nancy says that she never saw any half so good. Sure it is as yellow as gold. Isn't it, Nancy?'

'It is, and it takes so little of it to make a pandy of tea' said my mother.

'Pat,' said James, 'I do not wish to say anything yet about your Cope. Why, we never heard of such a thing in the States, but if the Cope can break up combines and bring prices down to a right level, then I am with you all the time.'

The airneal was in Peggie Davie's that night. James Durnion enjoyed it very much. I called the Committee outside and told them that it was best not to wait too long, that we would go over to our house and hold the meeting there. Over we went. I pulled the table out to the centre of the floor. We had not enough seats, but I had some bits of planks outside and I stretched one on each side of the table, across the chairs and we all sat down. John pulled out the copybook and read the minutes. I signed them. James Durnion stood up and said, 'Mr. President and gentlemen, I came here tonight to thank you for the great honour which you have conferred on me. Not only have you conferred an honour on me, but you have conferred an honour on that famous townland of Croveigh, that gave birth to my great father, Liam Durnion, who was driven from his native land by the cruel landlords.'

'Hear! Hear!' we all shouted.

'I guess I am not worthy of such honour,' he continued. 'However, unworthy as I may be, I accept it on my own behalf and on behalf of the great country where I first saw the light, the United States of America.'

We gave him great applause. Then James took a list of names out of his pocket and put down six half-crowns. John took down the six names. Then James put down ten shillings and gave me two other names. Then he put down three pounds for six others. When the names had been taken down, John Gillespie got up and shouted, 'Up America!'

The first item John had on the agenda was the consideration of getting a new house for the Cope. Brown said, 'Damn the better house you can get than where you are.' I said that I told Sally that the Committee would like to have the Cope here, but that Sally said she would not go to the wee house as it was too lonely.

'What the hell are you talking about?' said Gillespie. 'Didn't Sally go with you to Scotland? She came with you out here and she will go with you anywhere you want her to go.'

While we were discussing the subject, who came in from the airneal only Sally and wee Annie. I said to her, 'I am glad you came. The Committee want to change the Cope to this house and we can go down the Glen to the wee house. They will build a fine new room for us when

The Committee. From left to right: Denis O'Donnell, Dan McGinley, Jimmie Bonar, Domnick Bonar, John O'Donnell, Dan Sweeney (Secretary), Paddy Gallagher (President and Manager), John Gillespie, Dan Deery and Johnnie Brown.

James Durnion.

the potatoes are shovelled.' I gave her a bit of a wink for fear she would forget my warning.

'I won't go down there,' said Sally. 'I don't want to be there with my children amongst the fairies (our eldest boy was around her skirts as she spoke), the loneliest place in the world. I won't leave my own house. Can you not get a place anywhere else?'

We all said 'No.'

'I can get a good house for you in a better centre than here,' said Sally, 'and it will save you a lot of carting from the station.'

'Where is that?' said Dennis. 'In Dungloe,' said Sally. 'I know Condy Doherty is going out again to Alaska, and he is a great friend of ours. I'll run in to-morrow and ask for it, and I will get it.'

'Well, indeed you won't,' said Gillespie. 'Do you think we are starting a Cope for the Dungloe ones? Every one of them would cut our throat if they got a chance, and it is me that knows that.'

All the Committee appeared to be against Dungloe, and I was very much disappointed. James Liam got to his feet and said, 'Ain't that a funny thing, Mrs. Gallagher, talking about changing to Dungloe? That is my dream now. I dreamt last night that I was at a council meeting in Dungloe, that the council room was as good as ever I was in at home in the States, that our council consisted of thirteen, and that we had a long discussion as to how we should arrange to transport merchandise for the community. Some members were for shipping, others were for rail and road transport. We decided by a bit of a majority to get merchandise by shipping. We went outside the door to have a look at our harbour and I saw a ship as nice as I ever saw in the States coming into Dungloe Bay. Mr. Gillespie was the captain, Mr. Brown was at the wheel and Mr. Dennis was first mate. I was at the discharging of the cargo. We had hundreds of carts bringing our merchandise to our great big store in Dungloe. When we had the cargo discharged we went back to our council meeting and got good eats. We came out through a big shop that belonged to us and saw our boys and girls serving the Croveigh and Cleendra people with the best of eats. I then awoke, and you guess, boys, I felt much broke.'

'Heavens,' said Gillespie, 'that is a damn good dream and you will see that day yet. I was always telling you, Brown, what we would come to, but what am I talking about, sure you could not see that far ahead of you.'

I was delighted. If I got James Liam in a quiet place I would kiss him. I said, 'The more I think of it there is something in what Sally says. If we were in Dungloe, we would save a lot of carting. See yesterday, John had to yoke the horse in the cart and go to Croveigh with two hundredweight of meal and two bags of flour, three miles the other side of the town. We had to cart it first from the station to here, a distance of seven miles, that was fourteen miles in all. If we were in the town, we would be only three miles from the station, and we would only have to cart it another three miles, six miles instead of fourteen. We would also be in the centre of the parish. We would get a lot of new members and we would show the big guns in the town that we were not afraid of them.'

'Who the hell said we were afraid of them,' said Gillespie. 'If you think that I am afraid of them, you are far mistaken,' he said. 'I'll be one of the first to yoke my mare and carry the goods back again.'

'Neither am I afraid of them,' said Brown.

All the Committee said the same. I told them that I never suggested any of them were cowards, as I knew they were the pluckiest men in the world.

I then said, 'I propose that Sally goes into the town in the morning, asks Con Doherty for the house and that we move in immediately if we get it.'

'I second that,' said Gillespie.

'I declare that carried unanimously,' said I.

Brown was going to say something. I was afraid and said, 'I now declare this Committee closed. Our honourable friend, Mr. Durnion, has a long way to go home and it will be late for him. We will meet after the airneal next Sunday night. Come, James, my father wants to see you before you go home. I will go over with you.'

As there was no sign of the others moving, I got nervous that they would hold a meeting on their own and upset what had been done. I turned back and said, 'Come on, boys, Sally wants to put the child to bed. Come on with us, Brown, it is on your way home.' They all got up slowly and Brown came with us. We parted with him at the cross-roads.

James and I went to my father's house. It was previously agreed on that James would stay that night there. My mother put on the pandy and gave each of us a cake and bowl of tea.

'Well,' said my father, 'what do you think of the Cope now, James? Isn't our Paddy a great man. When Doney Gallagher made his first pair of trousers he told me and Nancy that he did not think it would be worth our while to rear him. Look now what he is doing for us!'

'Yes,' said James. 'I guess he will do some good if he

just keeps straight ahead. I think, Pat, there is something to him. We did good business to-night.'

'What did you do? asked my father.

'We changed the Cope to the town,' said James.

'Sure you are not saying that you are taking the Cope out of Cleendra?' said my father.

'That is so,' said James.

'Did Paddy agree to that?' asked my mother.

I answered, 'Mother, I and all the Committee agreed to change it as it will save a lot of expense. We will send the van out to Cleendra, and you will get all the goods from the van.' I had to stop speaking as I saw the tears roll down my mother's cheeks.

'Dammit,' said my father (no one spoke for a few minutes)- 'Doney Gallagher might not have been so far wrong after all.' He went on his knees and started to say the Rosary.

When the Rosary was over, I went to the door and said 'Good-night. Good night, James.'

'I guess I will be with you' said James.

No one asked him to stop. When we got to our house I told Sally that my father and mother were raging and did not ask James to stop for the night.

'Poor souls,' said Sally, 'I was more afraid of them than the Committee. Isn't it a good job I aired the bed for James? Did you get any supper?'

'Yes,' said James, 'had I known what was coming to me I would not have had eats there.'

James was up early next morning and Sally was with him.

Before the next Sunday we were in the town (Dungloe) in Condy Doherty's house. We were much disappointed at first, as we did not get a customer, only Sally's people and some of their friends on the Fair Hill, but the country people began to come to us, the Cleendra and Croveigh folk especially.

We held our next meeting in the corner of the grave-yard. We had not room in Condy Doherty's house. Niece McCool, Finn's brother, was last in the graveyard praying at his father's grave. When he went outside he saw one of the town lads standing behind the wall trying to hear what we were saying. He turned back and came over to us and said, 'Paddy, are you holding a meeting? This is no place for you. Come all of you down to my house; you can hold the meeting in the room and on one will hear.'

We all went to Niece's house and went into the room. The table was in the centre of the floor with a nice green table-cloth on it. We sat around the table on cushioned chairs. John produced the minute-book and read it. I signed it. We had applications for fifteen new members. Then Gillespie got up and said, 'Boys, my sayings are coming true. Look at the fine room we have today for our meeting. Some of you would not be in here if you could help it. The half of you cannot see the length of your own nose ahead of you.'

He opened his waistcoat, put his hand in the inside pocket, pulled out a bundle tied with a lace and handed it to me, saying, 'Here Paddy, you might need this before the next meeting. I am at your back, my boy.'

I picked up the bundle, put it in my pocket and thought no more about it. I went over to Madgie's and had my dinner.

I went out home in the evening, when I remembered that Gillespie had given me something. I took out the parcel and opened it. What do you think was in it? - one hundred and fifty pounds. I nearly dropped. I went immediately to Gillespie's house and told him that he should not have given me the money, as he did, that he should have told me what was in the parcel and John would have put it on the minutes.

'Do you think I am a damn fool?' he said. 'Every one of the Committee, when they would go home, would tell it to their women and they would clatter it all over the parish. Keep it. Do not say another word about it. If you do not want it this week, you will want it some other time. My boy, my dream is coming true. We will have our ships coming in some day with cargoes from Scotland.' I asked him did he know how much was in the parcel.

'Damn well I know,' he said, 'there is near one hundred and fifty pounds in it. That's what I had in the Post Office when I drew it. I am not sure whether I took any of it out. I think I did not.'

'Well, John, I'll lodge it in the bank tomorrow and John Charlie will take a note of it. We need not tell the Committee.'

'What would you give it to the Bank for?' he asked. 'Sure I gave it to you.'

I explained as well as I could the convenience of the bank and he agreed.

The next evening when I went home, I met Sally at the door and she was crying. She had the child in her arms. She said, 'Wee Annie is very sick, she can hardly breathe.' I rushed in and saw our lovely child gasping for breath. I kissed her, ran out and cycled to Dungloe. I brought Dr. Gardiner out as quickly as I could, but Annie died the second day.

It is only a mother or father who can understand what it is to lose one's dear one, after a few day's sickness. Sally and I were as sorry as any father or mother ever was for losing a child. Although she was not three years of age, it was one of the biggest funerals that ever left Cleendra.

The night after she was buried I went out unknown to Sally, knelt on top of the spink, prayed for a while hoping God would send her back to me.

The week before she got ill, I was in a field that I bought from Peggy Manus, working with potatoes, when I heard the voice calling, 'FATHER'. I looked around and saw my wee Annie trying to climb on up the stone ditch. Well, well, men and women may have pleasant hours but, I am sure no man ever felt as happy as I did at that moment.

# CHAPTER EIGHT

## *Opposition to the Cope*

We never rightly heard what took place at the Traders' meeting that day as Mr. C. was not there, but we know it was the last meeting the country traders attended. The following Monday was a Fair Day and our store was packed. The Lower Rosses people did not come to us for a good while, but boys, when they did come, they came with a rush.

About this time a number of people began to take an interest in our Cope. AE had an article in the *Irish Homestead* now and again. Trade improved wonderfully, until Condy Doherty's store got too small. We then rented the billiard-room, which was under the courthouse, from the landlord, and moved into it. The town people were angry with us for taking from them the place they used to have 'for debating and lecturing for the good of the farmers,' as they said. We were glad to get it, no matter how much we inconvenienced them. We were only concerned for the good of the Cope. They called us 'grabbers,' and they kept a sharp eye on the door to see if anyone who was in debt to them would enter the Cope.

I remember a fine old man coming in one day. He asked me for a good pair of boots. I sold him a pair. When he went to the door he saw one of the shopkeepers watching our door.

The man turned to me and said, 'Can I get out the back door?'

I had a lot of egg-cases against the door, but I removed them and let him out. He did not say why he wanted to go out that way, but I knew he was afraid of being seen.

About this time I received a letter from Mr. H.A. Law, to say that many people from the Dungloe district were asking him to recommend them for the JP – ship, but that he would be very glad to put forward my name to the Lord Chancellor if I would give him permission. I wrote back, thanking him, but stating that I had no ambition for the job and requesting him not to put my name forward.

When we had our first audit, we were out on the right side and had sufficient profit to pay a dividend of one shilling and sixpence in the pound on members' purchases. Our turnover was £490, and our wages' bill was nil. We wrote to the Irish Agricultural Organization Society to say that our annual meeting would be held on a certain date.

We had a letter back to say that Sir Horace Plunkett and Mr. Anderson would attend our meeting. The Committee was delighted. I went to Mr. Hanlon, Clerk of the Petty Sessions, and told him that Sir Horace Plunkett was coming to our annual meeting, and that I would be very grateful to him if he could give me the Courthouse for the occasion.

He said, 'I will give you permission to hold your meeting in the Courthouse. I consider it a great honour to the town that such a distinguished gentleman as Sir Horace Plunkett is coming to visit us.'

'Thank you very much, Mr. Hanlon,' said I. 'Will you please give me the key so that we may get the place fixed up.' He handed me the key and I went into our store; the Courthouse was on the floor above us.

The night before the meeting we were making great preparations; John and I remained in the town until after midnight. When we were coming into the town next morning, all the big stones along the road were plastered over with posters telling the members of the Co-op. to make sure and be in the Co-op. before twelve noon that day, as any member who did not call before that hour would not be eligible for dividend; at the bottom of the poster was 'By Order of the Committee'. These posters were everywhere in the two parishes, and on the Co-op and Courthouse doors. They were bogus.

The meeting was timed for three o'clock, and at about ten o'clock, while I was in the little office under the stairs, Mr. Hanlon came to the door and said, 'Paddy, I want you to give me the key; I was called to the 'phone now, and one the Magistrates said that he heard Sir Horace Plunkett was going to address a meeting in the Courthouse, and that he would not allow any Unionist meeting to be held in Dungloe for sapping the nationality of the Rosses people, and further that no such meeting could take place without the Magistrates' consent.'

The key was lying on the desk in front of me, I caught it and put it in my pocket, and said to Mr. Hanlon, 'I don't give a damn for all the Magistrates in the Rosses; we will hold this meeting today as we arranged, and it will not be a Unionist meeting, it will be a Rosses meeting. Surely John Gillespie, Johnny Brown, James Durnion, Dennis O'Donnell, John Charlie and myself are as Nationalist at heart as the Morly Magistrates you are talking about. The majority of them are like yourself – Unionist suckers.'

'Give me that key,' he said, 'how dare you? It is not in Glasgow Green you are now, you impertinent brat.'

I was getting a bit ruffled myself. I made to strike him, but he turned and went out to the 'phone; I do not know what he said.

About noon I shut the Co-op. and went for my dinner. There were some customers waiting at the door when I came back, and as soon as I went inside I heard a noise in the Courthouse. I listened, and one of the customers said, 'That is the carpenter; he was breaking the lock on the Courthouse door when we came here.'

I jumped across the counter, and ran up the stairs, and found the carpenter with a new lock, hammer, and screwdriver in his hands. I said, 'What are you doing here?'

'Oh!' he said. 'Their Worships ordered me to take off the old lock and put on a new one; they will not allow any Unionist meeting to be held here today.'

For the second time that day I plucked up courage and hit out. He ran into the street.

When this was over, our members began to mobilize, and indeed I was very glad. If the town fellows got mobilized first, we would not be able to dislodge them. Before three o'clock all our members were present. John was out with the van. He told the members whom he met that the posters were only another trick of the traders. Not one of the members mentioned dividend that day. We heard afterwards that the traders were of the opinion that our members would rush to demand their dividend, and that we would not have the money to pay them, and so there would be skin and hair flying amongst us.

I am not sure if that was their object. Whatever it was they did not succeed, if anything it only helped to make our meeting more successful for the Courthouse was packed, awaiting the speakers.

Sir Horace and Mr. Anderson arrived in good time, and e had a splendid meeting. I was called on to make a speech. I was shaking like a tree when I arose, and as far as I can remember this is what I said:

'I am glad to have here today such a great Irishman as Sir Horace Plunkett. No matter what lies are told about us in the Rosses, we are not Unionists! We are good Nationalists, trying to take the people of the Rosses out of the clutches of the Gombeenmen, and I am glad to tell Sir Horace Plunkett that already our members are showing an independence that is surprising to their enemies. Our van went into a new district last week. After it had passed out of sight of a big merchant's house, who is also a J.P., he followed it, and when the women who were at the van with their baskets of eggs saw him they ran home, and one of them smashed all her eggs. I hope that in a short time these women will show as much independence as the Cleendra women. Thank God no Cleendra woman will run today from a Gombeenman.'

James Durnion got up and said, 'Neither will the Croveigh women run.'

Several others shouted that the women of their townlands would not run either.

I was not able to say another word. When Sir Horace got up to speak there was tremendous applause for him. He spoke for threequarters of an hour, telling the advantages of the Co-operative Movement. He told of the many struggles he and Father Tom Finlay had to get the Co-operative Movement started, and that from now on he was sure it would be plain sailing. He got a great cheer.

Mr. Anderson also got a great reception.

The following day I wrote a letter to Mr. Hugh A. Law to say that after the action of the local Magistrates in trying to prevent the holding of the meeting I would accept the J.P.-ship. I was appointed a short time afterwards.

Feelings became very embittered between us, and the traders kept continually circulating the story that the Cope was a Unionist dodge, and that its object was to split the Nationalist Movement for Home Rule, and further, that it was subsidized by funds from the Orange lodges, and that it had inveigled a priest into it to help divide the National forces. These stories, while they did not do us any harm, did us no good. There were only four families in the town who would speak to me. I got very bitter, and every opportunity I got I hit back.

We continued holding our meetings in Niece McCool's. Niece and his sisters, Anna and Sheila, were very kind to us, and insisted on us having tea at their expense after every meeting. This became embarrassing to some of the Committee, especially Dennis Sean and James Liam.

I got a letter from Mr. Anderson, Secretary of the Irish Agricultural Organization Society, with a cutting from the *Irish Homestead* stating that the Pembroke Trustees were prepared to give a free grant of £300 each to the six most successful Co-operative Societies in Ireland for the purpose of building halls for education and recreation. He advised us to apply. When I read the letter to the Committee, John Gillespie said, 'Now, boys, you see my talk is coming true, we are going to have a grand big hall where we can dance our fill, and Brown will have plenty of room to sing them songs of his, and James Liam will be able to make all the speeches he likes there.'

Rev. Fr. Tom Finlay, S.J.

It was agreed that we apply for the grant, and at our next meeting we had a letter back to say that our Society was one of the six selected. The Committee were delighted. We got our members to clean the foundation, and we advertised for tenders by putting a notice in the Co-op window. When the hall was completed we were handed the key, and on the following morning a large poster was plastered across the door, 'The New Orange Hall', in very large lettering.

At the next Committee meeting John Charlie pulled the *Irish Homestead* out of his pocket and read a speech made by Father T.A. Finlay, S.J., on a Co-operative Society in the south of Ireland. When he had finished reading we all began cheering. James Liam proposed that we should invite Father Finlay to open our so called Orange Hall. I think we all seconded, so it was agreed that John should write to Father Finlay and invite him to perform the ceremony.

We got a reply in due course to say that Father Finlay would come to Dungloe to open our Hall. We got posters out, and had them posted up in all the available places in the two parishes and Sean Micky went out in the small hours of the morning and plastered them on the traders' doors. They retaliated by circulating that Father Finlay was an Orange priest; the last place he was seen was in Lisburn with a Mr. Harold Barbour, who had an Orange Co-operative Society right in the centre of the town.

The priest arrived, and Gillespie proposed that I should take the chair. James Durnion seconded, and Mr. Daniel Sweeney, the Roshine teacher, acted as Secretary to the meeting. I tried to make a speech, and as far as I can recollect this is what I said:

'Men and women of the Rosses, I am very glad to see such a big gathering here today to welcome Father Finlay. Look at this man; surely none of you are in doubt now that he is anything but a real Catholic priest, and not an Orange priest.'

I sat down; nobody spoke, and the clergyman looked at me and seemed embarrassed. Then James Liam was on his feet in the centre of the hall, 'Reverend Father Finlay, ladies and gentlemen,' he said, 'I am sorry our President did not give a better explanation in his introductory remarks. Why, your Reverence, our opponents have been circulating the story for the past few weeks that you are not a Catholic priest, but an Orange priest. I guess you know that none of the real Catholics of the Rosses believe a God-damn word – Oh! excuse me, Father' – and James sat down.

Father Finlay got up with a smile on his face, and said, 'I hope I have discharged my duties this morning as a Catholic priest by saying Holy Mass in your Church. I can assure you that I consider helping the farmers of Ireland to join together for their mutual advantage, let them be Catholic, Protestant, or Orangemen, is in keeping with the teachings of the Church.'

Then he went on to explain the objects of the Co-operative Movement and said in his opinion Sir Horace Plunkett was one of the greatest Irishmen of his day, and that he, Father Finlay, was glad to have the privilege of working with Sir Horace.

The meeting was one of the most successful ever held in Dungloe; all the Cope members were delighted, yet the Dungloe people with a few honourable exceptions continued to call our hall the Orange Hall.

Mr. Daniel Sweeney became our Secretary after John Charlie left us, and we could not have found a better or more loyal man. I sometimes felt rather ashamed when reading the glowing articles that were written by AE, Marie Harrising, and others, in praise of my work, and not one word mentioning Dan Sweeney's invaluable assistance.

When it was still doubtful whether we would sink or swim, the secretary of the Traders' Association sent a petition to the Commissioners of Education, pointing out to them that the National teacher of Roshine School was giving the use of the school to a new socialist body that was corrupting the Rosses, and furthermore was actually acting as secretary to this illegitimate group calling itself a co-operative society.

A copy of the letter was sent by the Commissioners to Mr. Sweeney. I do not know what his reply was, but I do know that he made up his mind immediately to throw in his lot definitely with the Cope. He was the father of ten young children. His only means of livelihood was teaching, yet he was prepared to sacrifice everything for the Co-operative. His wife was his equal in every way.

The first week after the opening of the hall, we had a very successful Ceilidhe, Irish dancing, singing, and story-telling. It reminded me of an airneal in Cleendra. Then he started an Irish class. The Roshine teacher, of course, helped us with this; his good wife, who was then teaching in Croveigh, Mr. Doherty, the Crowhey teacher, Miss Rodgers, who was an assistant in Dungloe School, and Miss Cannon, the Meenbanid teacher, were also actively engaged in this work.

None of the traders or their employees would come near us, and the local priests, for some reason which we could never understand, were opposed to us. They, along with the traders and some country supporters, built an opposition hall which they called the Parochial Hall.

On one occasion we had an all-night dance in our hall. We had a good committee and the dance was properly conducted. It was held on Friday night, and the custom at that time was for all dances to continue until daylight. Imagine our surprise the following Sunday when we heard the priest denouncing us from the Altar. He declared that no dance could be held in the parish in future without the consent of the priests, and that he was referring particularly to the dances that were being held in the Co-operative Hall. Some of our members were very angry, and wanted to call a special meeting and retaliate by not paying any dues. At this time I was living in Dungloe, and the following day my mother came in from Cleendra and appealed to me not to fall out with the priests.

I met the curate a few days later, and I saluted him as usual, but he did not acknowledge me. I told Sally and she was very hurt, and put her head in her lap. I went out again and I was very sorry for telling her. After about half an hour I went in, and I was sure she was crying.

I said, 'Sally, I have made up my mind that we will go back to Scotland. We cannot live here with so many people against us. When I open the Cope in the morning, I will commence to sell out, and when I have all sold, I will give Gillespie and the others their deposits, and pay every penny that we owe. If I have not enough I will sell the Cleendra land.'

She looked up at me, but with no sign of tears, and I shall never forget that look.

'Paddy,' she said, 'you are a coward!'

Before I had time to answer, she put the shawl round her heard, and went out of the door. Packie followed her. I looked out to see where she was going and she turned round the corner. I went as far as the corner, and I saw her passing up by the Barracks, and going into her mother's house.

During her absence I think I must have been speaking to myself, saying, 'Paddy, you are a coward!'

After dark, Sally, Packie, and Madgie came in. Sally said, 'Paddy, why did you not come over to my mother's. Madgie had the tea waiting for you. Did you not make a drop for yourself?'

I told her that I had not.

She said, 'God save us, you are lost.' She popped on the pandy and made tea. When we were all sitting at the table she said, 'Paddy, you know I did not mean what I said before I went out. I know you are not a coward, or never were. Don't forget to order the spraying material to-morrow. You told Rosie to remind you if it.'

When I opened the Cope the following morning, the first thing I did was to order the bluestone for the spraying of the potatoes, and when I came in for dinner that was the first thing Sally asked me, 'Did you order the spraying material?'

At that time there was a Mission in Dungloe. I went to one of the Missioners, and when I had made my confession I told him about the attitude of the priests towards the Co-op and myself in particular.

He said, 'My dear child, we are all human, and liable to err in temporal matters.'

He then gave me absolution, but I still knelt there.

'Father,' I said, 'will you not give me some advice? Is it better for me to leave the Cope?'

His answer was, 'Fight your corner. God bless you!'

On my way down the street I really thought I was the biggest man in Ireland. I think if the Pope denounced the Cope I would not have wavered in my determination to go on.

I was nominated as a candidate at the next County Council election, and an unusual campaign commenced. Meetings were held all over the electoral area. I spoke as well as I could outside the chapels after Mass on Sundays.

There was an election address written for me and I got it out on posters. It caused a great deal of bitter feeling between the traders and ourselves. They used the address, or 'The Cope Man's Pamphlet', with great effect, pointing out to traders outside Dungloe area that if they did not make a determined stand now and crush the Cope, the Cope would very soon crush them; that the Cope would open a store at each shopkeeper's door. This resulted in all the traders acting as election agents. They had their own relations to help them, and they drew up a list of all who owed them money. Then they visited these people and said, 'Before you vote for Paddy the Cope you will have to pay this account; if not we will have it handed over to Narahole (James Sharkey).'

Sharkey was a very useful bailiff for the traders. His procedure was this: all traders had a blue book containing documents which appeared to the ordinary person like a process; the trader gave these to Sharkey with the amount of the account, and a certain amount for the expense of the supposed decree. He would watch for his victim coming out from the chapel on Sunday, tell him he wanted to speak to him, take him to a close, and show him the blue paper, saying, 'This is a decree that was got out against you at the last Sessions in Lifford (Lifford is about forty miles from Dungloe). What are you going to do about it? If you do not pay me I will go and seize your stock.'

If the debtor could raise the money or a portion of it, he would do so, as it was considered a great shame to have the bailiff coming to your door. No matter how poor his victim might have been Sharkey never failed to carry out his threats. It was never known for a prosecution to have been taken against him for such seizures. Of course, the trader and Sharkey selected their victim.

The shop-assistants were even more embittered against me than their employers. I remember a boy called Dono-hue, who was a shop-assistant in Dungloe, at one of my meetings. Immediately I began to speak, he and some others began booing me. I knew he was the son of a police-man, so when they got tired booing me, I pointed to him and said, 'Look at Donohue booing me, the man whose father carried the battering-ram in Gweedore to tumble the tenants' houses.'

Most of the people turned to look at him. I was certainly pleased; I thought I got most of the cheering.

I was severely heckled at another meeting I addressed. One man said, 'You are a friend of Sir Horace Plunkett, and that Orangeman, Barbour, from Lisburn,'

Again at another meeting I was loudly booed when I began to speak. I retaliated as well as I could. I annoyed my opponents and they made a rush for me. Gillespie was there on horseback and he whipped his horse in through the crowd.

Big James shouted, 'Fall in, Hold the line!' and in a few minutes a crowd of the youngsters formed a guard around me. James shouted, 'Hold the line! Hold the line!' The echo of his voice resounded from the spinks. My opponents made no further attempt to upset the meeting. I finished my speech; the town lads hoisted me on their shoulders and carried me out of the crowd.

On the way home I asked James why he shouted to the crowd to 'Hold the line.' He said, 'Do not talk about the line for your life.' I noticed that the young lads were marching four deep in front of him. I asked him if he would come into our house that night. I said, 'Sally will be glad to see you. I cannot thank you half-enough for the good support you have given me today.'

'I cannot come in to-night Paddy,' he said, 'I have a little important business to attend to.'

I asked him if he would come in the following night. He assured me he would.

Sally and I were very glad when James arrived the following night. I sent down to Anna for a 'wee drop,' and while Sally was boiling the water in the wee paddy for the tea, James and I helped ourselves to the whiskey.

James said, 'Here's to your health Paddy, and I hope you will win the election.' Sally gave each of us a good bowl of tea and plenty of bread and butter.

I then said to James, 'I am still wondering why you were shouting, "Hold the line," yesterday.'

James looked at Sally. He did not answer for a few minutes, then he said, 'Och, that was only a word that came to my mouth at the time.'

I knew by the way he hesitated that he did not speak the truth. I winked to Sally and I said, 'Oh Sally, I nearly forgot, Madgie was in the Cope today and she said she wanted you and Packie over to her house to-night.'

Sally got her shawl, took Packie in her arms and went over to her old house.

'Now James,' I said, 'What was in your mind when you were shouting, "Hold the line".'

'Well Paddy, I will tell you, but you must promise me that you will not tell it to a living soul.' I promised, but I am free to tell it now.

He went down and bolted the door, and when he was seated beside the fire again, he said, 'That is one of the words we use when we are drilling in the glen.'

'Who is drilling in the glen,' I asked.

'The lads and I,' he replied.

Then I said, 'What are you drilling for?' 'For the coming fight,' he said.

I was greatly annoyed, and I said, 'James dear, there will be no fight, we are all of the same people and are blood relations, and you must throw that wild idea out of your head. If I thought there would be one drop of blood spilt over the Cope, I would leave the country in the morning'.

James leaned back on the chair, he coughed and then said, 'Our fight will not be a Rosses fight, it will be a fight to free Ireland! Are we not long enough under England? I was glad you gave that shot yesterday to Donohoe's son, the bloody "peeler" that carried the battering ram in Gweedore, to tumble the houses on the poor people. It is only the other night I heard my father talking about that. He said he remembered the day well, it was the 17th April, 1861, on a Monday morning, the Sheriff and Theobald A. Dillon, R.M. and the police force left Letterkenny for Loughbarra. When they reached Loughbarra, the first house they called on was that of Mrs.

H.A. Ward, a widowed woman who had six daughters and one son. Dillon ordered the policemen to throw the widow and her family outside the door, and they did as they were told. He then ordered the Crowbar Brigade to tumble the house. They tumbled forty six houses and left two hundred and forty one people on the hillside.

'Now Paddy, we're teaching the young lads what the English have done for us. Our airneals in the glen are different to your airneals in Cleendra. We do not let the youngsters mix with the old people. We take them to some barn every night. You need not be afraid that they will join the British army, we are teaching them to love Ireland. What do you think of the lads now, Paddy? They are not going to be lost. They are going to be great Irishmen.'

I said, 'James I do not agree with you, neither do I agree with what you say about the Englishmen. I was working with months in England, and I never met nicer or more honest men. I also worked under an English gaffer in Glasgow, on the Great Western Road when they were making the underground railway. I never met a nicer or more just man. And as to the Glenveigh evictions, your father only mentioned one name and that was Dillon's. I never heard of an Englishman called Dillon.'

'Och,' said James, 'I should have said that Dillon was a Roscommon man, that was what my father said.'

'Och James,' I said, 'I thought you were a sensible man. Who is drilling in the glen?'

James proudly answered, 'Did you see my company yesterday, how quickly they fell in, and kept you safe from the enemy?'

'Sure they are only school lads,' I said.

'That is the stuff,' said James, 'They will soon be men.'

'James,' I said, 'I hope you will give up the idea of putting military ideas into the children's heads. Those lads will be going to Scotland and England in a few years time with their heads full of military notions. They might enlist in the British Army and sure that would break their poor mother's hearts.

James was silent for a few minutes, then he said 'Paddy, it is your idea that no effort should be made to get rid of the English rule in Ireland that has bled us white. Did you ever hear your father telling about that English murderer Ould Phillip, who shot John Veldin of Cleendra on the rock at the Green Island, for cutting a creel of wrack to manure his praties, and the ould murderer was never even summoned. It was no wonder the people were not able to keep the black crows from picking the eyes out of the dirty blackguard when he died. Sure that was a parable from God on the dirty brute.'

# CHAPTER NINE

## *The Cope Man in Court*

A few weeks later I was served with a summons to appear at the next Petty Sessions to show cause why I should not be put under a rule of bail to be of good behaviour to all His Majesty's subjects, and quoting some Act of Edward the Third.

I thought it was a joke and paid no more attention to it. The day of the Session came along. I went up on the bench and sat beside the old Head.

A few cases were called and dealt with. The Chairman was the Resident Magistrate. Imagine my surprise when the clerk, Mr. Hanlon, announced that the next case was the Traders against Patrick Gallagher, Esq., J.P.

Edward McFadden, solicitor, appeared for the traders. He was a big burly man. He looked up at me sitting on the bench, and said, 'Come down here, sir, and stand over there!' – pointing to the dock. I was dumbfounded. I did not know what to do.

Mr. McFadden appealed to the Chairman to put me in the dock.

'Under what Act do you want me to put Mr. Gallagher in the dock?' said the Chairman.

Mr. McFadden reached for his bag, and pulled a book

out of it. He opened the book and read the following Acts.

OFFENCE OR CAUSE OF COMPLAINT.
Sureties, of the peace and good behaviour Cont.
Of Good Behaviour – of whom required – Person whom Justice of the Peace shall have just cause to suspect to be dangerous, quarrelsome, scandalous, common quarrels, and common breakers of the peace : rioters, those who lie in wait to rob, or are suspected to do so, or who assault or attempt another or put passengers, in-

STATUTE.
34 Edw. 111 c.1. and the Commission.

EXTENT OF JURISDICTION
Justice of the Peace has a discretionary power to take sureties of all such, and others whose behaviour may reasonably be intended to bring them within the meaning of the statute, as 'Persons of evil fame.'

When McFadden stopped reading, John Gillespie rushed up, shoved his fist under McFadden's nose, and said, 'You are telling damn lies. There never was an Edward Third. Micky Neddy never mentioned his name in Roshine School.'

One of the police made a rush for Gillespie, but sergeant Murphy blocked his way.

'Put that man out,' shouted the Head.

'Sergeant, get your men to keep order, please!' said the R.M.

The chairman read the section over several times before

he turned to me and said: 'Mr. Gallagher, I must ask you to go down and stand over there in the dock until your case is decided.'

I did as I was instructed.

McFadden then proceeded: 'Your Worships, I have a hundred witnesses to prove my case if necessary but I am convinced that when you have heard the evidence of even one of them you will put this blackguard under a rule of bail. You must see that he will no longer disgrace decent people.'

'I will not hear you, sir' said the R.M., 'unless you call your witnesses immediately.'

McFadden then called Jim Brady to the witness-stand.

'Now, Mr. Brady, tell their Worships what this man said.' Brady pulled a paper out of his pocket and began to read; he got as far as – 'I was present' – but then he could only stammer and could not get another word out.

If you had seen McFadden's face! It got as red as a turkey cock.

By this time I was less excited, and I was beginning to enjoy the proceedings.

'Can you tell us in your own way what you have to say,' said the R.M.

'Hand me that paper,' said McFadden to Brady. 'Now, did you hear that man in the dock say anything that would anger the people?'

'I did,' replied Brady.

'What did he say?'

'He said the traders were a pack of Gombeen men.'

'What else did he say?'

'Give me that paper, sir,' said Brady.

'Go down!' roared McFadden. 'Is Charlie Harkin here?'

'Here, sir!' said Harkin. 'Come up to the witness-box,' said McFadden. 'Now Mr. Harkin, you were present at the meeting along with Brady. Tell their Worships what you heard.'

'Wait!' said the Chairman. 'Mr. Hanlon, swear that witness. The last witness was not sworn. Call him back and make him repeat his evidence on oath.'

Hanlon called Brady back and handed him the book, saying, 'Repeat this after me.'

'I am not going to swear by the book,' said Brady. 'I never did, and I will not now.'

Harkin was then called, he took the book and Hanlon said, 'Repeat these words after me: I swear by Almighty God –'

Gillespie began to laugh, and Brown shouted, 'Three cheers for the Copeman!'

There was a rousing cheer.

'Clear the Court!' said the Head.

The Chairman pleaded for order and the case proceeded.

'Now, Mr. Harkin, you were at the meeting the last witness referred to?' said Mr. McFadden.

'I was.'

'You heard that man over there making a speech?'

'I did.'

'Did he say –'

'Now, now, Mr. McFadden, I will not permit you to lead the witness,' said the R.M. 'Let him tell us what he heard Mr. Gallagher say.'

'Mr. O'Connor,' said the Head, 'I cannot understand your interrupting the eminent solicitor, Mr. McFadden. You will keep us here all day if you do not allow him to put the case properly before us.'

'Am I the Chairman or are you?' retorted the R.M.

'You are the Chairman,' shouted Gillespie.

The Head roared to the sergeant to 'put that man out.'

'I can only act on the R.M.'s instructions,' replied the Sergeant. 'Now, sir,' said the R.M. 'Will you please tell the Court what Mr. Gallagher said.'

'He said that the Gombeen man was the ruin of the country,' replied Harkin.

'What else did he say?' asked McFadden.

Harkin began to scratch his head. 'Oh, now that I mind it, he said he would kill Gombeenism in the Rosses before long.'

'Come, come,' said McFadden, 'tell us what else did he say?'

'I did not pay much attention to him,' said Harkin.

'When he said he would kill Gombeenism, did the people get very angry, and was there going to be a fight?' asked the Head.

'Stop!' said the R.M., 'you have made a most improper remark. Have you anything else to say?' he added, addressing the witness.

'There might have been murder that day,' said Harkin, 'you must put him under bail, he is a bad man.'

'Get down,' said the R.M. 'It is you who should be the prisoner.'

Harkin walked out of the witness-box, but the R.M. called him back, and asked me did I want to question him.

I answered 'No.'

McFadden then jumped to his feet (the floor shook under him). 'Now, Your Worships, you have heard the witness on oath state that he was present at a meeting which the man in the dock addressed, and did his best to excite the law-abiding people of the Rosses to commit a breach of the peace which might have led to murder, and we know that when you have one murder you will have reprisals. The evidence has not been contradicted, or disputed. You cannot leave a man like that (pointing at me) at large. I am not authorized to ask you to put him in jail, where he certainly should be, but you must put him under a rule of bail, and make it a substantial one. It will take a heavy bail to shut his mouth.'

Mr. McFadden then sat down quickly, the floor giving another shake. The R.M. then said something to the old Head, and the other two Magistrates, who were traders, but I could not hear what they said. They left the Bench, and adjourned to the Star Chamber. They remained inside for a good while, and when they reappeared you could have heard a pin drop in the Courthouse. The Magistrates took their seats. The R.M. proceeded: 'The Magistrates by a majority have decided to ask Mr. Gallagher to apologize to the traders, and if he does so, they will give his case their most favourable consideration. Let there be no misunderstanding. This decision is not unanimous. It is the decision of the majority. Mr. Gallagher, will you apologize to the traders?'

'Indeed, I will not!' said I. 'I stated what I believe to be true, and I will repeat it while things are as they are.'

The Magistrates held another consultation, then retired to the consulting-room for a few minutes; they returned and seated themselves again.

The R.M. said, 'By a majority, the Magistrates have decided to put Mr. Gallagher under a rule of bail, to be of good behaviour to all His Majesty's subjects, and particularly to the Rosses traders, for twelve calendar months, in the sum of ten pounds by himself, and two solvent securities of ten pounds each.'

Brown shouted from the centre of the Courthouse, 'Me and Gillespie will bail you, Paddy.'

I said, 'Thank you, but I want no bail, neither will I give any.'

There was a lengthy consultation on the Bench this time. No one could hear what they were saying. There was not a murmur in the Court. They retired to the chamber again, and this time they remained inside for a long time. They reappeared, and sat down very carefully, indeed, you would think they were going to sit on tacks.

Then the R.M. spoke. 'By a majority of the Magistrates the verdict is, that Mr. Gallagher goes to Derry jail for one calendar month. In making this announcement I wish to say that I am doing so as presiding Chairman. I do not agree with the decision. I am sorry I have to leave now, as I have an appointment in Letterkenny which I must keep.' He turned to the ex-Head.

'You as the senior Magistrate will take the chair. Mr. Hanlon will make out the warrant.'

The ex-Head took the chair. I left the dock, and was beside him on the Bench before he had time to open his mouth.

'Next case, Mr. Hanlon,' he said.

'The King against James Wright,' called out Mr. Hanlon. One of the policemen who was already sworn (the policemen were sworn in a kind of a hand-shake business) came forward to the witness box.

'Where is the prisoner?' said the Head.

'Are you there, James Wright?' said Hanlon.

Wright went into the dock.

'Now, Constable,' said the Head, 'we are ready to hear you.'

'Your Worships,' said the policeman, 'in the execution of my duty on the fourth day of July, the Dungloe Fair Day, I saw the prisoner hit another man a box, and he was going to hit him again when I caught hold of him. He gave me a blow in the chest which stunned me for a moment, and then, Your Worships, before I got time to draw my baton, he hit me on the jaw and knocked me down. I am not myself yet.'

'What have you to say for yourself, you young blackguard?' said the Head.

'Nothing,' replied Wright doggedly.

I said that I had known young Wright from his childhood, and he would not harm a midge when he was sober, but that he was very quick-tempered when he had too much drink. I proposed that he should be acquitted under the 'First Offenders' Act,' although I knew that he had been convicted several times.

'You are let off under the First Offenders' Act. Go down!' ordered the Head. 'Next case, Mr. Hanlon!'

I took an active part in each case that was brought up, and whatever I said was agreed to. I was never more surprised in my life. I learned afterwards that I had frightened them by refusing to give bail. This had been the verdict they wanted, so that I would lose the J.P.-ship.

When the business of the Court was over, Mr. Hanlon handed up the warrant for my committal to the old Head, who handed it back to Mr. Hanlon saying, 'I am not going to sign that document.'

'You must!' said Hanlon. 'You are the Chairman now, and it is your duty to sign all committal warrants.'

The Head rose from his seat; I gave his coat a pull 'Come, Old Hack!' I said, 'Have the courage of your convictions. Sign the bloody thing.'

He pulled away from me and went out to the hotel to have a few quick ones to steady his nerves.

I went downstairs to the store to serve a few customers, and to my surprise the Co-op. members began to gather in; the news of my trial was already all over the parish. Gillespie and Brown were in, and I think it was they who had sent out the messengers. Gillespie said that Sally wanted to see me down at the house.

I went out with him and Brown; we met Dan Deery on the way, and he said:

'You are not going to jail and leave the Co-op. in charge of the youngsters?' (John Charlie was not in the Co-op. at the time).

I told him that I was, but that the Co-op could carry on all right till I got back.

We went into the house, and Deery said, 'Mrs. Gallagher, advise Paddy here to have some sense. He is thinking of going to jail and leave the Cope business to the youngsters. Sure half the parish will bail him.'

Sally looked at me and said, 'Paddy, I would rather see you carried in on a stretcher, then to think you would satisfy them brutes by going under bail for them.'

That decided the issue. Neither the Committee nor any of the others ever hinted that I should go under a rule of bail afterwards.

Sally had a fine chicken cooked for me, she was going to make sure that I would not be hungry going into jail. I had a good feed, and we went back to the Cope to give some final instructions to my wee assistants before I should be arrested, as I expected that I would have been taken to the Barracks before night. Some time later Mr. Hanlon came in, and told me that I had the magistrates in an awful fix.

'None of them will sign the warrant,' he said. 'They are afraid that their verdict was illegal, and that you will get your own back on them. The Head is in a hell of a state.'

Then Hanlon explained that I would be free until the R.M. himself signed the warrant, for of course the Resident Magistrate will have to sign the decision of the majority of the bench. Hanlon was certain that he had not an appointment to keep in Letterkenny or elsewhere, but left on purpose.

So then I gave the assistants a hand to serve the customers. We did a roaring trade that evening. The following day there was no sign of my being disturbed either. On the third day, Mr. Hanlon came into the Co-op. after post-time and told me that he had a letter from Mr. O'Connor, the R.M., asking him to post the warrant to his address at Buncrana, because he was compelled by the rules of the Court to sign it. I said to Hanlon that I hoped the warrant would not be back until the following Tuesday, as I had received a letter from the Scottish Co-operative Wholesale Society Ltd. in Glasgow, stating that their Secretary and three of their Directors would call on us on the following Monday, and I would like to be there to meet them. Mr. Hanlon said that he would write to Mr. O'Connor and tell him that I expected important visitors on Monday, and if he could hold over the warrant I would be very much obliged.

The Scottish representatives arrived on Monday, and they remained overnight in Dungloe at my request. My trial of the previous week was not mentioned to them. They left Dungloe on Tuesday morning.

Mr. Hanlon came into the Co-op. after post-time that day and informed me that he had the warrant back and he would have to send it to the Barracks, and that likely the police would arrest me in time for the two o'clock train to Derry.

I gave some final instructions to Rosie, Sally's sister, who was helping me in the Cope. I went home to say goodbye to Sally.

About twelve o'clock Constables Healy and Moore came to the door and said that they had a warrant for my arrest, and assured Sally that it was a most painful duty they had to discharge. I walked off with them.

When we arrived at the Barracks one of the Rosses magistrates who was jarvey for the police was standing beside his car, a fine new whip in his hand, and he all smiles.

'Mr. Gallagher,' said Healy, 'you and I will get up on this side. Constable Moore will get on the other side with His Worship.'

'Well, by my soul, I will not sit on that man's car. I will walk it,' I said indignantly.

I started off for the station and the police followed. The jarvey used the new whip on his horse, and turned him home.

Although it was not known when I would be arrested, I was surprised at the number of people who gathered to see me off at the station. We were in good time for the train, and if I had been going to America, I could not have got so many handshakes. As the train steamed out of the station I waved my red handkerchief to the convoy on the bridge and they all waved back to me.

Sergeant Kirk, the weights and measures man, came into the same carriage; he was going to Letterkenny. Our first stop was at Crolly Bridge; at the time there was no station at Kincasslagh Road. When we arrived at Crolly, the proprietor of the Crolly Hotel-a Paddy Gallagher also, but no relation – and Mr. Thomas Hamilton, the excise Officer at Dungloe, were at the station. They slipped into our carriage. As soon as the train moved out one of them produced a bottle of whiskey and three glasses. He gave me the first glass, and offered each of the constables a glass, which they refused, stating that they were not drinking. Mr. Gallagher then handed a glass to Sergeant Kirk, saying, 'As a matter of fact, Sergeant, had we know you were on the train, we would have brought another glass for you.

The Sergeant said, 'Thank you, Mr. Gallagher; I am a pioneer, I never tasted liquor in my life.'

'Bedamned to you all,' said Hamilton, 'you will not take it now, and likely you will be full before night. What about you? Are you a pioneer also?'-looking at my glass which was empty.

He insisted on filling it up again, and he and Mr. Gallagher drank the two glasses which the policemen refused. When we reached Gweedore Station Mr. Hamilton put two of the glasses in his pocket, and let the other glass and the remains of the bottle on the seat beside me, despite my feeble protests.

Nothing of further interest occurred until we reached Letterkenny, but immediately the train moved off from the station, Healy said, 'Mr. Gallagher, give us a drink out of that bottle.'

I reached him the bottle.

'Why the devil,' said he, 'did they take the other two glasses with them? Sure they knew we would have had a drink only for the Sergeant being in the carriage.'

'Stop your talking,' said Moore. 'Shove round the drink; one glass will do us damn well. I thought Kirk would never leave.'

Healy took the first himself and filled it up again for me, but I insisted on Moore taking it as I had had two between Gweedore and Crolly. We then had turn about, and had the bottle finished by the time the train slowed down at Pennyburn Station.

When we came out on to the street there were a lot of jarveys there, and when they saw the policemen and a prisoner they thought they were on a 'dead cert'.

'We will take no car,' said Healy, 'we will walk it, as we are in no hurry.'

We walked up the Strand, and when we came to the Guildhall, Moore said, 'We will go in here and see what kind of stuff they keep.'

We went into the pub which is right opposite the Guildhall on the corner of Foyle Street – I think the name at that time was McCool. We went into a snug in the corner and got plenty of meat pies and drink and remained there until half-past nine. The bar tender told the police they were taking too much drink, and the jail would be closed at ten o'clock.

'Damn the jail; we will never hand Mr. Gallagher in. I do not care if I am dismissed in the morning,' said Healy.

'Right!' said Moore, 'I am with you every time. Put them up again!'

Their friendliness made me want to go straight into the jail to safeguard them. After some argumentation we went staggering up Shipquay Street and along Bishop Street. As we came up to the big gate of the jail there was a warder going in by a small door in it.

I don't remember it all very well. I know I was taken into a room, and I know my pockets were turned out. I am clear enough about a big man dressed in civilian clothes who entered. He held the warrant in his hand. I staggered a little and one of the warders shouted at me, 'Stand at ease!'

The big fellow said, 'You are not to speak to this gentleman like that! He is not the ordinary type of prisoner, he is one of His Majesty's Justices of the Peace.'

'Well, sir, he was handed in to me like any other prisoner,' said the warder.

He began to search my pockets again calling to the man with the book, 'A metal watch, have you that down? Six shillings and eightpence – have you that down?'

'Yes,' said the other fellow.

That was all they found on me. (When I was leaving home Sally made me take a pound, but when I left the pub I had only six shillings and eightpence.)

Then the big man said to me, 'Mr. Gallagher! Surely there must be some mistake somewhere. I see by the committal warrant that you can get off if you give bail. I think you should not come in here amongst the criminals.'

I tried to answer, but he saw I was not in a fit state to give any explanation. He then turned to the warder and said, 'Give him the best cell you have, and something to eat.'

The warder hooked me off to the cell.

'Your Worship,' said he, 'what would you like to eat?'

I told him that I was full enough. My bed was a plank about a foot from the ground, and an army blanket folded at the foot of the bed. It was not long until I was fast asleep. Next morning the warder told me that the big man was the Governor.

On Wednesday I was called out to do some exercise, but I felt too bad to stir. I was only three days in jail when I was told the Governor wanted to see me. I was brought to his office. He was sitting at the table when we went into the room, but when we entered he jumped to his feet, and picking up a telegram from the table he read:

'Dublin Castle sixty-one. To the Governor, Derry Jail. Release Patrick Gallagher, J.P., of Dungloe immediately. By Order of the Lords Justices.'

He then reached his hand to me and congratulated me on my release. I marched out.

I sent Sally a telegram telling her that I was freed by order of the Lord Lieutenant, and that I would be home on the last train. I thought it was the Lord Lieutenant instead of the Lords Justices. I went to Miss Conlon's and had a good dinner. I then went to Charlie O'Neill's. It was lucky for me that I had made a stand in Miss Conlon's against a bottle of whiskey, or I might have forgotten about Sally and the last train.

When I arrived at Gweedore I saw some fires which I took to be lime burning in the kilns. When the train reached Crolly there were a good few fires there too, and from Crolly to Dungloe I saw that there was a fire at every second house, and you would imagine Arranmore Island was all ablaze. I heard afterwards that Captain Hugh Rose O'Donnell's wife of Arranmore set fire to a tar barrel in front of her house, and if the wind had changed, nothing could have saved the house from being burned.

Dungloe Station was crowded with people. I had some difficulty getting out of the carriage. I was carried shoulder high to O'Gorman's car, and Peadar O'Donnell and his lads led the procession with lighted torches (turf-soaked in paraffin oil and stuck on the prongs of hay-forks) with the wee band right behind them. When we reached Dungloe I was surprised to see that the windows of seven of the houses were illuminated with candles: of course Mr. Brennan's was the most brillant; Anna spared nothing. All the other houses were as black as night. The Co-op. Hall was splendidly lit up, and when we arrived there the band ceased playing.

James Liam took the chair and made the speech of his life welcoming me back, and throwing in a word of praise for the youngsters who had carried on the Cope so well during my absence. Several of the others also spoke, and they insisted on me saying a few words. At the following meeting of the Society we had applications for forty-three new members.

One of the traders began to whisper that some of the Derry fellows had bailed me out, but as far as we could hear it was only one of them who tried to circulate the story. Nobody could have been more surprised than I when the Governor of Derry Jail read the telegram from Dublin Castle, ordering my release.

After my conviction I had written a letter to the Rev. Father T. Finlay, S.J. I do not remember now what I said in that letter, but the substance was, that the local magistrates sentenced me to a month in Derry Jail, because I would not go under a rule of bail to be of good behaviour. I expressed the hope that by going to jail for a month I would not bring any disgrace on the Co-operative movement.

At the time Father Finlay was on holiday in Doochary, and the day I was arrested he was out fishing. Miss Bailey from Castletownroche, County Cork, who was teaching Domestic Economy under the United Irishwomen in Dungloe, left her class and cycled to Doochary; she went up the river to where the priest was and told him that I was in Derry Jail. He rolled up his line, and went back to the hotel. He was too late for the train at Fintown. On Thursday he went back to Dublin. After my conviction on Tuesday, a report of the trial had appeared in *The Derry Journal* on Wednesday, and in large type it had shown that the R.M. was against the conviction. Father Finlay got a copy of the paper, and this is how he told me the story at a meeting in Dungloe afterwards.

'I went up to Dublin Castle, and asked for the Lord Lieutenant. I was told he was not in. I then asked when he would be in, handing my card to the porter. He took it and came back in about five minutes. He said that the Lord Lieutenant was in London. I asked him, "Who rules Ireland in his absence?" He went inside again, and when he returned, he said, "The Lords Justices." I said, "I want to see them." He told me that they did not sit on Fridays, but that they would be there at ten o'clock the following morning.

'I left the Castle very much annoyed.

'The next morning the porter was waiting for me to arrive, and immediately brought me into a great big room. There was a young man there sitting at a desk; he got up and knocked at a door, walked inside, came out instantly, and beckoned to me to follow him.

'There were four men sitting around a table. They were the Lords Justices. One of them said, "Well, Father Finlay, what can we do for you?" and I asked him to release Patrick Gallagher J.P., Manager of the Templecrone Co-operative Society Ltd., Dungloe, from Derry Jail immediately.

'"Here is the report of his unjust conviction, and here is his letter to me. You must release him. I came from Donegal on Wednesday, but I could not see you yesterday."

'Each of them read the report in the paper, and your letter to me; they then held a short consultation and one of them rang a bell. The young man came in, and the Justice who had rung the bell said, "Take down this – To the Governor, Derry Jail. Release Patrick Gallagher of Dungloe immediately. By Order of the Lords Justices.'"

Amongst the people who conveyed me to the station was Mrs. Gardiner – Dr. Gardiner's wife. Boys, but she suffered for that act. The Gombeen men held a meeting the following day and decided to boycott Dr. Gardiner. They invited a young doctor into the district, and it was said, I do not know what truth was in it, that they went sick in their turn in order to keep him. To the doctor's credit be it, as soon as he got to know the circumstances he packed his kit and skinned out.

The Gombeen men were not to be beaten. They got another doctor from Cork. He was immediately christened the Gombeen doctor. He remained in Dungloe for several years. When anyone got ill, if there were in the traders' books they had to take the Gombeen doctor. If they were free they would take the Cope doctor (Dr. Gardiner).

I think of all the lousy tricks they did the boycotting of Dr. Gardiner was the lousiest.

On 17 September 1911, I was presented with a clock. I have no idea of the value of it, but I would not part with it for any money, unless it was to save the Cope from bankruptcy. It bears this inscription:-

*To*
Patrick Gallagher Esq., J.P.
*Chairman of the Templecrone Co-operative Society.*
*From a few of his friends in the movement*
*in recognition of his devotion as a Co-Operator*
*and his fortitude in bearing the unjust imprisonment.*

That was a big day in Dungloe. Father Tom made the presentation, and amongst the people on the platform were: Lady Mary Plunkett, and the author, Shane Leslie. My father, mother, my Aunt Saldy, and Uncle Donald were there. I think everyone in Cleendra that could walk was in the hall that day. After the presentation, Fr. Finlay explained how he had me released from prison.

After the meeting was over, Sally had lunch for us. We could not take my father or mother or any of the Cleendra ones to the room, as it was too small. I got in a bottle of whiskey and a bottle of wine, but none of the distinguished party touched it. My father, mother, Peggy, Saldy, Donal, Gillespie and Brown were in the kitchen. Sally was between the kitchen and the room attending to the table. She came from the kitchen laughing, and whispered to me, 'Paddy, your father is getting impatient, he said, "Damn but, Sally, they will be there all day"'. The next thing I heard was my father, Gillespie and Brown went up the town to Anna's. We were then living in the bungalow, which we are now using for our factory. When the party left and bade good-bye to all in the house I went along with them to the corner. We met my father, Gillespie and Brown coming down the road. All the party shook hands with them. When my father got hold of Lady Mary Plunkett's hand, he stared her in the face and said, 'Damn but you are a handsome girl, as nice as Nancy was when we were married, and she was the most handsome girl in the parish.'

When the visitors left, I went back to the house. They were all sitting around the table having a feed. I sat in along with them and had a second helping. I think you get more good of the bite you eat with your own people than with strangers. The men had their glasses before them. I filled them up. My father said, 'Sally says that none of the gentlemen touched the drink.' I said, 'That is so.' He replied, 'They must be a poor kind of gentlemen that would not take a drop of that good whiskey, of John Power's. Here's to ourselves.' They emptied their glasses.

He then said, 'Give us another drop Paddy, until we drink your good health. I hope the rascals will soon put you to jail again!! The next clock you will get you will give it to us. The thing we have is too fast for me.' Sally said, 'Oh, Pat that is a terrible thing for you to say to Paddy, sure if he goes in again it will kill Nancy. Sure she was on her knees, until she nearly wore them altogether praying for him while he was in that bad place. God save everyone on it. Sure Paddy, you never were bad and I hope never will be, but if they put you in again, some people will be saying that you are bad.' My mother said, 'Sally, do not be afraid of that, sure no one could say Paddy is bad, look at the good holy priest that was in this house today, and the other nice ladies and gentlemen. Don't be afraid Paddy, you are sure to have luck.'

I then put another wee drop into the glasses for the men. I did not offer any wine to the women, as I knew they would not take it, and we had no egg-nog to offer. Brown lifted his glass and said, 'Damn but I would go to jail myself for a few days to get such a nice clock and a feed like this.' Gillespie said, 'So would I, but we will not let them send Paddy to jail again. There is always the danger that something might happen. I am sure if there is any shame left in the other bucks, they will never put him in again. They should go and bury themselves in the midden for ever the dirty ……..! All of them remained in the house until after midnight. It was like an airneal on Cleendra, story-telling and singing.

Brown sang:-

*Good luck to all the people*
  *Who around Dungloe do dwell,*
*Burtonport, Kincasslagh*
  *And Mullaghduff as well;*
*Success to Paddy Gallagher,*
  *That honest man we know,*
*He built a famous harbour*
  *On the banks of sweet Dungloe.*

*He built his bonnie harbour,*
  *He built it trim and neat,*
*He borrowed not from Council,*
  *He asked nothing from the State;*
*He runs a weekly steamer,*
  *With freights so very low.*
*And lands the best of cargoes*
  *At the harbour of Dungloe.*

*Good luck to Paddy Gallagher.*
  *This man of brains and skill.*
*He now is grinding lots of meal.*
  *In the famous Dungloe mill;*
*He is giving good employment,*
  *Long may his factories grow,*
*Good luck to Paddy Gallagher.*
  *From the town of sweet Dungloe.*

*Good luck to all the bonnie maids,*
  *Their sweethearts straight and tall,*
*Who dwell around sweet old Dungloe,*
  *'Mid the hills of Donegal;*
*Long may the Rosses flourish,*
  *And just before I go,*
*I drink long life to Gallagher,*
  *On the banks of sweet Dungloe.*

196

# CHAPTER TEN

## *A Visit to London*

At one of the airneals in Cleendra, when I got up to go home, Donal said, 'What the hell hurry are you in Paddy? Sit down there until we have a wee chat.'

Denis:- 'Paddy, there is too damn much singing, dancing and story-telling going on here, let us have a bit of crack.'

I could not refuse and I sat down beside Donal. He hit me a clap on the knee with his hand and said, 'Paddy, I'll bet you that pipe, and it is full of tobacco, that your mother did not tell you about the wetting herself and Mary Brown got last night coming home from Glenties, with their bundles of rags and yarn. God bless me, if you saw them when they came into our house, I was sure they were nearly drowned. The water was running out of their clothes. I told Brown, he is there now (Can he deny it?), that if I was on your committee I would make you get some knitting for our women.'

My father said, 'Donal, what you say is true. When Nancy came home I thought she would never do a day's good, but she is hardy, look at her now- the handsomest women in the house and Mary Brown is lying with the cold.'

My other said, 'Pat will you ever have sense? You will shame Paddy talking like that.'

'No, I will not,' said my father. 'The going and coming to Glenties is not near as bad now as it was before aul Balfour built the Gweebara Bridge in 1896. Glory be to God, I'll never forget the fright our Mary gave the Cleendra knitters the year Nancy and I were married. There was no bridge in them days.' I'd better tell you the conditions that prevailed in the Rosses in those days, and then tell you the remainder of my father's story.

The Glenties firm was a Gombeen firm and amongst their activities was the buying of yarn and distributing it amongst the women knitters of Glenties and the Rosses areas. They gave goods (mostly drapery) in exchange for the work. They allowed the knitters at the rate of one and threepence for one dozen pairs of hand-knitted socks, (there were no machines in those days). The most they would give at any one time was four dozen, but the Rosses women never took more yarn than sufficient to make two dozen – four was too heavy to carry on their backs. The Cleendra women always went in squads. If any one had not their lot finished the others would help so that they would all go off together.

Gweebara is on an estuary running in from the Atlantic to Doochary, a distance of twenty miles. The Rosses women always went by Gweebara and crossed when the tide would be out. The distance was sixteen miles. There was no bridge until 1896. If they went round by Doochary it would be twenty-four miles, as they had eight miles to travel before they reached Gweebara. It was difficult to judge when the tide would be out, especially on dark days when they could not see the sun (there were no watches nor clocks in the Rosses then). Hardly a year passed but one or two of the Rosses women were drowned crossing the stream. Often they had to wait for hours before they could wade across. Patrick McGill, the writer, told this story much better than I can tell it. He called the firm Fairly McKeowns. They have not left a chick nor child behind them. They left plenty of money, I suppose when they could not take it with them. There is another firm in Glenties now in the knitting business, but they are gentlemen. They give good employment  and pay the workers well, God bless them.

I'll now resume my father's story:-

'Mary was fond of dancing. God she would put pleasure on you when dancing a hornpipe. Well, there was a dance to be in Falmore in John Bonnar's house, and Mary did not want to miss it. She had to go to Glenties with her three shillings' worth of knitting along with the rest of the women. She told me when leaving to wait for her, that she would be back early and be with me to the dance. I thought it would be impossible for her to be back in time. Well, as I was getting ready, polishing myself up to look my best, when Nancy would see me, who do you think came marching in but Mary. She threw her shawl and her bundle of yarn in the bed. My mother put on the pandy and had bread, butter and milk quickly ready for her. Mary washed her feet and face, combed her hair, caught her shawl, threw it over her shoulders and said, "Come Pat, I am sorry for keeping you waiting but you need not be afraid; Nancy will wait as long again for you."

'I said, "Where are your boots?" She answered, "Damn the boot do I want." She gave me a wee pluck. My mother was very annoyed and told Mary that she would be dead before she would reach the dance. Off we went. When we reached the top of Cleendra Brae, I said, "What happened your boots, Mary? Did the heels fall off them?" Mary said, "When they took my socks, marked the price in the book and gave me yarn for two other dozen, I whispered to Sheila Hohnie that I was going home, that I wanted to be at the dance in Bonnar's. Off I went. When I came to Gweebara the tide was not half out so I stripped off, tied my clothes round the thread with a cut of the yarn and with another cut I tied the lot high up on my shoulders. I was afraid to take the boots as they were heavy. I left them on the rocks where we always took them off. I am sure Sheila will bring them home. I plunged into the tide, it was running strong and it took me a half- mile out of my way. I was glad none of the others were with me as I fear they would not make it as the tide was running very fast."

'Well, when the others came to the rocks the tide was out and Mary's boots were sitting on the rocks. Sure what could they think but that she was drowned. I never saw Mary dance better than that night. Not a boy tramped on her toes. Next day she told me that she never felt so fresh after a swim.

'Anyway I heard Sheila say that the women went on their knees and said the Rosary and most of them cried all the way until they reached our house.

'My mother said to them, "What kept you? Sure Mary is home a long time, herself and Pat are dancing now I'm sure. I wanted her to rest herself but she went jumping out on the door."

'Sheila had Mary's boots in her hand and let them drop. She fainted but soon came to herself again. We should forgive old Balfour for passing the Coercion Act because no one was drowned at Gweebara since the bridge was built.'

The Cope went into the knitting business shortly after this. It all started out of a talk we had after a meeting. Johnny Brown began telling how sorry he was for my mother and his wife a night or two earlier when he went to meet them on their way home from Glenties with thread for knitting socks.

We all agreed that it was a terrible pity that such conditions should exist, that women from the Rosses should have to travel a distance of sixteen to twenty miles each way for a parcel of clothes for which they would be charged a pound or thirty shillings, and which are not worth half the price, and to make it worse had to make up the money by knitting socks which they would only get credited with at one shilling and sixpence a dozen pairs. It took them over a year before they could get another bundle of rags.

'Ah, damn it, Paddy,' said Gillespie, 'you must stop this slavery.'

James Liam said that it was up to us all to put an end to such a state of affairs. He pressed me to take a subscription of twenty dollars towards any scheme I could conceive.

I told them I had no idea where to buy yarn at the right price, or where I could sell the socks when they were made.

'I'll tell you where to get the yarn,' said Brown, 'I'll send you in the address in the morning. There are tickets on the yarn which Mary had with her, with some name on it.

The next morning, one of Brown's youngsters came in with a ticket: 'Patons & Baldwins. Registered in Great

Britain.' I wrote to Patons' people in Alloa for five pounds' worth of good yarn that would make good socks. In due course I had a pro-forma invoice. I did not need to go to the Roshine school-master this time to get him to explain what a pro-forma invoice was, for God knows we were well used to them. I sent off the money and got the yarn. A few hours after I received it, it was in the hands of the knitters. It caused me a great deal of trouble, as one-third of our members did not get any, and I had no available cash to send for more yarn.

The first dozen I got in, I offered to several Dublin houses, but none of them would offer me a penny. It was the same with the Belfast houses. Any of them that did reply stated that they were getting their requirements from their usual suppliers. I finally got a firm in Sligo to buy them. Sir Josselyn Gore-Booth was the owner, a brother of the Countess Markievicz. I sent for more yarn and at least kept the Cleendra women from ever going to Glenties again.

About this time, the Swiss put ladies' handknit long coats on the market. Some person drew my attention to an advertisement in *The Daily Mail,* with an illustration of one of these white handknit coats. I wrote to Patons asking them to post us three pounds of the best white yarn they manufactured. They sent it on by return without the cash, no pro-forma invoice, and gave us a month's credit. (We deal with them still, they are a grand firm). One of our members' daughters knitted the coat. Then I did not know what to do with it. I stuck it in our wee window, and the following day I sold it to a passing tourist. I made a profit of six shillings and threepence on the deal. By that post I sent another order for twenty pounds of the same quality yarn.

The following day I had a letter from Miss Spring Rice, of Foynes, near Limerick, to say that there would be an Aonach held in the Agricultural Hall, Westminster, London, and that on behalf of the United Irishwomen she was taking a stall for the purpose of bringing Limerick lace before the public, and, if the Templecrone Co-operative Society wished to exhibit any hand-work at the stall, she would gladly divide it. I read the letter to the Committee and we had a lengthy discussion as to whether we should exhibit or not, and if we exhibited, who should go, or, how many should go?

Gillespie, said, 'We'll all go. It will be the day of our lives, and we might never get the chance to see London again.'

'Let's talk sense,' said Dennis. 'I hate that foolish kind of chat.'

'You be damned,' said Gillespie, 'you never had any pluck. I am going anyway, and I don't mind paying my own expenses.'

I said that I feared the expense would be too high, even for one, that London was a long way off, and that it would mean a week, or maybe two weeks there. Johnny Devenney had private means, he was always well off, and he proposed that I should go, and nobody else and that he would pay all expenses. They all agreed and gave Johnny a great cheer.

On Monday morning I sent a telegram to Messrs. Patons, Alloa, the sense of it being that if the twenty pounds of white super yarn was not on its way, to rush it through quickly with another ten pounds, and added a word about us going to the exhibition. I had a reply back at 1 o'clock, saying 'Railing order to-night.' I was rather disappointed;

I thought they would have said more than that.

We had the yarn in good time, and I got the girls to make fifteen handknit sports coats, as they were then called. All the girls were good figures, but we selected one, who we thought was the best, as a model for fitting the coats on. Every one who would come around would examine the coats on our human model, and criticisms would come from all angles.

Sir Josselyn Gore-Booth's man called with us to sell ready-mades and shirts, and to buy socks. I told him that I was going to the Aonach in London with our sports coats. He said that he had been in Manchester the week before, buying suitings and shirting cloth for the firm, and that it was a great city entirely, having huge business houses, several of them as big as Dungloe. He advised me to break my journey there on the way to London and gave me several addresses where I should call. He told me that if I took a through return ticket to London, I could remain in Manchester one or more nights. He advised me to stay in the Victoria Hotel, which was a good centre, and for my life not to sell my samples, as I could not go to London without them.

I thanked him for the information and made up my mind, there and then, to have a shot at Manchester. As he was leaving, he turned back and said:

'One other advice before I go. Do not travel steerage on the boat; go saloon. The cost will be very little extra and you will get a good bed for a halfcrown. All commercial men go saloon, and you never know who you might meet on the boat. It might be possible that you would meet a buyer. In any case, take my advice, never go steerage.'

I again thanked him and told him that I would act on his advice. My recollection of steerage in the past was not pleasant.

Meantime, I was getting ready for the road. My friends thought that I should wear a homespun sports suit, knickerbockers of course. Joe Breslin made the suit. Sally put a good deep pocket on the inside of my waistcoat for my money, and made two nice pairs of handknit dark grey stockings for me. She had a grand time getting me rigged out. She bought me two ties, six dickies, and two shirts, all new, in the Cope.

The morning I was leaving, she saw Gillespie coming to the house with his best suit of clothes on. Sally said, 'Good gracious, here's Gillespie.'

The car was at the door waiting to bring me to the station. The driver took out my three parcels. I had my samples in two of them; my dickies, ties, stockings and two handkerchiefs, and a cooked hen in the third paper parcel. I bade goodbye to Sally and Packie in the house. I wanted to shake hands with Gillespie, but he said, 'Wait until you are on the car.'

When I sat on the side of the car, ht got hold of my hand and I thought he would squeeze the life out of it.

'God bless you, Paddy, and I hope you will have luck,' he said.

When he drew away his hand I found that he had left a paper in mine. I knew that he did not want any person to see it. I put it into my pocket and did not look at it. When I reached the station I bought a return ticket for London. When the train left the station I pulled the paper out of my pocket and saw that it was a pound note. I felt vexed that Gillespie was not with me. I could not think of anything until I reached

Letterkenny only Gillespie. Such a man! Big as he was, I thought he was not big enough for his great heart that shone as bright as the sun on a good day in June.

I was in Belfast in good time for the boat. The three parcels were a bit awkward to carry. Every few yards I travelled I met a boy who would insist on carrying them, but I held on until I got on board. I saw people booking their berths. I booked a berth, too, the first of my life.

Then a porter got hold of my three parcels and put me into a nice little room. There were four beds in it, two on each side, one on top of the other. He asked me what time I wanted to be called in the morning. I told him to call me in time for the first train to Manchester.

'Right, sir,' he replied. 'Will you want breakfast?'

I said that I would not. I had still half the hen that Sally put in along with my dickies when I had left home.

I thought it was too early to go to bed so I decided to take a stroll around. I was much surprised at the grandeur of the rooms. When I wandered into the diningroom, the sight nearly left my eyes gazing at the variety of food that there was for a hungry man to choose from. I was not hungry, however, as I had had a feed of Sally's hen between Lisburn and Belfast. What a difference between the people sitting there and those in the steerage. I was taking it for granted that the steerage was the same as the Derry-Glasgow boats. I went to a sailor and asked him if I could see the steerage. I handed him a shilling for a drink. He took me over the hatchway and told me to go right up to the bow of the ship and then go down the nearest stairs. I had no difficulty in finding my way.

I was glad to discover that the accommodation was a hundred times better than the Derry-Glasgow boats. There was a good, broad seat along the side and it was nice and clean. Of course, there were no beds. I went back to the dining room and had another look around. I then went off to my bunk. I said a few prayers but did not fall asleep. I kept thinking why I should have such a comfortable bed and the men and women in the steerage having no place to lay their heads, and maybe none of them with a hen in their bundles.

I was up in good time in the morning and got the first train to Manchester. I enquired at the station for the Victoria Hotel. A porter pointed out the place to me. It was right opposite the station. Another lad got hold of my bundles. I asked him, 'What is your charge?' He said whatever I liked. I handed him a shilling, and he was in the hotel before me. The door of the hotel was a revolving one and I had some difficulty getting in. I went round with it two or three times before I got clear. Luckily no one saw me. When I went up the stairs, I asked the first man I met if I could get lodgings for the night.

'Do you mean a room?' he asked.

'Yes,' said I.

'Go over there and enquire,' said he.

I went to a large window where there were three ladies at their desks. I said, 'Please can I have rooms?'

'Yes,' said one of them, 'how many do you want?'

I said I wanted one. She shoved a great big book over to me and said, 'Sign there.'

I followed the example in front of me and got over that part of the performance without a hitch.

'Number two hundred and three,' she said.

Then one of the porters got hold of my parcels and took me to the lift.

By this time the papers were getting holed and part of the knitted goods were to be seen. When I got into the room, I immediately went out to look for parcelling paper and string. I could not find any shop selling such articles. Eventually a small draper gave me sixpence worth of paper and twopence worth of string. I went back to the hotel to put the garments into new parcels and had a look at the parcel that contained my dickies and the remainder of the hen; the leg of the hen was sticking out a little bit and somehow I thought that funny.

I finished the remainder of the hen to the bones, rolled them up in a paper, went back to the station, and left them in the lavatory. I returned to the hotel. I had a shave and a wash, put on a clean dickie, and went out with my two parcels of sports coats. I enquired the way to Messrs. Byhands, and in the end I reached it, for sure enough, there it was, the name 'BYHANDS' in huge letters over the door. In I went. The first person I met was a fine big man in a green uniform. My first impulse was to ask him if he was an Irishman, when I saw the green rig, but I did not ask the question. I asked him to please show me the way to the buyer of the ladies' sports wear.

He said, pointing to the stairs, 'Right up, fourth floor.'

I went up and made enquiries at the head of the stairs for the sports wear buyer. I was told that he was not in, but that if I stood in the queue I would see him when he arrived. I went into the queue. There were four in front of me, and in less than ten minutes there were five others behind me. Each of them had a nice case on the floor beside him. They were all dressed in black swallow-tailed coats, with grey striped trousers. They wore great big castor hats (I think I could have put most of my samples in them), umbrellas hanging on their arms, and a pair of gloves in each man's fist.

In about twenty minutes the buyer showed up. The first in the queue went to his counter. He opened his case and put some kind of goods on the counter. Then he took out his book and did some jotting. The next man did not open his case at all. The third opened his case and did some writing. The fourth was a long time with the buyer. I could not see his samples as there were high boxes between us. When he came away, I stepped forward. The buyer looked at me. I think he was looking at my homespun suit and grey cap.

'What do you want?' he asked.

'I want to sell you some nice hand-knitted ladies' sports coats, made in Ireland,' I said.

He had another look at me and my parcels and said, 'Not buying this week.'

I made an effort to say something, which I cannot now remember, but before I got time to open my mouth the man behind me in the queue came right between the buyer and me and was opening his case. The buyer must have signalled for him, although I had not noticed him. What could I do only walk out. So off I went.

I remembered some other names that Sir Josselyn Gore-Booth's man had given me. I got to one of the houses and asked for the ladies' sports coats-wear buyer. The porter, who was wearing a great navy coat with brass buttons-I could not see his trousers-asked, 'Are you buying or selling.'

I said I was selling.

'He won't see any agent after eleven o'clock,' he said, 'it is ten past now.'

I told him that I was not an agent, but a manager.

'Cuts no ice,' said he.

He looked a pleasant fellow, so I said:

'Sir, it is my first time in Manchester. I do not know much about how to get in touch with buyers. I would feel grateful if you would give me any advice.

'Can't,' said he.

As I turned to walk away, he said, 'You must look a commercial man. Call on buyers before eleven o'clock.'

I returned to the hotel with my two parcels. I left them in the bedroom and sat a while thinking. 'You must look a commercial man,' I kept saying to myself. I went down to the door to have a look around, and I thought I could still hear someone saying, 'You must look a commercial man.'

I went to the station and enquired for the first train to London. It was not until three o'clock, so I went up by the hotel to Market Street. I passed a shop with men's nice black suits in the window. I stopped for a moment and went in. Before I had time to say 'Good day,' a smart young man came to me. He was all smiles and said, 'Good morning. What can I do for you?'

'I am thinking of buying a commercial suit,' I said.

'Oh, yes,' he replied, 'I have just what you want.'

He went into a room and came out with a black suit, which he told me was the best commercial suit in Manchester. I said that I wanted a suit with little grey stripes in the trousers.

'Oh, I am sorry; I know now what you want. You want a good suit made to measure.'

He brought me out a web of cloth with grey stripes in it.

'That's what you want,' he said.

I told him that I could not wait to get a suit made to measure as I was bound for London by the three o'clock train.

'That's all right,' he said, 'I'll have a suit ready at two-thirty, if you call back.'

He took my measure and I told him I would be back at that time.

'That will be all right,' said he. 'The custom of the house is cash with order and the price of a first-class commercial suit is seven pounds ten.'

I handed him the money and went back to my hotel.

I returned at the appointed time. The suit was on the counter when I went in. The salesman told me that he had to get the tailors to work dinner hour and had to pay them double time, but that he was not going to charge me for that. The house would stand the loss.

When I tried on the suit back in my room I found it was a bad fit. I then decided to remain the night in Manchester. I went round to the draper, wearing the suit, and pointed out to him where it did not fit; the coat being far too long and narrow.

'Perhaps the cutter made a mistake and gave me the wrong suit,' he said. 'He is so busy that he might have mixed up your suit with some of the others. Wait a minute until I see.'

He went into the room and came out with another coat.

'Come in here, please,' he said.

He took me into a little office.

'Try this coat on,' he said.

I did so, but it was too wide.

'Wait a minute,' he said again.

Then he went back and came in with another coat.

'I think this is yours,' he said. It fitted me all right. Boys, wasn't I green ..…!

On my way back to the hotel I saw a suitcase in the window of a shop. I went in and bought it. I put my samples in it when I reached my hotel, and put my homespun suit, dickies and stockings in the parcel.

I then decided that I would have a try the following morning at Smith & Jameson's. I came downstairs and went out for a ramble. I kept walking convenient to the hotel. While passing along I saw a shop window which contained only hats. I made up my mind to go in and buy one. I could get none to fit me as my head is a bad shape, a kind of bullet shape, and what was wide enough for me was far too long but the salesman assured me that he could make the hats fit any shape of head. He got a wooden-shaped head, and by manipulating screws he could make it almost any shape or size. He put one of the hats that he tried on me on to this and began to screw. After a time he took it off and put it on my head. It was not much out. He placed it on the dummy once more, and this time it was perfect fit. He took me over to a mirror to admire myself, and then asked me if he would parcel it up. I told him I would wear it, and I stuck my cap in my pocket. I was walking out of the door, when he tapped me on the shoulder.

'Excuse me sir, you did not pay for the hat.' I paid him, and went back to the hotel.

I sat in the lounge for a good while. I was not content; I was thinking about the morning. I had a feed of cold ham and chicken, and went to my room. I said my prayers and went to bed, but I could not sleep, though I counted several times 'a hundred sheep going through a gate'; I think it must have been the comfort of the place that overpowered me. Oh, how I longed to be at home again. As far as I remember it was the most miserable night I ever spent. I would rather a hundred times have been back in the Randy Rows, waiting my turn with my pal to go to bed. I fell asleep only when it was dawn.

I was up early, washed, shaved, put on another clean dickie, and put on my hat. Overnight it seemed to have reverted to its original shape. I did not know what to do. I decided at any rate to wear it until I would see the buyer at Smith & Jameson's. I had to walk very steady for fear the hat would fall off.

I was there long before they opened. There was a boy at the door with a brown suit on. As far as I could see, his job was to push the door around. I asked him for the ladies sports coat department. He said, 'Fourth floor, turn left up the stairs.'

I went as directed. The first person I met I asked to show me the buyer. 'Not in yet,' was the answer I got. When I was there about fifteen minutes others began to arrive. I heard one of the men behind me in the queue say to another, 'There he is now.' I thought I would take a chance, so I walked over to the man he had indicated, with my suitcase in my hand, but with no gloves or umbrella. He looked at me.

'Are you the buyer?' I said.

'I am,' he replied.

I told him that I had nice samples of ladies' sports coats and that I would be very glad if he would buy them.

'What house do you represent?' he enquired.

'My own,' I said.

'Where is your own?'

I said it was in Dungloe. 'Never heard of it,' said he. 'Let me see your card.'

I told him I had no card.

'Where is Dungloe?' he asked.

'In Ireland,' I said.

He began to laugh. 'Put them on the counter,' he said, 'and I'll have a look.'

He walked away. I scattered the samples on the counter and began to feel a bit happy. He soon came back and examined every garment thoroughly. He called a young lady over and she also examined them.

He took some notes and said, 'I am very sorry I did not see your samples last week. I would have given you an order. I fear I am over-bought now. I must sell what I have bought before I add to my stock. Good morning.

He went to the other end of the counter. The man who was next to me in the queue passed my by and went down to him. I packed up as quickly as I could and went downstairs feeling very downhearted. I was thinking that I was in very bad luck. When I was near the foot of the stairs on the second floor, I must have given my head a bit of a shake back, because I saw my new hat tumbling down the stairs in front of me. I tried to stop it with my foot, but I must have got excited, for the next place I saw it was on my leg. I had put my foot right through it. Indeed, had I not been at the bottom of the stairs, I surely would have tripped and might have broken my neck. On my way to the hotel I thought of this, and I think I felt rather sorry that I had not. I punched back the crown and put the old thing under my coat. I went into the first draper's shop I came to and bought a new cap. When I arrived in my bedroom I stuck the remains of my hat in the fireplace. I packed up, came downstairs with my bag and parcels and left them with the porter. I told the waitress that I was leaving by the three o'clock train for London. She went to the office and came back with my bill. I put my hand in the inside pocket of my waistcoat and took out the money. I had sufficient in the first draw to pay the bill. The waitress came back with the receipt and threepence change. Sir Josselyn's man had told me that I would find tipping an expensive item in England, so I was on my guard. With all that, the girl had been so nice to me that I decided to give her a shilling. I dived again into my waistcoat pocket, but damn the shilling or anything else I could find. I searched all my pockets, but I hadn't a cent. I thought at first that I must have lost my money, but on further recollection I remembered how wildly I had been spending it. In my excitement I picked up the three pennies and put them in my pocket. I put on my cap and went to the porter for my bag and parcel.

Off I went to the station and was there two hours before train time. I am sure I was the most wretched man in Manchester. I knew that if I could get to the Aonach before it closed, Miss Spring-Rice would not see me stranded. As soon as the train moved off, I picked up my parcel, went into the lavatory, took off the commercial suit, and slipped into my homespuns. I went back to my seat far more comfortable.

It was near nine o'clock when the train reached Euston station. There were plenty of porters at the station. As I was getting out of the carriage, one of them had my bag out of my hand as quick as lightning. He then made for my parcel saying, 'Want a taxi, sir?'

'No,' I said, 'give me my bag, please. I am sorry I have

no money to tip you. I have not a cent in the world only three pence. If you tell me the way to Westminister Hall, you can have that, and welcome.'

'Keep your threepence,' he replied; 'you have a long way to go. Go out through the gate, turn to the left, go on to the end of Southampton Row until you come to an old church. Any policeman will tell you what bus will bring you to Westminster Agricultural Hall, and the fare is threepence.'

I had not long to wait until the bus came along. I hopped in and told the 'bus-man that I was going to Westminster Agricultural Hall, and that I would feel obliged if he would put me off at the nearest place to it.

'Threepence,' said he, handing me a ticket.

Such a relief. I was afraid of my life that it might have been fourpence. It was a long distance and I began to get afraid that he had forgotten all about me. I kept watching him. I popped into the first vacant seat I saw at the door and asked the conductor had I far more to go. He said 'Third stop.' When we came to the third stop, he signed to me and I jumped out.

I enquired the way from the first policeman I met and he directed me. He told me it was fifteen minutes' walk. I began to run, stopping at every corner to ask the way. When I came to the entrance, there was a man at a turnstile demanding a shilling entrance fee. I told him that I was sorry I had no money, but that I was sharing a stall with Lord Mounteagle's niece and I would pay him to-morrow.

'Sorry, I cannot let you in,' he said.

I reached him my bag and told him he could keep it if I did not return.

'Very well,' he said, 'I'll let you in.'

I went inside and commenced to look for stall number thirty-two. The Hall was brilliantly lighted, and there was a great crowd of people present. Some of the stalls were closed, others selling their goods. I found number thirty-two. Miss Spring-Rice had gone, her exhibits covered up, and the portion she had reserved for me had two bare shelves. I opened my bag and spread out the sports coats. Before I had them all out, three ladies came to me asking the price. I heard one of them remark, 'Isn't it a beauty?' I chanced my arm and said: 'Thirty shillings.'

'It's worth it,' she said, opening her bag and handing me a brave thirty shillings.

What a relief! I felt as if I had not a poor friend in the world.

One of the other ladies said, 'I did not come prepared to buy. I'll be here tomorrow and buy one of those beautiful coats.'

By this time most of the people were moving out, so I decided to pack up and bring my case with me. When I went to the man at the turnstile, I handed him a ten-shilling note and he gave me my change. He told me that if I wanted an exhibitor's ticket I could go to the office round the corner in the morning and get a card that would admit me free. If only he knew how little concerned I was about a free entrance at that moment!

I picked up my parcel and enquired from the first person I met about a hotel. I was told there was none near at hand. In the end I was directed to a hotel near the Houses of Parliament. When I went to the door, the porter looked at me. He reached for my bag and parcel.

'Follow me to the reception-room,' he said.

I followed him. I had not far to go. There were half a dozen clerks there. I said to the girl nearest me that I wanted one room. She looked at me in my homespun sports suit, and the nice stockings that Sally had made me with cap to match.

'Sign here,' she said.

I signed my name in a kind of scrawl that I am sure none of them ever read since. I could not read it myself.

The porter took me to my room. It was magnificent. I was nearly afraid to move round in case I would spoil it. I had a much-needed wash and went downstairs to the lounge. Heavens, such a sight! Every two, three or four were sitting round little tables, with different kinds of glasses, some not much bigger than thimbles and others as large as small saucers. The women had hardly a stitch on them from their waists up except a little strap on each shoulder like a pair of braces, to keep a wee bit of cloth halfway up their breasts. My first impression was that I was in a bad house and the sooner I was out the better. Out I went. I met a policeman and told him that I was staying in that hotel – pointing to it – and asked him if it was all right.

'The best hotel in London,' he told me.

I went in again and sat down amongst them. I thought there was not a person in the room but had a good look at me. I did not sit very long, but retired to my room and slept soundly that night.

I was up early the following morning and had breakfast. I asked for the bill and paid my brave seventeen and six for bed and breakfast (almost a week's wages, which was eighteen shillings). I went to Westminster Agricultural Hall. I arrived there at 8.30; it did not open until ten o'clock. I went to the office and got a card that admitted me free of charge. After the officials I was first there. I had my knitwear on the shelves long before Miss Spring-Rice arrived. She had a great welcome for me and asked me when did I come. I told her that I came the night before, but I never mentioned about the sale. She had her end of the stall nicely fixed with beautiful Limerick lace. She helped me to rearrange the sports coats. We stood by until one o'clock, but no one came near us. Then Miss Spring-Rice told me to go and have some lunch and that she would go when I came back. She told me that there was a restaurant at the back of the Hall. I went there and had a nice meal for one and sixpence.

When I came back, Miss Spring-Rice went for her lunch. After that we stood at the stall until six o'clock but not a single person came near us. My partner again told me to go and get some dinner. I was feeling hungry and went off. I travelled a good bit before I came to an eating-house. I went in and asked for sixpence worth of bread.

'Take a seat,' said the attendant. 'The waitress will serve you.'

I sat at a table. The waitress came along and handed me a menu. I said that I only wanted sixpence worth of bread.

'This is a restaurant,' she said; 'it is a baker's shop you want.'

'This place is all right,' I said. 'I am in a hurry. Please give me a few slices of bread.'

She came back with two think slices on a plate. I think I could have eaten them in one bite.

'Four more of those,' I said.

She went off and came back with the other four. She slid them off her plate on to mine.

'What are you going to have to follow?' she asked.

'This will do,' I said. 'How much is it, please?'

She commenced to write the bill. I was going to ask for some paper to wrap the bread in, but she looked at me very boldly and left the bill on the table, saying, 'Pay at the desk.' I took my handkerchief out of my pocket and wrapped it round the bread. I picked up the bill and paid at the desk. The amount was sixpence.

I went back to the Hall. On my way back, when passing a stationery shop, I went in and bought a packet of note-paper and envelopes, intending to write home for some money. Miss Spring-Rice went off for her dinner when I got to the Hall. She told me it might be possible that she might not be back, and that if anyone came along to buy lace I could sell it, as the prices were plainly marked on all the pieces.

About 7.30 a lot of people came in, and quite a number of them had a look at our stall. One very small lady came to me and asked if I was from Ireland. I told her that I was.

'I love the Irish people,' she said. 'My father was an Irishman. I have never been to Ireland, but I hope to be there some day.'

She examined a few pieces of lace. She then picked up one of the sports coats and examined it. She questioned me for I am sure fifteen minutes as to how such beautiful work could be done by hand, who made it, and a hundred other questions which I never could remember. By this time there were at least nine other ladies standing watching her. She whipped off some garments she wore and was into the sports coat while you would be looking round you. She asked every one of the others what they thought of it. They all agreed that it was a beauty, but that it was a pity it was a little too big. Then the little woman took it off, and put on her own wrap again. She opened her bag and handed me two pounds, saying, 'You are selling your goods too cheap.'

The price marked on it was thirty shillings. I reached her a ten-shilling note, but she refused it, saying: 'Keep that please, give it to the girl who knitted it,'

I thanked her as well as I could. I reached for a piece of paper that was on Miss Spring-Rice's stall to wrap it, but she said, 'It is all right. It is a shame to hide such a beautiful garment. When are you going back to Ireland?'

'I will be here till Saturday. Likely I will be going back on Monday or Tuesday,' I replied.

'Good night,' she said, 'I'll see you before you go.'

Off she went.

In all, I sold six pounds fifteen shillings worth that night and did not sell a pennyworth for Miss Spring-Rice. When I closed the stall, I left all the goods just as they were, including my parcel, and pulled a cover over them. Miss Spring-Rice had assured me that there was no danger as the place would be locked up.

When I went out about eleven o'clock, I asked the first policeman I met if he could direct me to a hotel that would not be too expensive. He directed me where to go.

I had no difficulty in getting to the street he told me of, and, sure enough, as soon as I entered the street I saw two hotels almost beside one another. I went into the first. I met a man at the door with a very short jacket on; the two breast-pieces were made of navy-blue cloth, a row of brass buttons on the sleeves, and the back made of moleskin. I enquired if I could have a room for the night, and he led me in through the hallway. There was an elderly man sitting at a little desk in a small office at the end of the hall, where you could hardly turn a cat. When he had a good look at me he asked me if I wanted a room. I said that I did, but that I wanted to know how much it would be.

'Four and six for your bed; six and six for your bed and breakfast,' he said.

'All right, that will do.'

'Bring this gentleman to number six,' he ordered.

The lad with the patched jacket said to the old man: 'No luggage, sir.'

The old man then asked me, 'Is it bed or bed and breakfast you want?'

I said, 'I'll take both.'

'Six and six, please,' he said.

I was in no hurry the next morning, as I knew the hall would not be opened until ten o'clock. However, I was there before it opened. Neither Miss Spring-Rice nor I sold a pennyworth until six o'clock. I went out for my dinner. The dinner was a few packets of cakes and a jug of beer that day, and every other day. When I came back to the stall, a nice-looking young man, wearing a tall hat, came to me and asked me if I was Mr. Gallagher. I told him I was. He reached me his hand and said:

'I am Erskine Childers. I had a letter today from Ireland from my cousin, Miss Barton, telling me that you were here. I am very glad to meet you and make your acquaintance.

'I would like you to come to my house tomorrow night to meet Mrs. Childers, and have tea with us,' he said.

I thanked him the best I could and agreed to go to his house. He said that he lived in Chelsea, but I was to remain in the Hall until he called for me. Miss Spring-Rice then arrived. I introduced her as well as I could. When Mr. Childers left, she questioned me to death as to how I had got to know him. She said that he was a very important man and that she was glad to be able to say when she returned to Ireland that she had had the pleasure of making Mr. Childers' acquaintance.

She sold some lace that evening. Shortly after Mr. Childers left, the lady who had saved my bacon the second night came to our stand along with two other ladies, and spoke to me in a kindly manner. She said that her friends came to buy some of my beautiful knitwear. They nearly bought up everything I had on the stall. While I was trying to get the garments into parcels for them, Miss Spring-Rice suggested to the ladies that if they left the coats on the stall until Saturday, she and I would be very thankful, as by taking them away the stall would look very bare. I approved of this. I had their money in my pocket. By then, I had in all over thirty pounds. I felt quite rich. I offered to give them their money back, but to reserve the garments for them until Saturday if they agreed. The little lady said, 'We will leave them with you, with the greatest of pleasure. You're Irish. Keep the money. Here is my card, 'handing it to me.

I read 'Mrs. Lillian Clark.' The next evening about five o'clock Mr. Childers came to me at the stall. We got a taxi at the gate (the first I ever was in) and did not stop until we reached Mr. Childers' home. When we went into the house, his wife was there, and I was surprised at the warmth of her welcome. I was not long there until five gentlemen came in. Mr. Childers introduced me to them, and in a short time we were sitting round the table. I got a bit mixed up here again. I watched the others to see what tools they were using. There was a fork, a bigger one, a knife, a bigger one, and a small blunt one. I did the best I could. Mrs. Childers made it so pleasant with her humorous stories which she kept telling while we were eating.

After the dinner was over, we went into another room. One of the gentlemen was called Basil Wilson. That is the only name I remember.

'Mr. Gallagher,' he said, 'we would like to hear your views on the Home Rule question.'

'It would be great for Ireland if we had Home Rule,' I replied.

'Why?' he asked.

'We would then have Home Rule,' I said.

I saw Mr. Childers laugh. Then another gentleman said, 'Mr. Gallagher, what good would it do Ireland to have Home Rule?'

I was in a bit of a fix and did not know how to answer. After some hesitation I said:

'Well, we could then manage our own affairs and make our own laws.'

'Who would make your laws under Home Rule?' he asked.

'Our own people,' I said, 'who we would elect to College Green?'

Another asked me 'Who would you elect to College Green?'

I told him that I did not know.

Mr. Wilson then said, 'Mr. Gallagher, what we Englishmen fear is that if we permit you to govern yourselves you will be far worse off then under English rule. Look at your own case. Is it not the men who sent you unjustly to jail who you would elect to an Irish Parliament?'

He gave me the surprise of my life; I never dreamt that there were men in London who you knew I was a 'jail-bird.'

Then one of the others said, 'Mr. Gallagher, your information is very interesting, but if you think for a moment, that is the greater reason why we should govern Ireland. You admit that your own men are worse than we are, yet you will not say a word against them, but you are always attacking us.'

I was in a bit of a fix again.

'One enemy at a time,' I said. 'Of the two we have, we consider the English by far the worse. Whenever the Gombeen man is fighting the English, we are with him in that fight, but as soon as we are rid of you, we will tackle him, and believe me, he will not last seven years, don't mind seven hundred.'

Mrs. Childers jumped to her feet and clapped her hands. I was proud. Mr. Wilson said, 'I am not disputing what you are saying, but it would be impossible for Ireland to finance herself without our assistance.'

I was in another fix, but Mr. Childers came to my rescue. He said, 'I think so far Mr. Gallagher must have satisfied all of us the great advantage it would be for Ireland to govern herself. It is hardly fair to go into finance.'

While Mr. Childers was talking, I remembered being at a meeting of the Land League in Broxburn, Scotland, where Jack Mulhern was making a speech, and I remembered a wee bit of it, where he said, 'Look at the Childers Commission Report where it is proven to the world that

Ireland is paying three million pounds a year to England over her just taxation. That was an English Commission.'

I said, 'I do not understand finance, but didn't the Childers Commission prove that we were being robbed of three million pounds a year in unjust taxation which money should be kept at home for our own use.'

They all looked at Mr. Childers and began to laugh. His wife laughed heartily. I had not the slightest idea that the Chairman of the Commission was Mr. Childers' father. There was a long discussion on several other points.

Mr. Childers took me back to the hotel in a taxi. On our way, he said that as that was my first time in London I should remain over until the following week, and if I did so that he would bring me into the Houses of Parliament on Tuesday. I agreed to stay over, and gladly accepted his invitation.

On Saturday about three o'clock I saw three gentlemen and a lady approaching the stall. One of the men wore kilts, which in a way were different to the style I observed in Scotland. The jacket and scarf were brown. Another man was frail with a black beard. The lady was also delicate with silvery grey hair. They came to me. The gentleman with the black beard asked me if I was Mr. Gallagher. I said I was.

'Let me introduce my friends to you,' he said, 'Mrs. Stopford Greene, Lord Skerrin, the Honourable Mr. Gibson – Lord Ashbourne's heir – and my own name is Roger Casement.'

They asked me many questions about Donegal, and especially about the Rosses. They knew a hundred times more about the rest of Ireland than I did. They looked at the sports coats and the Limerick lace. Mrs. Stopford

Greene was much interested. I am sure they remained at our stall for nearly an hour. When they were bidding me good-bye, Sir Roger Casement gripped my hand tightly and said, 'I have been told you are doing good work for the people. I hope you will not forget the language. Ireland will be lost if she does not preserve her language. Look at Bulgaria today, she is the admiration of the whole world, and why? – because she preserved her language.'

As they passed out of my sight, I was left spellbound. I thought I was in Cleendra Glen in the fairies' castle. I must have fallen asleep then. When I was tapped on the shoulder by a tall, frail old man I awoke with a start.

'Are you Mr. Gallagher from Dungloe?' he said.

I said that I was.

'I am Sammie Boyle from the Lower Rosses,' he said.

I was certainly delighted to meet him. I had often heard of him at home, and I knew his sister well, Mrs. Jamsey Sweeney, one of the finest women who ever left the Rosses. She, her husband and family were living in London.

'Minnie (Mrs. Sweeney) told me that she heard you were here,' he said, 'and that Jamsey would call for you and bring you out to the house tonight. He will be here after closing time.'

He then began to talk about home. He was in the Customs and Excise in London. If I were his brother his welcome for me could not have been greater. He said that he would be out in Jamsey's before me. When I told him that I would not be going home until the middle of the following week, he took out his card and wrote the address of the Army and Navy stores on it. He told me that he would meet me at the centre door at five o'clock on Monday and introduce me to the sports-wear buyer. I was delighted.

About eight o'clock Mrs. Clark and her friends arrived. By this time I had the last article sold. I first of all showed them the garments they bought and then parcelled them up as well as I could. When I had them ready, I remembered that Mr. Boyle was to take me to the Army and Navy Stores on Monday, and now I had not a sample to show. I stood still for a moment and did not know what to do. Then I decided to explain my difficulty to Mrs. Clark.

'Oh, that will be all right,' she said, 'I know the buyer well, and I'll go along with you and bring the coats with me that my friends and I have bought. What times will you be there?'

'Five o'clock at the centre door,' I told her.

As they were leaving, Mr. Sweeney came in to me. It was he did three months in Derry Jail because he would not drive the police to the Gweedore Evictions. I knew him well before he left home. I cannot describe how glad he was for me, or I for him. I bade good-bye to Miss Spring-Rice and thanked her for her kindness and the help she had given me. She had not sold all her lace. She was continually worrying, thinking she was not getting on so well as she expected, to enable her to help the Limerick girls who were, she said, the best lace-makers in the world.

I went out with Mr. Sweeney to a taxi that he had waiting. When we arrived at his house his wife was as delighted to see me as he had been himself. Sally and her sister, Madgie, were the first two she enquired about. I am sure she asked me about every one in the Rosses. We sat up until two o'clock in the morning. Mr. Sammie Boyle remained until one o'clock talking about home. Oh, such welcome. I told her a little of my experiences in

Manchester, but I warned her not to write to any person at home. I did not tell her about the hat. I knew well she could not keep that story.

'Why did you not wire,' she said, 'and Jamsey and I would have met you at the station?'

I said that I did not know her address.

Then she told me that if I had wired home for money when I was in Manchester that they would have wired back all the money I wanted. I did not know until then that you could get money by telegram.

I wanted to get to the city early on Monday. Mr. Sweeney's house was in Chapham Common. It all appeared a city to me, but when in Sweeney's, they often talked of going into the city. Mrs. Sweeney would not let me go. She wanted me to stay a week with them.

I got away about three o'clock, and was at the Army and Navy Stores before five o'clock. Mrs. Clark was there, and on the minute of five o'clock Mr. Boyle arrived. We went right in. The sports department was on the first floor. Mr. Boyle introduced me to the buyer, and I think Mrs. Clark gave me a second introduction. She put the samples on the counter. The buyer looked at them most carefully and said to me:

'What about delivery?'

I said that I did not know. He looked at Mr. Boyle and Mrs. Clark and then said, 'If I give you an order, will you deliver?'

'I surely will,' I replied.

'When?' he asked.

I said I did not know until I would go home, that we had no yarn and did not know how long it would take.

'It is a most unsatisfactory way to do business. I'll give

you a trail order and I'll leave it to you to deliver as early as possible.'

He wrote out an order for a dozen of each of the five numbers that Mrs. Clark had brought in. I thanked him and we walked out.

Mr. Boyle said, 'We will go into this café for tea.' I never heard the name café before. In we went. It was the nicest eating-house that I ever was in. He handed me the menu and asked me what would I have. I could not make head or tail of it, and said that I did not feel hungry, that I would have just whatever he was having. Mr. Boyle I am sure knew my difficulty. He gave the waiter an order for both of us. Mrs. Clark had something different every time. I think, in all, we had six rounds. Mr. Boyle said to me, 'I am sure you feel strange in this city. You know their business methods are quite different to ours at home in the Rosses. They must have everything in proper order. I venture to make a suggestion that when you are here you appoint an agent, give him your samples, he will call on the buyers and take the orders and send them on to you.'

'I suppose that is what I should do, but how can I appoint an agent?' I asked.

'Sit there with Mrs. Clark until I come back,' he said, 'I will not be more than ten or fifteen minutes.'

He went off. Then Mrs. Clark said, 'Mr. Gallagher, I do not agree with Mr. Boyle. You have nothing to do but show your beautiful garments and you are bound to sell them in every house you go into.'

I immediately thought of my faults in Manchester. I was beginning to think that only for herself and Mr. Boyle I would have drawn another blank in the Army and Navy Stores.

'I am afraid I would not be successful. It is a long way from Ireland to London, and I hate to be away much from home,' I said.

'Twice a year will do you to come to London,' she replied, 'and it will do you good. Look at the successful sale you had at the Aonach. You could sell a ship-load of that beautiful stuff of yours.'

Mr. Boyle then returned. 'I was back in the Army and Navy Stores,' he said. 'I just met the buyer at the door as he was going home and he gave me the name of one of the best agents in London. He says that he will sell stacks of your stuff if you do your part, make all the goods up to sample and deliver on the date you have agreed to. The agent's name is Elkin. Well, I'll meet you at this door tomorrow at five o'clock. I'll 'phone Mr. Elkin first thing in the morning and I have no doubt but he will be here to meet us.'

'I shall be here too,' said Mrs. Clark.

I said that I was very sorry but that I intended going to the Parliament tomorrow at that time.

'I knew the first sight I got of Mr. Gallagher on Wednesday night at the Aonach that he was a superior person,' said Mrs. Clark. 'I was attracted to him immediately. I pride myself in being one of the best judges of human beings in London. I never make a mistake. I'll feel honoured if you will get me a ticket. I am sure you are going to make a speech and I would love to listen to you.'

I felt rather embarrassed and did not know what to say. While I was thinking of an answer, Mr. Boyle remarked, 'I did not hear of a by-election, Mr. Gallagher. When were you elected?'

'I was not elected,' I said; 'there was no by-election Mr. Erskine Childers is coming for me tomorrow night at five o'clock to bring me into the Houses of Parliament.'

I saw Mr. Boyle smiling. I was a little upset. Mrs. Clark came to the rescue and said:

'Mr. Gallagher, here is my measurement' – handing me an envelope – 'I want you when you go back to make me a coat according to those measurements. When I get it I'll do Oxford Street every day for a week. Send me your address and I will get cards printed. Every person who asks me where I got it, I'll hand your address. I am sure you will get more orders than you can turn out.'

I took the envelope, put it in my pocket and thanked her. She gave me another of her cards for fear I would lose the first one.

'Mr. Gallagher, Minnie and Jamsey will be waiting for us. I promised sure to have you out before seven o'clock,' said Mr. Boyle.

'No, no,' said Mrs. Clark, 'you are both coming with me to the theatre (I forget the name now). Harry Lauder is there tonight. Mr. Gallagher must see him. We will be in good time for the first house, looking at her watch. 'You will be back with your friends before ten o'clock.'

Mr. Boyle agreed immediately. I said that I would do whatever he did. As soon as we went outside, Mrs. Clark signalled to a taxi-man; he took us to the theatre, which I am almost sure was somewhere near Trafalgar Square. Mrs. Clark, in addition to paying for the taxi, bought the tickets in spite of Boyle's protest. I enjoyed the show immensely. Harry Lauder certainly was very good. When the performance was over we went out, and having bade good-bye to Mrs. Clark, hired a taxi to Sweeney's.

We had another great night talking about the Rosses.

Boyle arranged to meet me at the Army and Navy Stores

on Tuesday at one o'clock. I was there before the time. He and another small gentleman came to me about three or four minutes after one. When he had introduced me to Mr. Elkin we went in to have some lunch. Mr. Boyle did the ordering for himself and me. Mr. Elkin, I think, took about the same. Then Boyle introduced the business.

'If you leave yourself in my hands,' said Mr. Elkin, 'give me the right stuff and a good commission, I'll sell your stuff.'

I said that suited me all right. Then he produced a long typewritten document and said, 'This is the usual agreement that is signed between manufacturers and agents. When Mr. Boyle 'phoned me I got it typed to save time. Will you please sign here, Mr. Gallagher?' handing me a pen which he took from his waistcoat pocket.

Mr. Boyle reached for the agreement. After reading it carefully, he said, 'Mr. Gallagher cannot sign that agreement until you alter it. Firstly, seven and a half per cent commission is too high. It would put up the price of the goods too much. He will give you two and a half per cent. Secondly, Mr. Gallagher cannot agree to give you the exclusive sale of all his products for the next five years. Alter that to read "the exclusive sale for twelve months for London at two and a half per cent commission." Make the alteration and Mr. Gallagher will sign.'

Mr. Elkin began to protest, saying that he was the man who would open all the good English accounts and that it would be most unfair, after he did all the digging, that some other one would come in and reap the benefit.

'If you can open all the best accounts then you have the ball at your own feet,' said Boyle. 'Mr. Gallagher is not such a fool as to drop a good man for a doubtful one.

Make the necessary alterations, please.'

Elkin made the alteration and both of us signed.

'Where is the copy?' asked Boyle.

'I forgot to bring it with me,' said Mr. Elkin.

'That will be all right,' said Mr. Boyle, reaching for the agreement, 'I am the arbitrator in this case. I'll hold the original. Here is my card. Make out a copy, sign it and give it to me. I'll give you the original.'

This was agreed to and I promised to send Mr. Elkin the samples as soon as possible.

When the waiter came with the bill, I reached for it, but Mr. Boyle was too quick for me, saying, 'We are not just as poor in London as you think. We are able to pay for a bite yet.'

There was no use in my protesting. They both bade me good-bye.

I went to the hotel, left my case there and booked a room for the night. I strolled around wondering how the police were able to control the traffic.

I was in the hotel about half-past four. Mr. Childers called for me. He had his taxi waiting outside. We then went off to the Houses of Parliament. I listened for about two hours to the debate. I did not hear anything which interested me very much; at least I can only now recollect one little incident, which was caused by myself. Some English member was speaking; he said something about Ireland, which I did not catch. Anyhow, another man got up and attacked him, and strange to say I cannot remember what he said, but whatever it was it appealed to me, and I turned to Mr. Childers and said, 'Damn but, the "Wee Terrier" is a bully.'

I thought I spoke so low that I could not be overheard, but I was immediately tapped on the shoulder by a lad wearing a blue uniform, with a lot of tapes across his chest, who told me that if I did not behave myself I would have to leave. I felt greatly embarrassed when Mr. Childers whispered to me that one was not allowed to speak in there. I did not say another word, until Mr. Childers said to me when we were in the taxi, 'That was Lloyd-George who was speaking, and to whom your comment referred. Did he appeal to you, Mr. Gallagher?'

I said that he had.

Mr. Childers replied, 'I have no faith in Lloyd-George; I feel he is not the friend of your country that he would try to make the people believe.'

I parted with him at the hotel, and I never saw him again. Her certainly was right about Lloyd-George.

# CHAPTER ELEVEN

## *The Minister Vanishes*

On my way home to Ireland I was quite happy with my Army and Navy order in my pocket, all my samples sold, and the prospects of getting work for our girls.

I had not written a word to anyone since I left, so that when I arrived at Dungloe about eleven o'clock at night Sally was in bed. When I knocked at the door she cried out, 'Who's there?'

'Paddy,' said I.

No door was ever opened quicker. Goodness, she was glad for me. She wakened Packie, got the fire going and had the pandy on top of it in no time.

On the following night the Committee met. Boys, but they were glad for me. James Durnion questioned me to death, but no matter how I told about the size of the houses, the control of the traffic, or the Houses of Parliament, it was not worth the talking compared with the New York skyscrapers, Broadway traffic, or the White House. Gillespie was very near getting angry with him. Brown was the first to ask me did I get any prospect of work. When I told them that I had sold all the goods and had an order for more, which I produced, Brown clapped me on the back and said, 'Bully man. Paddy, with God's help we will put down this slavery.' Gillespie was very proud of himself.

The next night, on my way out to Cleendra, I had to pass Gillespie's. I had a pipe for him that I had not intended the other Committee men to know about, so I went into his house to give it to him. He caught my hand and the tears came rolling down his cheeks. He did not speak. He sat on the chair, took a knife out of his pocket, filled the pipe with the brown tobacco, which I had also brought him, got a coal with the tongs and was in the act of putting it on the pipe when I stopped him by saying, 'It is a wooden pipe, you will burn it.'

Neither of us had a match (I don't smoke). I got a piece of paper, and when he had the pipe lit he said, 'Paddy, all I can do is smoke your health.'

And he did.

I told him I was going to see my father and mother and he said that he'd come with me. When we went in I think they were as glad for me as the first night I came home from the Lagan. I was not long in the house until all the Cleendra folk gathered in. Of course there was no singing or dancing that night while Paddy the Cope cast a spell on them with his wonderful stories about England.

I went out fishing every evening after I closed the Cope. Sometimes I came in with a nice little lot, and other times without any. I decided to have a day's fishing with the rod and line on Loughaghnish. There are a hundred lakes and loughs in the Rosses within a radius of eight miles from Dungloe, with brown trout in all of them, and in some of them there are sea trout and salmon, all free fishing, but of them all, Loughaghnish can boast of the biggest brown trout. It is the only lough I ever fished with a board, and I got some nice catches on it.

I cycled to my father's house one day, and after helping myself to a good drink of milk, I proceeded up the hill to the lough, and began casting along the shore on my father's side. It was not very long until I landed a nice trout, about two pounds, and while I was taking him off the black and teal, I saw a tall man coming towards me, walking very quickly. He wore a mackintosh and a black hat, and when he was within twenty yards of me, he shouted, 'What are you doing here?'

I waited until he came nearer to me. I took off the fish on the hook, and was admiring it.

He again said, 'Did you not hear me when I asked you what are you doing here?'

I replied that I was fishing. He looked very cross, and I stared at him. I then knew that he was the Maghery minister. Although I felt annoyed and my temper was heating up, when I saw the minister I decided not to say anything; but he ordered me to get out of the place, that I had no right to fish on the lough, as it was only gentlemen who permission to fish on it. He said that he would report me if I did not leave immediately.

I had another look at him, and I said, 'Only for respect for the collar you are wearing, I would put you into the lake. How dare you order me off my father's land. Would you please go now, and do not dare cast on this side of the lake. You can fish on any other tenant's land as far as I am concerned, but if ever again you put your foot on our property we will have you summoned for trespass.'

He walked away without answering me. He did not cast until he crossed the ditch to Denis Houston's land. I was feeling a bit upset, and when he was out of sight I rolled up my cast, and went back to my father's house. I told my father what happened, and he was very much annoyed, and told me that it was not right to vex the minister. I tried to explain, and said in my opinion that Mr. Orr had no legal right to trespass on our land, but that I would be the last to prevent him, if he did not interfere with me.

'Glory be to God, Paddy,' said my mother, 'I think you are all changed since you went to London. What harm was the poor minister doing? Sure your father never tried to stop anybody from fishing on his land, and if you will take your mother's advice you will go to Maghery before you go back to Dungloe and ask the minister for his pardon.'

I tried to explain the position as best I could to my mother, but she could not understand.

I wanted to get away to Dungloe, but my mother would not let me go until I had tea; she had the pandy on the fire, and while you would cough she had three big bowls ready for us. All the others were away on the roads. She cut up a nice scone and took a lump of nice fresh butter out of the press. I enjoyed the feed, and when we were about half through my mother again appealed to me to go to Maghery and beg the minister's pardon.

'Paddy,' she said, 'you do not know what harm you may do us. I would not like your father and I to be put out of the house in the end of our days. Sure you know the power the ministers have. You remember my brother Donal telling you the night before you went to London how another minister put your father's people out of Maghery.'

I then realized my mother's uneasiness. I finished my tea, and when we were all sitting around the fire chatting, I tried to make my mother see the days of evictions for whims were over and that neither minister, landlord nor all the bailiffs that ever Ireland reared could evict us or any other body, so long as we paid the rent.

'That's right, Nancy,' said my father, 'Paddy is telling the truth. I heard Father McGlynn saying the same thing about thirty-three years ago, and I heard Micky Neddy telling it at this fireside. Indeed, Paddy, I am glad you did hunt him, thanks be to God for such a change in the world. Sure that is also the reason we have no fear of our good-looking daughters that the old landlord would take them from us. Musha, but it is different to the time when we were youngsters.'

I then asked my mother if she was content now, and she said, 'Maybe I am. Who did you say made them laws, Paddy?' I told her Michael Davitt was the man whom the Irish people should thank.

I said good-bye to them, went outside, and began pumping my bicycle. I heard my father say:

'Nancy, Paddy is right. He must be a great scholar. He said the same words that Father McGlynn and Micky Neddy said. Paddy is the only other scholar who ever told us that. God knows, Nancy, there are no scholars at all now. If Micky Neddy had stayed at home, his scholars would be the smartest men in the world.'

I could not help laughing, and the next thing I heard was my father's step coming towards the door, but I was around the corner before he reached it.

The next day the story went around that the Cope-man had a row with the minister at Loughaghnish, and that the Copeman was going to throw the minister into the lake. A short time afterwards there was a terrible hubbub in the Rosses. The Rev. Mr. Orr invited the Rev. Mr. McEnerney to have dinner with him at the rectory in Maghery on the 22 March 1914, and while Mrs. Orr was preparing for the dinner, Mr. Orr got his fishing-rod and basket, and passed out through the yard, met his man Paddy John, and told him that he was having a dinner-party, and that he was going out to Loughaghnish to get some trout for the dinner. The Rev. Mr. McEnerney arrived in the evening but there was no sign of Mr. Orr returning, and when it was getting dark, Paddy John went out amongst the neighbours saying, 'God bless my soul, Mr. Orr went to Loughaghnish for some trout for the dinner, and he has not come back yet. Mrs. Orr is in a bad way about His Reverence.'

The story went through the district like the shot of a gun, and all that were able got ready to go out. The night was very dark, some carried lanterns, others had turf soaked in paraffin oil, while some carried sticks with bags which were soaked in paraffin. Away they went up the hill towards the lough, a distance of about one and a half miles. When they arrived at the lough they lighted the turf and the bags and began shouting, 'Your Reverence, come here! Mr. Orr, come here! Minister, come here!' but there was no response. Paddy Lanagan suggested that they should go round the lough as he might be stuck in some bog and not able to free himself. They went around the lake, a distance of about four miles, but there was no sign of the minister. They then decided to abandon the search until morning, and the following morning at daybreak they all went towards the lake again.

A message was sent to Dungloe, and the police were on the scene very early in the morning. It so happened that I was out in Cleendra on the evening of the twenty-second, to see my mother, who was not keeping well, and although I remained out until after nine o'clock I did not hear a word about Mr. Orr being missing until the following morning, when two of the police knocked at the door. Sally asked who was there, and one of them answered, 'Is Mr. Gallagher in? We want to see him.

Sally said, 'Get up, Paddy, there is someone at the door. It must be that your mother is worse.'

I pulled on my trousers and went to the door, and saw the two brave policemen.

One of them said, 'Good morning, Mr. Gallagher, I just want to ask you a few questions.'

'All right,' I said.

He asked me if I had been in Cleendra the day before, and I told him I had; he then asked me what I was doing out there, and I said that that was none of his business.

'Now, Mr. Gallagher,' he replied, 'we are only doing our duty, and you being a magistrate, should know that we have to do what we are told. We would like to know what you were doing in Cleendra yesterday.'

'Oh, nothing in particular,' said I; 'I just went out to see my mother, who is not keeping well.'

The policeman who was doing all the talking asked me if I had been near the lough, and I told him that I had not.

'Did you by any chance see the minister?' he asked.

'No,' I said.

'Did you hear he is missing?'

'I heard nothing about it,' I replied. 'What happened to him?'

The policeman said, 'He went out to the lough after eleven o'clock yesterday morning, and did not return. The Maghery people were all out searching for him all night, and they could not find any trace of him. We thought that you might have met him, and that is the reason why we are bothering you so early in the morning. The Head, Sergeant, and all the other constables went away out at daybreak. We are hopeful that nothing happened to him.'

They went away. One of them went to the Barracks, and the other remained in sight of my house until I opened the Cope, and then he kept in sight of the Cope until he was relieved by the other fellow. The story spread throughout the Rosses, and there were many theories as to what happened to the minister. The most prevalent rumour was that he met with foul play by the Catholics, that he was an active supporter of the Ulster Volunteers, and on that account the Catholics would not hesitate to murder him. But during this time what do you think all the Catholics were doing? (There were no Protestants within four miles of the lough). Every man, woman, boy and girl, who lived in the neighbourhood of the lough were out searching for the missing minister, from the first light of dawn on the cold wet morning he was reported lost.

At last Anthony Henry found his hat, fishing-rod, and basket on the brink of the lake in the long heather. He shouted, 'He is here!' and the echo of that shout resounded from the spinks, and all who were searching came running to the spot, but they could see no sign of the minister.

'We will all kneel down in God's name and say the Rosary,' said Anthony, 'and if he is down there, he will rise.'

They went on their knees and said fifteen decades of the Rosary, and then Anthony recited as much of the Litany for the Dead as he could remember. I often heard John Frank say that you would hear Patrick Paddy John miles away answering Anthony when he was reciting the Litany.

By this time the police arrived on the scene. The Sergeant

asked if there was a boat near hand, and they told him that John Conleen had one, and off they went for John's boat. John was in bed, and he did not know that the minister was lost. When he heard the noise around the house, he jumped out of bed, and called Speed (his dog). He took the dog in his arms and went up to the attic with him. He was sure it was the police looking for unlicensed dogs. Mary pulled on her skirt, threw a wee shawl round her shoulders, and went to the door, which she opened, saying, 'We have no dog here; you can come in and search if you like'; but when she saw it was Patrick Paddy John who was at the door she did not know what to say.

'Where is John?' said Patrick. 'The minister is lost in the lough, and we want John's oars and pins to search for him.'

Mary called John and told him that it was only the Maghery boys looking for the oars to get the minister; that he had drowned himself. John shoved down the ladder from the attic, which he had pulled up after himself and the dog; he went out with them and got the oars and pins in the byre, and off to the lough with them. They rowed the boat to the far side where the people were waiting for the minister to rise.

The police then decided to go back to Dungloe and get some drags made at Paddy Roarty's forge. While they were in the forge Denis McShea came along with the horse and a cartland of goods for Johnny Edward's shop in Meenacrosh. He stopped outside, unyoked the horse, and led him into the forge, saying, 'Paddy! Put on a slipper for me because I am in a hurry. They are short of some goods in the shop, and John Peter warned me not to waste a minute'.

'You bedamned,' said Roarty, 'you do not be in such a hurry when you go into the pubs, and I have more important work to do than shoeing your ould horse. These gentlemen' – pointing the red-hot iron to the two policemen who were standing by – 'must get their turn first. They want this grappling to try and lift the minister from the bottom of Cleendra lough. He was drowned there yesterday.

Denis blessed himself and he went deadly pale. One of the policemen rushed over to him; he thought he was going to faint, but after a while he got all right and said, 'May God help me, sure I met his ghost at the crossroads yesterday. I might easily have known that he was not alive; he was walking so fast, and every step was as long as two. He was only touching the ground with his toes; and what I never saw on him before, a cap with a big peak on it, and it pulled down over his eyes. He never said a word to me and it is the first time he ever passed me without bidding me the time of day.'

'Away with you out of here,' said Paddy.

Denis left the horse in the forge and made the first rush to Kenny's. Anna was in the bar. As he entered the door he shouted:

'A glass of your best, Anna, quick, or if you do not I will not be alive to drink it.'

Anna poured out her usual big glass. Denis reached for it and slugged it over.

'Oh, Anna, I am done,' said he. 'I met the minister's ghost. Something is going to happen, and he repeated the story he told in the forge.

Anna called Kenny. He came into the bar. Anna gave Denis another drink and told him to tell Kenny what he had seen. The story was repeated, but Kenny was not a believer in ghosts, and began laughing.

Meantime one of the police went to the Barracks and reported Denis's story. Kenny was the only person who believed in the truth of it, except that he did not believe that it was a ghost that Denis had seen. He said that Denis had seen the minister in real flesh and blood.

In any case the police called a halt and did not carry out the programme of dredging the lake.

It happened that Jimmie, our vanman, was out on the Derrydruel district that day delivering goods. When he came home he heard of the drowning.

'Damn the drowned he is,' said Jimmie. 'As I was going to Denis's I saw the Reverend Mr. Orr coming up the road. When he came near me, he pulled the cap down over his eyes and went behind a turf stack until I passed. When I looked round I saw him going up the road like hell.'

This confirmed Denis's story, so the scene shifted and the minister was tracked and the suspicion growing up around me was cleared away.

# CHAPTER TWELVE

## *The Trouble*

From 1918 to 1921 I had a miserable time of it. The Black and Tans were worse than savages let loose. They were murdering, ravishing and burning.

There were £28,000 deposits in our Society, all Rosses money. Some people had £5, others from £50 to £300. Every day when I opened the paper I would read of Co-operative Societies being burned out. I did not know the minute the Cope would be set on fire too, and as the ordinary insurance did not cover us against military acts, I felt most miserable. I got out a special insurance policy against military destruction. It only covered us for three months and the premium was £500.

The price of the goods began to go up and we had not sufficient capital to run the business. We were shipping flour and general goods from Liverpool. We had an overdraft in the National City Bank. Mr. Smith Gordon was manager. I applied on behalf of the Society to give us a further accommodation of up to £10,000. Mr. Smith Gordon, whom I knew personally, wrote back and asked me what I wanted so much money for. I said in reply, that I was anxious to get a cargo of generals from Liverpool. It was a common term in business to use 'generals' for general goods, at least I thought it was all right. In any case, Mr. Smith Gordon gave us the overdraft up to £10,000, and wrote me a personal letter. I am very sorry I haven't got it now, but as far as I remember the following is more or less what he said:

'Dear Paddy,

Your application for an increase of your Society's overdraft up to £10,000 has been granted by my directors. I would be grateful if you would advise me the hour of the ship's arrival as I am anxious to meet some of the Generals.'

It was only when I read the letter half a dozen times that I saw the silliness of mine. I did not, nor could not think of replying. The next time I was in Dublin, Mr. Smith Gordon said, 'Paddy, I never heard of any great deeds done by your cargo of Liverpool Generals.'

Another day a carter came from Fintown Station with a box to our factory. The box was labelled 'machinery', but when we opened it, what do you think it contained? – thousands of rounds of ammunition : .303 rifles, bayonets, revolvers and other war material. The military were then stationed in the Parochial Hall, and the officers in Sweeney's Hotel. I put the lid on the box again, and warned the workers who saw it 'to keep their mouths shut.' I was not in the Volunteers, and got no advice about the consignment. I went down the town and I met one of the Volunteers. I told him that I wanted to be put in touch with Peadar O'Donnell, 'the author'; Josie Sweeney – now Major-General Sweeney; or, as an alternative, Jimmie McCole, now Captain McCole, but I could not get in touch with any of these.

I waited until midnight; then John Conleen and I took the Cope lorry, put the stuff on it, and we did not stop until we landed out in Cleendra, where we hid the whole consignment near the holly bush at the fairies' home. The following night Packie got in touch with Bernard Sweeney, a brother of Josie's, and they went out to Cleendra and lifted the stuff. I do not know how it was distributed, but I was thankful to be rid of the responsibility. It was certainly an anxious time.

Things were getting a bit hot in north-west Donegal. Mr. Hunt, manager of the Londonderry & Lough Swilly Railway Company, wrote a letter to some of the merchants advising them to call a meeting of the Rosses and Gweedore traders, telling them that if they did not bring pressure to bear on the young irresponsible blackguards and compel them to stop interfering with military supplies sent by his line, he might have to close down the line. The traders burned Mr. Hunt's letters and as far as I know not one of them was acknowledged. Shortly afterwards the military made a raid on the Rosses. They came in hundreds, by land in their lorries, and by a gunboat to Arran Roads. They took the same passage in their motor boats that Napper Tandy took on the 12 September 1798, that is through the bite at Rutland, and landed at Burtonport. They arrested a great number of prominent men, young and old, and without any formality of trial interned them in Ballykinlar.

The Cope had the only lorry in the Rosses. They robbed the lorry of the magneto and carburettor and some other vital parts. I made a fuss over it. A Major Something wrote to me and said that if I called with him at his headquarters in Letterkenny he would give me the parts of the lorry that his soldiers had taken in Dungloe. As soon as I got the letter, I cycled to Letterkenny.

As I was entering the town a British Soldier presented his gun at me and shouted, 'Halt.' I came off the bicycle. He said, 'What is your name?' I told him. The next question, 'What are you doing here?' I said, 'Here is a letter from your Major asking me to come for the magneto.' He read the letter, (I never saw it since and I do not remember the name of the Major). He then said, to two other soldiers, 'Bring this Shinner before the O.C.' They marched me up to the Asylum, which was then the Military Headquarters. As soon as we passed through the gate I heard a shout, 'Paddy, where the hell are they going with you? Come over here until we have a chat. It's a long time since I saw you. How are they all at home? I am glad you are coming to stay with us.'

The speaker was Paddy Mulholland of Keadue (about three miles from Dungloe). To be fair to the British Soldiers they passed on and seemed to enjoy the incident. Heavens! If it was the Black and Tans they would smash his head. Paddy and I worked together in 'Tarbrax Mine' in Scotland. He was then a smart handy man but the poor man had a nervous breakdown and so was in the Mental Hospital.

I was taken into one of the cells. Then an officer came in and said, 'Well Shinner, what are you up to? Did you search him?' he asked the others.

I had nothing on me only a few shillings and the letter signed by the Major.

'Oh,' said the officer, 'you are the man we are looking for. We have got you easy.'

The news spread through Letterkenny that the military had Paddy the Cope arrested and that he was wounded. Willie Kelly, solicitor, was soon on the scene, and he was permitted to see me. He told me that he was almost sure that if I signed the necessary military undertaking he would get me released.

'For heaven's sake, Mr. Kelly,' I said, 'do not mention any undertaking. I would disgrace the Rosses if I did such a thing.'

He had a notebook in his pocket and I asked him for a leaf of it, which he gave me. I wrote to Sally, telling her and the boys not to be uneasy, that I was going to be taken by the military to Ballykinlar that night, but that I would be in good company along with the other prisoners. I said that I was not as old as some of them and that I was accustomed to hardships and could easily stick it. I sent another note to Leo Brennan, our Secretary, telling him as well as I could to carry on.

Mr. Gregson, of Messrs. Spillers & Bakers, Ltd., Cardiff, England was in Letterkenny that day, and he met Willie Kelly coming back from the Asylum. They had a consultation. Both drafted some kind of document and went to the Asylum and got in touch with the officer in charge. Mr. Gregson was a great talker. He told the officer that he was making a serious mistake in arresting Mr. Gallagher, the manager of the Templecrone Co-operative Society and Messrs. Spillers & Bakers' (Cardiff) agent for the Rosses. He said that they were after shipping a cargo of flour to the Templecrone Co-op., and that if Mr. Gallagher was not there to look after it the cargo would go to loss. He pulled out his card and handed it to the officer, saying, 'If anything happens to our flour, our Managing

Director, Sir Arthur Nicholas' – I think that was the name he gave; I am not quite sure – 'will raise the question with the Government.'

I was taken out and put sitting in one of the tenders with a bunch of soldiers around me, their rifles at the ready. I knew our destination was Belfast. The lorry started, and while the gates were being opened I heard a bugle sound. Whether there were other signals or not I do not know, but the lorry backed again to where we started from and we remained there for about two hours. Then there was a further order shouted, and I was told that I was free.

I walked towards the gate when I thought of the parts of the lorry, and turned back to ask for them. Another soldier took his gun from his shoulder and presented it at me. I turned and made for the gate. No one interfered with me. When I came down as far as McCarry's Hotel, Mr. Willie Kelly, Mr. Robert Gregson, and several others were there. It was only then that I got to know of Kelly and Gregson having been in the Asylum on my behalf. They told me that before they left, the officer gave them a definite undertaking that I would be released, but that he would have to wire to Dublin and get permission.

We went into McCarry's Hotel and had some refreshments. Mr. Gregson decided to take me home in his motor car. We feared to take the usual route as we heard that there was a lot of Black and Tans raiding between Ballybofey and Doochary. We went round by Donegal and Glenties and on to Dungloe.

Sally did not know of my being in trouble. The letters did not arrive until the following day. Gregson was in great form. If you heard him tell what he came through! He was the best storyteller I ever heard. He frightened the wits out of Sally, and he seemed to enjoy telling about the fuss of the bullets flying around us and he doing eighty-five miles an hour. He said that when he came to a trench outside Donegal, which he knew was there beforehand, he put his foot on the accelerator, got the car up to a hundred miles an hour and jumped the trench. I never met any man who could tell a story with Mr. Gregson.

A few days afterwards, A Colonel Moore, who was stationed in Belfast, on the advice of the big Unionist merchants of Londonderry, decided to blockade the Rosses and Gweedore. No one knew better then the Derry merchants that from April to August there never was more than a week's provisions in these districts, and that all the supplies came through Derry. They advised Colonel Moore that if he prevented provisions leaving Derry for north-west Donegal by rail, the rebels would be coming on their knees begging for mercy. He issued a military order forbidding the railway to carry any goods to north-west Donegal in June 1921. Immediately the order was issued, Owen Doherty, owner of the fishing-boat Orient Star, and his crew from Gweedore, left Bunbeg and went into Derry Harbour for a cargo of provisions for Gweedore and the Rosses. When the cargo was loaded, the military came along and made him unload again, so he had to go back light. The Orient Star is now trading between Galway and Arran Island. Food was running short and there were hundreds of cases of eggs which we could not move as the military had all the roads leading into the Rosses blockaded. I went to Carrigart to look for one of the steam drifters, and one of our boys, Neil O'Donnell, went to Gweedore. I failed in Carrigart but Neil succeeded in Gweedore. He told me that I could get the s.s. *Better*

*Hope*. I went to Gweedore the following morning, met the owner, Archie Dunlop and chartered the *Better Hope*. I had her in Burtonport that night, loaded her with eggs and moved out to a creek in one of the islands. The following morning Paddy Sweeney and I went aboard and set steam for Glasgow. The next day we took shelter in a creek at Downings, and as darkness set in we moved off again. All lights were out. We were at Rathlin Island at dawn. We took no cover, went right up the Clyde, and berthed at the docks near the Co-operative Wholesale Society at Morrison Street.

Here again the Scottish Co-Operative Movement came to our rescue. They gave me everything I asked for. They loaded the ship and did not ask me for a penny of cash. I could not then, or now, find words to express my great gratitude to the Scottish Co-Operative Movement. Once again they showed their human element and their honesty, no bargaining about prices, and everything of the best at the lowest possible figure. When I told some of the managers of the different departments that our part of Donegal was blockaded by the military, the expressions they used were as strong, if not stronger, than any I ever heard at home. I remember one of them who was very much annoyed saying, 'If the average Englishman or Scotchman knew how the bloody bastards of politicians are treating the Irish there would be a revolution, and the sooner the better. Think of it! I fought in France for the freedom of small nations; at least that is what we were told we were fighting for; and now to think the London Cabinet is trying to starve our neighbours because they want to manage their own country. What the hell do they know how you should manage your country.'

Paddy Sweeney remained in Glasgow with his brothers.

We left Glasgow on the morning of June 23, as soon as the dock gates were opened. We sailed down the Clyde. I took my turn at the wheel. Every ship we met – and we met plenty – we thought might mean the end of our journey. I said my three Hail Marys going to and coming from Glasgow many a time. The skipper and owner, Archie Dunlop, never showed the least sign of fear. Some of the young lads said that if they had a few good guns they wouldn't give a damn if we met the entire British fleet. I am sure one of them did not care what happened, one in particular, John Gallagher; I think he was disappointed that there was not some kind of a scrap. I believe I was the only coward on board. I was frightened, not so much about myself, but I feared the cargo might not reach the Rosses.

However, we met with no difficulty. When we came through Innistrahull it was beginning to clear. We went into a creek in Mulroy Bay, and anchored there, and as soon as darkness set in, we heaved our anchor, and steamed for Burtonport with all lights out. We reached Rutland Island before dawn. I sent Gallagher ashore with a note for our secretary, Leo Brennan, telling him where we were and that we would be in Burtonport that night and if he thought the coast was clear to bring plenty of help for discharging at nightfall. Gallagher arrived back with a note to say that it was a bit risky, but it would be worth taking the chance. He said there would be plenty of men at the pier as soon as darkness set in.

We heaved anchor and sailed into the harbour. Boys! I was delighted to see the crowd that was on the pier. There never was a ship discharged so quickly at any pier in the world as the *Better Hope* that night at Burtonport.

I might here mention that we got to know afterwards that we were not in much danger of being chased or sunk by a warship as the blockade only applied to Derry. We, however, were still in dread until we had the cargo discharged at the pier.

It so happened that two days afterwards we had a cargo of flour in from Cardiff. The Derry merchants got alarmed. I do not know whether it was true or not, but we heard that they again approached Colonel Moore and urged him to blockade all ports in Ireland as well as Derry. The military had to consult the Government in London, and they would not agree. Then the Derry merchants called a meeting of the Chamber of Commerce and appointed a deputation to interview Colonel Moore at Belfast, and urge him to lift the blockade if he could not blockade all other ports; that the Derry trade was being diverted, and that they were already suffering. The blockade was lifted the next day, but from that day to this Derry has never regained the trade she lost.

We ship regularly into Burtonport, Mr. Thomas J. McBride into Bunbeg. Isn't it wonderful how the wheels of the world came round? Thomas J. McBride is now using the Bunbeg Stores (which the landlord used in the past for storing and shipping the people's food in the Famine days) for storing the cargoes of food and other goods for the people. The Cope is doing likewise with the Burtonport Stores, and I hope that in the very near future we will be doing the same in Killybegs, as we are now owners of the Killybegs Stores.

After the blockade the White Cross Society gave a grant of £6,000 for relieving distress in the Rosses. Dr. Kennedy, the Secretary, called with me and told me that the Society would give a grant to our Committee if we would agree to use it to relieve the hardship in the Rosses. I came to the conclusion that this would create some jealousy amongst the local traders, and that it would be better to have a more representative committee. Dr. Kennedy agreed, and a local committee was formed from the most prominent men in the Upper and Lower Rosses, including the clergy.

We sent a scheme for work to the White Cross, which they approved of. In the scheme we made provision for the erection of a pier at Dungloe for the convenience of the Rosses and island people, to take their corn to Dungloe mill, and their turf home. There was no engineer on the job. Kenny Brennan and I were there daily. When the pier was completed in 1923, I made up my mind to get the Cope goods in by sea. I did not want to get a pennyworth through Derry if I could help it. I told my Committee so, and, as usual, they approved of my suggestion. Off to Liverpool I went searching for a light draft boat. After some enquiry I chartered the s.s. *Glenmay*. Her draft was eight and a half feet loaded, carrying capacity, 150 tons. The charter was for six months' fortnightly sailings from and to Liverpool and Dungloe.

When I got home I called a special Committee meeting. I told them that I had chartered the s.s. *Glenmay* for six months, to come in every spring tide with a cargo of goods for the Cope. John Gillespie got up and whistled *The Flowers of Edinburgh* and danced a hornpipe. He then caught me by the two hands and said, 'Paddy, you are welcome back. Long was I waiting to see our own ships coming in. Now, boys, you see my talk has come true. What do you think of that, Johnny Brown?'

'Damn but, it's great,' said Johnny.

John sat down and James Liam said, 'Mr. President I am delighted that we will very soon see our own ship coming into Dungloe with the Cope goods. Out in Croveigh we did not believe we were getting much benefit from the money given by the White Cross Society, and we were blaming you for allowing so much of the money to be used in building what many people were calling "a dry-land pier". It will be a different story now when they will see their goods coming direct across the water. Now, Mr. President, it gives me great pleasure in proposing that you fix the day of the first cargo to arrive at Dungloe on the next Fair Day, and the world will be at the fair. They will see a sight they never expected.

Gillespie seconded it. I said that I was sorry that I could not fix her for the Fair Day, as the tides on that day would be neap, and the *Glenmay* could only come in on the top of spring tides as we had only nine feet of water at the pier. There was great disappointment amongst the Committee then.

I then told them that when I was in Liverpool I made enquiries about granite sets. I was introduced to a man who told me that he was an agent for several quarries and that he would have no difficulty in selling all the sets we could produce. The Committee were delighted, and we started to make granite sets. We had granite everywhere around us. Practically all the Upper and Lower Rosses are all grey and red granite with a covering of six or eight inches of soil in some places and three or four feet of bogland in other places. George Russell (AE) in describing the Rosses, says, 'It is a country where the bones of the earth stick through its starved skin.'

We advertised for a set maker.

The first arrival of the s.s. *Glenmay* with a cargo of 'generals' was a great day for the Rosses. There was a large crowd of people on the pier and on the surrounding hills watching her coming up the bay, where there was never before seen a bigger boat than a twenty-four-foot yawl. For the two days that she was at the pier, old women from miles around came to see her.

They never before saw a ship.

The night she landed at Dungloe, I was, naturally, a bit excited. Brown waited on the pier for me until I was coming home. He reached his hand and gave me a warm handshake.

'Come on, Paddy; we will go into Anna's, and I will give you a glass of the best in the house. Damn but, I am very proud of you. You are the bully man,' he said.

'No, Johnny, thank you,' I replied, 'I will not touch or taste it until the *Glenmay* sails out the bay. You know we will have a big day tomorrow discharging her.'

Johnny was not pleased, and he said, 'If you do not think it worthwhile to go in with me, you can go. I will go in myself'; so I changed my mind and said, 'I will go in with you.'

'Bully man,' said Brown, and in we went.

When we went home to sally, who do you think was there but my brave Gillespie. He got up and put his arms around my neck, and kissed me several times before he let me go, and then he pulled out Sally from the corner, and both of them danced a hornpipe, while Brown sat on the table and lilted for them.

When they were tired Gillespie told Sally to give me a drink. She handed him the bottle which he had brought in a short time previously.

Sally got the tea ready, and when we were finished, Gillespie said, 'Now, Brown! Look at what we have come to. Yourself or any of the others could not see a finger-length before you. Only for myself and Paddy and James Durnion you would be stuck with the fairies out in Cleendra yet. Come on, John, let's go home. Paddy go to bed! We will have a big day tomorrow. We will be in as early as we can. Paddy! Good night to you and Sally and Packie and God bless you all.'

And off went Gillespie and Brown.

Unfortunately there was some jealousy, and one man in particular who would make an innocent man believe that what he said was true, if you did not know him, said, 'What does Paddy the Cope know about shipping? This will break his neck. She is now on his dry mill-race, and she will never go out. Look at the clouds. The wind is going north; there will not be five feet of water in that race when she is unloaded.'

He prophesied wrongly: she floated on the top of the tide and went off to Liverpool for her next cargo, and for the six months she never lost an hour for want of water; but she gave us many an anxious moment, as it was just 'touch and go' several times. We sent out two cargoes of sets to Liverpool and we never got a cent for them. This was the only English firm that ever let us down over our twenty years' dealings with the English people. Some time ago I was told that he was not an Englishman, although he could speak English fairly well. Would you believe neither 'AE' nor any other writer ever wrote a scrap about this big blunder on my part, and not one of the Committee ever blamed me. When we gave up hopes of getting anything for the sets, Johnny Brown said, 'That is nothing to worry about. I went two harvests to Scotland. Each time I had a pound away with me and I had not a cent coming back. I could not get work.'

'What signifies one pound,' I said, 'compared with five hundred?'

'Well, Paddy,' replied Johnny. 'Maybe a pound was worth more to me in them days than five hundred pounds to the Cope to-day.'

'Let us hear no more about our loss,' said James Durnion.

'If you were in the States, why, overnight some men lose thousands and millions of pounds. They never grumble, they make it up again next time.'

With the growth of the Cope we got new ideas. Our factory was growing. We needed power. There is a river flowing along the foot of the town. The landlord harnessed some of its power to turn a mill-wheel. Our old oil engine was giving trouble. The mill-wheel and the river that turned it began haunting my dreams. I picked up odds and ends of information. In the end I made up my mind we must buy the mill and the water rights. But a whisper would stir the merchants. The thing to do was buy first and let the Committee in on the news, when enthusiasm could bubble and cause no harm. Leo Brennan and I put our heads together. When the documents were ready for signing the Committee was called together. The Committee gave us their blessing. The news was let loose. The merchants made a rush, but they were late. We had the documents in our safe before they got their breath.

The first thing we did was to erect a power house, put in a turbine, and a Greenhill Mill for making our own maize meal. We took the power to our factory, bakery, and Cope, gave free lights to the Catholic Church and the Protestant Church, and Dungloe Street, and gave lights of more than two units to the houses in Dungloe at eightpence per unit, one light for three shillings per month, two lights for five shillings per month. Now, looking back on it, twelve years previous to that there were not twelve householders in Dungloe who would have bid the Copeman 'Good morning'; but that it the way of the world.

# CHAPTER THIRTEEN

## *A Trip to America*

In December, 1928, Miss Mary Ann McGuire, a great friend of ours, who was then living in Dungloe, and who is now proprietress of Carrigart Hotel, decided to go to the States. She had previously been there. She was also interested in knitting. I made up my mind to go with her, if the Committee would agree. In fact I had made all arrangements before I asked permission from them.

At our Committee meeting on the 11 January 1929, I told them that I would like to go to America. I had a nice range of samples to show the American buyers. I said that since I started the Cope in 1906, twenty-two years ago, I had never had a holiday, and that would like to see my sisters, cousins and other relations again. None of the Committee spoke, for what I thought, a long time. At last Johnny Brown said:

'Paddy, I would rather you put the idea out of your head. If only you could know how uneasy we are when you go to England, and you never away more than seven or eight days. God bless us, if you go to America, you might be away seven or eight weeks. If anything went wrong in the mill, or the factory, what would we do? And who knows what might happen to you between here and America?'

'I agree with you,' said Dan Deery, 'many a one went to America and never came back.'

I was beginning to get very uneasy by this time, after all my preparations. I was also beginning to get ashamed because I had told many of my friends that I was for America on the sixteenth. Suddenly John Gillespie jumped to his feet. I was almost sure that he would oppose my going.

'Go, Paddy, my boy,' he said. 'Don't mind Brown. I'll come in every day and help the staff to carry on. Sure we let you to jail, why should we not let you to America? Boys, when you come back, we will have a big night. Don't forget to see Nellie Wan, and tell her that John Gillespie was asking for her.'

'Will you call and see my Willie in Philadelphia,' said Durnion. 'Here is his address. I had this letter from him on Christmas Day with a cheque for forty dollars. I have not changed it yet. Here it is to you, Leo. I want it changed.' Our good secretary,

Dan Sweeney, one of the Roshine schoolmasters, had previously resigned, and Leo Brennan, our present secretary, had taken his place.

I then asked them if they agreed that I should have a holiday after my twenty-two years' service.

Gillespie said, 'You know damn well, Paddy, you are going to get your well-deserved holiday.'

'To make sure that no one will be complaining again,' said James Durnion, 'I propose that our President gets his well-earned holiday in my country, the glorious United States of America. He will come back a new man with grand ideas in his head. God bless him. I guess we will be a bit lonely during his absence. I tell you now that it will be worth it.'

'I second that,' said Gillespie. 'I'll pray to God night and morning while you are away for your safe return.'

'We all will do that,' said Brown.

I said, 'It is proposed and seconded that I get a holiday. Is there any amendment?'

'There will be no amendment,' said Denis. 'We all wish you all sorts of luck. When do you intend going Paddy?'

'On the sixteenth,' I said.

'I'll be down before you go away with Mary's address. God, Paddy, won't she be glad to see you. We are not going to bid you good-bye. We will see you before you go away,' said Denis.

When the meeting was over, James Durnin called me aside and said, 'Mr. President, I am glad you are going to see the States. I'll be in again before you go away. Take that with you and put them up for the boys. Let them see that there is stuff in old Ireland yet.'

He handed me two pounds. I made no protest. If I had, he would be annoyed.

On Friday night, January 15, all the Committee came to our house, and nearly everyone in Cleendra. There was not room for them all, so we went to the factory. Oh! Such a night! Singing and story-telling. Do you mind this? Do you mind that? I had tears in my eyes now and then though I'm damned if I knew why.

All remained till two o'clock in the morning. I could not take one-tenth of the presents that were given me.

When Brown was leaving, he got hold of my hand. I'll never forget that handshake from that strong, bonny man. His lips moved but he did not speak. When he let go of my hand, he just walked away.

Gillespie came next. He got a hold of my hand and

said, 'Good luck, Paddy'. He put his other hand in my pocket and walked away. I knew he put something into my pocket.

When I went into the house after bidding all of them good-bye, Sally and Packie were crying.

'I'll not go at all if you are going to be in that state,' I said.

'You must go now, Paddy,' Sally said. 'It's not your going. It's just everything. Aren't people fine?'

I put my hand in my pocket and got Gillespie's five golden sovereigns.

We went to bed and were up early the next morning. We motored from Dungloe to Derry. As I entered the motor that was to bring us to Derry, I was surprised to see every worker in the factory, and every member of the staff coming to bid me goodbye. Such a change since the first time I went to the Lagan.

Jim was in St. Columb's College in Derry. I went to see him at the college.

We got abroad the tender at Derry Quay at eight o'clock. We were alongside the s.s. *Caxeronia* at Moville at 10.30.

We berthed at Halifax on Saturday, February 2 and got a permit to go ashore. Halifax, as it appeared to me, is a wretched old city built on the side of a hill, old houses, icicles as thick as your legs hanging from the roofs. I saw children on the streets in rags. I never saw any of the Rosses children so poorly dressed. On the other hand, I saw men dressed in fur coats just like London ladies. It was bitter cold.

The reason we called at Halifax was to discharge 4,000 cases of liquor. One of the sailors told me every case would be in the States in twenty-four hours. While the discharging was going on I did not see a worker who had not a pair of gloves on. I could not understand how they could work with so much clothes on.

On Sunday, the third, we left Halifax at 10 a.m. It was very cold but I could not leave the deck. The scenery was magnificent sailing along the Nova Scotia coast.

On Tuesday, the fifth, we sailed up the Hudson by the Statue of Liberty, and berthed about 10 a.m.

After a day in New York I went to Elizabeth, New Jersey, to my cousin, Sally Tully. Oh, such a welcome? We were in each other's arms, when in walked her sister, Lizzie. She pushed Sally away, and she got hold of me. I thought she would never let me go. Then Tully came in. Mick was in the American Navy. Margaret and Madgie were in Pittsburgh.

Before I had time to tell them some of the messages their mother sent with me, the neighbours began to come in.

I intended to stay one night, but I had great trouble getting away from them after the third night. I then went to Bayonne to see Sally's sister, Mary, then Mrs. Bonner. I will not try to describe the welcome I got in Bayonne.

I left for Pittsburgh, going out to my sister Mary, who lived in Homestead. There were, I am sure, at least fifty Rosses boys and girls with us to the station. I was presented with a return ticket.

I got the train at New York at 10.30. I arrived in Pittsburgh at 8.30 a.m. on Sunday morning. I had made enquires during the night from the railway attendants about a connection for Homestead, and I was told that there was no Sunday service. When I got out of the train I followed the crowd. I intended to get a taxi, as the distance was only about seven or eight miles. Long before I came to the entrance I saw my sister Annie (she was home about ten years previously), she was watching for me, but did not see me until I was beside her.

'Hello, Annie!' I said.

She did not speak, but just put her arms around me. I would have been much more comfortable if there had been no person near us. Then two handsome young girls put their arms around me and kissed me.

They were Annie and Mary Kelly, my sister Mary's daughters. It was to her Peggie sent the passage money many years ago. There was John O'Donnell also, an America born, a relation of ours, with his car.

When we got into the car, Annie said, 'Paddy, only for you spoke I would never have known you, you have got so fat. I could never imagine meeting a fat Cleendra man. You are the first. Wait until Mary sees you, she will get the surprise of her life.'

When we landed at my sister Mary's, she rushed to the car, and you can imagine for yourself the welcome she gave me. I could not describe it. We went to Mass later, and when we came outside after Mass, the number of people that I knew who came to welcome me was surprising, and the crowd of others whom I did not know was astonishing. I am sure they held us up for about an hour.

I went back to Bayonne and spent a few days there, calling on friends. Charlie's house was packed every night. Half of the people who called could not get in.

The ship was sailing from New York on the next day. Well, the train from Bayonne was packed with Rosses people to see me off. My cousins from Elizabeth, Dinnie Gallagher and several others were there.

The passage was a pleasant one. When I landed in Derry,

Sally, Packie and Jim were there meeting me. Sally told me that Johnny Brown was dead and buried. It made me very miserable at losing such a good friend.

The following night I went out to Cleendra. I called with Mrs. Brown. She put her arms around me and she cried and cried. It was different crying to the Americans. Her cry was a sore one and a good right she had at losing such a fine man.

The airneal that night was in our James's. You can imagine the many questions I was asked about our people in America. It was the saddest night I ever spent in Cleendra only when my father and mother died, as every now and then someone would mention Johnny Brown's name.

# CHAPTER FOURTEEN

## *Harbour Dues*

At our Committee meeting in January 1936, it was decided that I should go to Holland to buy a cargo of cement and some other goods.

I arranged to go the following day. I was rather disappointed at no fuss being made about my going. Of Course, Gillespie and Brown were dead and James Durnion was confined to bed. He never had a day's health since 1928 when he did three months in Sligo jail for non-payment of rent. He was over seventy years and in receipt of the old-age pension at the time.

I left Dungloe by motor car, and got the train at Fintown Station. I had a new suitcase and in addition to the suit on my back I had another in the case, but devil a cock or hen had I with me this time. I had also some hosiery samples to show to a few London houses that we were doing business with.

When I arrived in London, the first business house I called in I told the buyer that I was going to Holland, and asked him for his advice, as I knew that he went to the Continent often on business.

He said, 'I am busy now, Mr. Gallagher. Could you arrange to meet me at lunch at one o'clock? I'll advise you then.'

'Certainly,' I said, 'if it does not inconvenience you.'

'It will give me the greatest pleasure,' he replied.

I had his order in my pocket.

We met at lunch. He told me to go to Cook's, get a return ticket, get five or ten pounds' worth of guilders, and if I went to Rotterdam to stay at the Atlanta Hotel, where many of the staff could speak English.

I had other calls to make and as I could not get away until the following day I decided not to bother about the ticket until then. That evening as I was going into Charing Cross Hotel, where I was staying, who do you think I met but James Doherty, a Rosses man. I had not seen him for years. Well, we were both glad for one another. We sat there for many hours talking about nearly every person in the Rosses and he telling me about his experiences out foreign.

When I told him that I was going to Holland, he said, 'I'll fix you up,' handing me his card.

I said I was delighted and so I was. I did not tell him that I had intended to go to Cook's the following morning.

Next morning I called at Doherty's office. He had my tickets ready, and handed me a hundred and twenty guilders, saying, 'Paddy, you can pay for all you use of them when you come back.' He wished me the best of luck.

I went with the boat train to Dover. As my passport was being examined, I heard, 'Hello, Paddy!' I turned to see if it was I or some other Paddy that was meant, and there at my back was big Barney O'Driscoll, owner of the Killaloe Slate Quarries. I tell you we were glad to see one another. I did not meet him since. He was going to Germany. My ticket was for Rotterdam.

I landed at the Hook of Holland, got off at Vlaardingen, went to the Co-Operative Superfosfaatfabriek (isn't that a big lump of a name?). I think it is the biggest artificial manure factory in the world. I bought 400 tons of superphosphate from them. I then went on to Rotterdam, booked a room in the Atlanta Hotel, went to a firm of brokers, Messrs. W.H. James & Co., Ltd., Korte Hoogstraat 36A, and chartered a boat called the m.v. *Beta* (M.V. is a quick way of saying motor vessel). The man I chartered the boat from was a fluent English speaker. He came to the hotel that night to see me, he was a charming man, his name was Broek.

I had very little difficulty in Holland. I only stayed there two nights. As soon as I arrived in London I went immediately to Mr. James Doherty's office. I had only to give him less than three pounds for the guilders. When I reached home I can tell you that Sally, Packie and Jim did put me some questions about Holland and the kind of people the foreigners are.

We had a special Committee meeting the following night. The only business we did was to discuss my journey to Holland, which had saved on the manures alone £225 for the people of the Rosses. In due course the m.v. *Beta* arrived outside Burtonport. She was drawing too much water to get into the harbour, which belongs to the Donegal County Council. I arranged to discharge her outside the County Council's property. When the Harbour Master demanded harbour and ship's dues I refused to pay. He reported it to the County Council by telephone. After some time he again approached me.

'Paddy,' he said, 'you must pay the dues. If not, I am instructed by the County Council to arrest the ship.'

'Devil a due or dues will I pay,' said I.

'All right,' said he, 'I have the ship now under arrest.'

I can tell you the excitement then got up. In less than two hours nearly every one in the Rosses heard that the ship was arrested, and it was added in some places that the Cope Man was under arrest also.

The Sergeant and the Guards were standing by all day. When the ship was unloaded the pilot went abroad and the Captain gave orders to loose the ropes. One of the wire ropes was looped round on a large granite stone. The Harbour Master sat on it.

'I have this ship under arrest and she will not sail until the dues are paid,' he said.

I loosed all the other ropes, went aboard the ship and asked the Mate was it possible to cut the rope. He said it was, handing me an axe and saying, 'When you find me putting a heavy strain on, hit the rope with the axe, right on top of the comen.'

I got hold of the axe, as I often did when cutting props in the mines in Scotland, and hit the rope on the comen, and to my relief it nipped in two, leaving the Harbour Master sitting on the loop end.

We sailed out through the same narrows that Napper Tandy had guided the French on 12 September 1798. When we passed the three-miles limit we stopped the engine, opened the seals that the Customs Officer had put on at Burtonport, and drank success to the *Beta*, and hoped she would soon be back again.

The Captain told me that I had not committed any illegal act by cutting the rope, that the ship was not legally arrested unless a Court Order had been issued and a notice nailed or posted on the mast. I tucked this bit of information in my nut thinking it might be useful some other day. I came back home with a wee drop in my hip-pocket for the morning.

The Harbour Master reported this little incident to the Donegal County Council. They have a Pier Committee. In any case, this Pier Committee held a special meeting. It began to look like trouble. It did not seem sensible to us that we should pay for bringing a boat into a shelter that was idle otherwise; it's as hard to know when to stop fighting as when to begin.

I called a meeting of my Committee, put all the facts before them. I said it might be a gamble, but in my opinion it was worth testing. Charlie Brown, a new member of the Committee – a son of Johnny's – said, 'Paddy, fight them for it. If you fail, no one will blame you.'

Phil McCauley, another new member, said, 'If I were you I would have legal advice on it.'

We all agreed that the two young fellows' advice was sound.

I wrote to Mr. Furlong, Solicitor, Letterkenny. He suggested to have Counsel's advice. Shortly afterwards I was on business in Dublin. I met Mr. Furlong and we went to see Mr. Basil McGuckin, one of the high-priests of the law. Mr. Furlong asked me to explain the case to Mr. McGuckin. I did so as best I could. He asked me several questions, which I was able to answer. He did not look for, or produce, any law book. I was a bit disappointed as I thought he would look up some authority and quote the laws for us, but not so. As soon as I answered his last question, he said, 'Mr. Gallagher, you have a sitter.'

He never said another word about the case although we sat a good while in his hospitable house.

On the way back to the hotel, I said to Mr. Furlong, 'Dammit, it is a wonder he did not, at least, give us his opinion.'

'Are you not satisfied?' said Mr. Furlong. 'Did you not hear him say you had a sitter, that is good enough.'

At the next Committee meeting I reported the result of my visit to Dublin. I said that the Counsel said we had a sitter.

'That's good,' said Brown.

'Damn good,' said McCauley.

The rest of the Committee were like myself, they did not know what a sitter meant.

The next ship that came in was on 1 April 1936. What ship do you think she was but the same pirate ship, the m.v. *Beta*, with a cargo of flour from Cork for the Cope. The Harbour Master demanded the dues but damn the cent would I pay.

Meantime, the Donegal Pier's Committee were looking up all the old law books from King John's time. They were as bad as the old Head. They were not sure of the law. Nothing happened.

The next Cope ship was the s.s. *Maria*, with 1,000 tons of cement from Denmark. The Captain was a Norwegian, and a rough-looking diamond. I went abroad and told him that if he was approached for ship's dues he was not to pay, that I would deal with the matter. He agreed.

Meantime, I heard that the Council's solicitor was on the 'phone to the Harbour Master. Anyhow the Harbour Master told me that it was his instructions to arrest the ship if I did not pay dues.

'Devil a due will we pay,' I said.

When the ship was unloaded and ready for sailing, the Harbour Master shouted to the Captain that he was acting under instructions from the County Council's solicitor, and his instructions were to arrest the ship if the dues were not paid; and he had her now under arrest.

I said to the Harbour Master, 'If the Solicitor is giving you these instructions, why do you not arrest the ship in a legal manner, nail a notice to the mast? Surely you should know the law by now.' I had my lesson off.

The Harbour Master did not nail the notice to the mast; he would be suspicious of advice from me. I then shouted to the Captain that if he was ready to sail everything was all right. He was ready.

I asked the Pilot's assistance to loose the ropes. He hesitated for a moment. I think he was of the opinion that if he did so he would be committing an illegal act. I loosened the ropes and out sailed the s.s. *Maria*.

From that day up to the present I have not been asked to pay a penny of harbour dues.

# CHAPTER FIFTEEN

## *Success*

I have been Chairman and General Manager of the Cope since it was registered. In addition to the granite-set blunder I made several others. During wartime, if I were any good I could have made as much money for the Cope as would leave it independent of deposits or banks. Prices were going up, and instead of following the prices, we were cutting. For example: we were selling the sugar two shillings and eightpence per hundredweight under the controlled price, and everything else accordingly. Most of the goods were controlled, and business houses could only get their quota. As there was nearly all the time a scarcity, the unscrupulous trader made huge profits, while we were only able to pay our way.

Some of our girls were earning six pounds a week in the factory, although we were not meeting direct expenses, but it was a pleasant time for me to see many of our workers getting twice my wages. I am glad to say that the same almost applies up to this day. I wish we could pay them more.

I am sure if I asked my Committee for £1,000 a year, they would not have the slightest hesitation in giving it to me. The only thing that is worrying me is that the Cope is not in a position to give employment to every one who is able to work in the Rosses.

In 1906 our Society was registered, fourteen members. We have six branches, Maghery, Lettermacaward, Meenbanid, Kincasslagh, Annagry and Burtonport. We have forty-four men and boys employed in them; in our bakery, thirteen; in our mill, two. We have working in our hosiery factory one hundred and fifty girls, between indoor and outdoor.

In 1906 our turnover was £490, no wages; 1907, turnover £4,692, wages £165; this year our turnover will exceed £100,000.

There is a great change in the Rosses since our Society was organised in 1906. In those days you had not the courage to ask how much you owed the business people unless you were able to pay all that was demanded from you. No one had a pass-book, all have pass-books now, and the business man who charges more than five per cent interest on overdue accounts is finished. Thank God the slave mind is gone. If it is in any other part of Ireland today, it is not in the Rosses.

We sell our knitwear, especially our gloves, in many countries outside the British Isles. We sell to some of the best houses in America, Canada, Australia, etc. We are nippling at hand-made carpets, which we are doing in our new factory at Annagry. So far we have made little progress, but we are hopeful we shall succeed.

When we opened our store in Cleendra we had only a very small house, twelve feet by thirteen. Dungloe was the capital of the Rosses, it had two hotels and five large business houses. We were in a bad centre out on the Maghery Peninsula and seven miles from the station. When we came into Dungloe we could only get one room on the ground floor, today we have by far the largest business premises in Dungloe, and I say, without exaggeration, that we do more business by far than all the others combined in Dungloe and the Upper and Lower Rosses.

The one thing that has been worrying me for a considerable time is that we have no pension scheme for our workers. The reason is that up to now we could not afford it. It is probably my fault. As soon as I imagined that there was a pound in sight I would borrow another in order to do something that would give employment to another soul. I hope, however, that I will hold the line until I see a pension scheme established so that our workers will be able to live in comparative comfort in their old age.

In housing, the people have taken advantage of the Government scheme for building new homes. I hope and pray that the Government will continue their housing schemes, and borrow all that is necessary. I cannot help thinking what would have happened to our Society in 1921 if we had not borrowed that £10,000 from the National City Bank. I am sure there would be no Society today and I shudder to think the conditions the people of the Rosses would be in without the Templecrone Co-Operative Society.

There is also a great improvement in the roads. Motor cars can now go to most of the houses. The Government has done a great deal of good work in rural districts, making new roads, draining swamps, but, of course, with the best intention in the world, no Government can make good land out of the wretched soil we have, consisting of bog, gravel and rock, and, unfortunately, we have no wealthy people amongst us to start industries.

With all that, our people are fairly content. Ninety-five per cent of the people are living in their own homes. The average valuation is only twenty-five shillings and the average rent now to the Land Commission is only fifteen shillings per holding. Then nearly all of them have two cows, their own milk, butter and eggs, and one or two of the family in Scotland, England or the United States of America. These people who are away never forget their fathers and mothers while they are alive. Ay, and after their fathers' and mothers' deaths they never miss a Christmas without sending a fat letter to the brother or sister who lives in the old home.

There is another wonderful change since my young days. A great number of our people who are in America, England and Scotland come home now for a holiday. If you saw my sisters and the other people's brothers and sisters coming home with boxes full of presents for us, you would feel glad and sad; glad to meet them and again sad that we should ever have been parted, and many a tear has been shed at such meetings.

In addition to the Rev. T.A. Finlay (who visited us often), Sir Horace Plunkett and AE, we had several other important visits form people who were interested in the Co-Operative Movement up here on the top of Ireland, amidst the bogs and rocks; most of the directors of the Scottish Co-Operative Wholesale Society, a few of the directors of the English Co-Operative Wholesale Society; all the directors of the United Co-Operative Baking Society; and that brilliant writer, Miss Marie Harrison, who wrote about Templecrone in the *World's Work*; Professor A. Victor Murray, of University College, Hull; Mr. Savel Zirand, New York Bureau of Industrial Research;

Mr. Darling, who is Registrar for one of the Indian Provinces; Mr. J.A. Stanilaus, of Madras; Mr. Amer, Egypt; Dr. Rashad, an important Egyptian official; also Mr. John P. Wallace, Assistant Editor *Wallace's Farmer*. This paper was then being run by Mr. Henry Wallace, grandfather of the former Secretary for Agriculture in the United States. And last but not least that charming and handsome lady Madame Gonne MacBride. She visited us during the Blockade, and has always been where help was required.

# CHAPTER SIXTEEN

## *Finale*

I got a letter one day from the United Co-Operative Baking Society, Ltd., 12 McNeil Street, Glasgow, to say that the directors of that Society were coming round our way on a visit and would be anxious to meet me.

I was glad to meet the people who had befriended us so stoutly when the local traders tried to crush us away back in 1907, and made their stay as interesting as I could. One of them remembered well the day our appeal for supplies came to them and gave me their side of the story. They called a special meeting of the directors, who decided unanimously to stand behind the puny Co-Operative effort in Donegal. I remembered so well the fever of the days of waiting for their decision, and the overwhelming joy the news of it finally gave us that I could only wish I could give each of them a leprechaun to take home with him in gratitude.

We talked that much of the early hard days that I got it into my head I would go back to Scotland and run around through some of the places where I had worked long ago. The Chairman and directors of the United Baking Society were more than kind to me and put a car at my disposal so that I might make my turas. Back at the Randy Rows I met Mrs. McMahal, with whom Sally and I lodged when we first went to Scotland. We then went to Winchburgh to see a Mrs. Boyle with whose mother I lodged forty-five years ago. She is as fine a woman as her mother and that is saying a big lot. You talk of hospitality … I only noticed the scenery once and that was one evening on our way by Loch Lomond, Lough Long and Lough Finn. There was a bloom from the heather like the glow of the blue bells along the Doochary river. I'll always remember it.

At West Calder I sought for Mr. Pratt, manager of the Co-Operative Store there. He was manager of the Pumperstown branch when Sally and I first joined the Co-Operative Society. Many a time he eased things by letting our account be overdrawn while we were finding our feet.

I came back home with my mind full of Scotland and of the changes in it since my day. Workmen have better times there now. Even unemployment has not such terrible terrors in it. There's more style – people think more of themselves maybe. I had to think too of the change in myself – there I was round Scotland in a motor car, sleeping at good hotels, eating of the best, the ghost of the man that wandered from farm to farm with straps under my knees to help keep up my trousers. And yet yon days were great days and I could sigh for them and the half-ounce of tea and the pennyworth of sugar, and the quarter-pound of bacon, the half-pound of onions, the Model lodge and the hotplate.

Scotland with its changes was still in my mind when I came back home. For the first time in my life I found myself remembering the far-off days. Many a time I recalled a happening, a laugh, a song, a wake, but this was different. I was remembering the countryside and measuring the old days against the new ones.

There are changes – big changes. The houses are different. They have been remade in the past few years. Nobody need fear the landlord if he puts in a new window or raises the second smoke. On the contrary, the Government give grants to improve old homes or build new ones. Children wear clothes that would not even come to us in our dreams when I was a child. They are better fed. They go to school until they are fourteen years. I doubt if a child in the parish does not reach the sixth class before he faces the world now.

There is no fear of the landlord or his agent. The bailiff is no longer a bogey man. The word 'eviction' is dead except in old stories. Not only is the landlord gone but the rent is almost gone.

People look on the law in a friendly way. The Guards are neighbours' sons in the eyes of the people. They pay dog licences in Cleendra. The Government is not a whip, but service that comes into people's lives with doles, relief schemes, and the like.

There is more money in circulation. A shilling was a big bit of money when I set out for the Lagan. You can meet a child with one in his fingers on a fair day now, instead of the halfpenny I would have been rich with.

And at the same time, thank God, people are discontented. The dole is good, and relief schemes are good, but young people need more. I suppose even the yellow meal that was given out as relief in the eighties of the last century was an improvement on the way things were before it, but nobody dare quieten people with yellow meal today. Who knows how soon it will be before the few shillings dole are as out of date as the meal!

Education is developing people's minds, and young

people expect that those who think themselves so fit to govern that they push themselves forward for offices, to find work for the youth so that they may set up homes for themselves.

The social changes are startling when you come to look at them. All the Big Bucks of my young days are in the dust. It is a rare thing to see a man touch his cap to anyone except a priest, and outside his office a priest counts for little more than the case he has to make. I have seen priests heckled on the election platforms as badly as ever I was.

The motor car which would have been expected to make new snobs has done the opposite. A couple of old age pensioners will charter a motor to take them in for their pensions or take them to Mass. It has an effect on people to find themselves astride the world like that.

With people's minds free like that, the road for the Co-Operative Movement is wide open. The sort of fight our Society had to make would not be forced on a Society anywhere today. The noise and excitement of the political struggle kept people's minds off co-operation, but any day now there will be a rush back.

Maybe it is a pity that when I was telling my story I did not keep our shop, and factory, and all that more on view. I should have brought them out, and put them on the scales month by month, so that the reader could see them growing. But that would not be easy for me, for I spent my time hunting off every shark that tried to savage us more than measuring and showing off. But other people kept an eye on us. George Russell kept an eye on us, and maybe the best thing I could do for you would be to copy out of *The Homestead* what he said.

*The Irish Homestead,*
Saturday, 11 November 1916.

## TEMPLECRONE
### STONE WALL COUNTRY

If the traveller visits the district he wonders how men ever came to settle there, what necessity drove them to make their homes in a region where the rocky ribs of earth break everywhere through its skin. Wherever the eye roams there is the brown of bog, the grey of rock, and the little patches of green which appear here and there are strewn with boulders like tombstones over human hopes long buried. There is not a tree where the earth could shelter itself from its own storms, and yet if we climb a hill we see multitudes of little holdings separated by grey walls of stone built up from litter of the fields, and these grey walls running into each other appear like a gigantic net-work of ragged lace let down from the heavens. Science later on may do something with these bogs, but now the visitor wonders how any person came to live there and he murmurs to himself something about 'Love and hope and man's unconquerable mind.' How, he asks himself, can these hundreds of little holdings, about five acres on an average, each with about two acres of arable land and that strewn over with rock, how can these support human life? What attracted people here? There is indeed a wild beauty here when the rain stops and the sun shines and the clouds scud over the sky and the world in an amazement of viv-id colour, the streaming roads are ablaze with glittering silver and the hills are blue and gold, the hollows where the shadows fall are purple and the little lakes gleam like jewels set in bronze; but that beauty is unprofitable save to the artist's eye, and we wonder whether these fairy flashes of colour, the harvest of vision, indeed, bring any compensation for the scanty harvest, yielded by the fields below that heaven of everlasting light. For truly the winds are tempests here and the rain falls in a passion as if it would wash away the earth and leave barer the rocks, and bog and field are ever sodden with moisture. But still here from a hill up over Dungloe one can see little cabins amid the network of stone walls, and there is not a spot which could be cultivated from the hillsides to the inlets of the sea which has not been utilised. How have these people lived? They have eked out the living the earth denied them by migratory labour. Almost every family has sent its men to Scotland and its girls have stood in the hiring fairs in Ulster, and after a season's work they returned, the men with ten or fifteen pounds and the girls with their lesser savings, and that hard-earned money enabled these families to pay their shop bills and eke out the produce of the potato patches and the milk of a couple of cows and the profits of raising a litter of pigs. A hardy folk these, continuously cheerful and battling against conditions which a good many people would have preferred going to jail rather than accept.

### Where the Gombeen Man was King

It is always over such poor districts that the gombeen man has reigned most successfully and as late as the beginning of this century the dynasties of gombeen men seemed powerful as ever. They straddle over the Rosses, dominating them as Apollyon in Bunyan's tale straddled quite across the path of the Pilgrim. They were the Bosses of the Rosses. The farmers were tied customers of theirs. Seventy-five per cent of the farmers were born in debt and were never out of it. It was not the policy of the Bosses that they should be out of debt. Never willingly did king liberate his slaves, and any man who asked for a full statement of his debt was looked upon sourly. Men were terrified even to ask what they owed. They paid what they could in November when they returned from their labour in Scotland, and there was almost always a running balance against them, and indeed before liberation came there was very little use in rebellion, because these gombeen kings of north-west Donegal were all intermarried, as the governing families in Great Britain are, and formed a caste among themselves. They only seemed to be in opposition to each other, but they had agreements about prices, and to exchange gombeen men was much the choice of a traveller whether he will go by the desert roamed by the lion or the jungle haunted by the tiger. They sat on the bench as justices of peace. They nominated county and district councillors and members of parliament. They boasted when the Co-operative Society was started that they could turn out every man on the roadside who was a member and, indeed, in times past they had evicted many. The landlord of this district had evicted none of his tenants. The gombeen men led the opposition to the landlord, yet had a monopoly of the evictions themselves. The rents paid to the landlord averaged between fifteen shillings and thirty-five, and the average valuation of the holdings was twenty-five shillings, but the tribute paid to the real reigning dynasties was greater by far. The landlord owned the land. The gombeen men owned the people, and the profits the gombeen men got out of the men was greater by far than the profit the landowner got out of his holding. Was it any wonder that the owners of the men were enthusiastic leaders of the movement against the owners of the land? Naturally they were anti-landlord, for there were twenty-five shillings on an average paid yearly out of each holding to the landlord which otherwise would have swelled the revenue of the Bosses of the Rosses.

## THE ADVENTURES OF 'PADDY THE COPE'

We could tell many pleasant incidents of the campaign. Once when Patrick Gallagher was making a speech he was interrupted by a trader, and his retort that he would attend to him presently was utilized to mean that the leader of co-operation intended to inflict bodily damage on the interrupter, and an information was sworn that the said trader was in danger of his life. The Bench had five traders and a Resident Magistrate. The five absolutely illegally ordered Patrick to find bail for his good behaviour which he refused to do, and the alternative was jail, which Patrick cheerfully accepted, but such a perversion of justice was reversed in a day or two and a wire came from the Lords Justices in Dublin ordering Patrick's instant release. His return was a great event in Dungloe. Patrick was met by crowds. The streets of Dungloe were illuminated and the hills were lit with bonfires as they are on St. John's Eve. But these little diversions, caused by the intrigues of exasperated enemies losing their power, never interrupted the real work of the Society. It won its way by good business management. 'Paddy the Cope' was not only a good fighter but a man of business of the type which is not unfrequently born on an Irish bog and ends his days as an American millionaire, with this difference, that 'Paddy the Cope' works for others and not for himself, and the Society and its well-being and the welfare of the farmers and their families he has more at heart than anything else in the world. Here we have a splendid instance of the democracy going into business on its own account and choosing its picked men, the aristocracy of brains and character, to manage its business for it.

# CHAPTER SEVENTEEN

## *Back to the States*

I might have been hanged for murder, only I met with two men who had much more sense than I. On 12 August 1917, Joe O'Donnell and I were invited by Mrs. Logue of Doochary to shoot on her mountain. The shoot on the land adjoining hers was taken by the Lord Mayor of Londonderry who had a bailiff watching his shoot. Joe had the best dog I ever shot over, he was named Simon, he was neither a pointer nor a setter, he was a blue grey, but boys he was the dog that could find the birds. As soon as he came about thirty yards from the bird, he stood as stiff as a poker and lifted his right hind leg. He never moved until you went alongside him, and would then walk along with you until the birds got up. If you happened to miss the bird, God bless me, Simon would frighten you with the look which he would give you.

We went into Doochary and got one of Mrs. Logue's boys to go with us to show us the mountain. When coming up the Corkscrew Brae, young Logue looked back and said, 'O'Donnell the bailiff is following us. You need not care, I know the boundary, and there are plenty birds on my mother's land.' When we reached the shoot, Simon went in, and about ten yards from the road, he stood, the hind leg went up. In we went, Simon walked a yard or two ahead of us, a pack of grouse got up and Joe took down one with the right, and one with the left. I got one with the right, but missed with the left. The seven that got away flew to our right and lit on the preserved property, Simon stood still until they lit, and then he began to move towards them. The bailiff coming up the road shouted, 'If that bastard of a dog crosses the border, I will shoot him.' (He had a gun with him). I shouted back, 'If you shoot Simon, I will shoot you.' Simon crossed the boundary, I saw the bailiff put the gun to his shoulder and fire at Simon, Simon squealed and went around a little mound out of our sight. I threw off the bag with the grouse in it and ran. I heard Joe call 'For God's sake come back Paddy.' The bailiff began to run, I shouted to him 'Stand you coward.' He was out of range. I followed him and was within two hundred yards of him when we came to Doochary, he ran into the barracks. I walked back up the Corkscrew, when I got to the top the anger was gone, I was crying for Simon. I then came to where Joe was sitting with Simon between his legs. Joe was patting him, he did not see me until I asked if Simon was still alive, he answered that he was all right except for a few pellets in his ear. Joe then blessed himself and said, 'Surely to God Paddy you did not shoot him?' I said, 'No, the coward ran into the barracks.' Joe then thanked God and His Holy Mother.

After a bit of a rest we got up again. I said, 'Come on Simon.' We crossed to where the bird dropped and Joe got two and I got two, the other three flew away. On our way back we put up another pack and Joe got two and I got one. I would not let Simon near the survivors of the first pack. We came home with ten and a half brace – twenty-one grouse.

At our Committee meeting on the second Saturday in September 1926, when the minutes were read James Durnion stood up and said:- 'Mr. Secretary, with my sincere regrets in parting with most of you, I tender my resignation. When I joined this institution, I did so, with the hope that I would help you to lift our fellow countrymen out of slavery, and out of the clutches of the gombeen men and landlords, under which they have suffered since the years of the famine 1846 and 1847. I now find that the institution which I am ashamed to be a member of, is worse than any gombeen man or landlord, that ever lived in the Rosses.' He then walked out. Consternation prevailed. I shed a tear or two. After a while I said, 'Gentlemen, what does he mean or what has happened? I know of nothing.' Johnnie Brown said, 'Paddy he told me before we came in that you acted the bailiff in sending your lorry up to Fintown to seize a poor woman's hay.' I said, 'That is not true, it is the first I heard of it.'

It happened that before the meeting was over the two lorry men arrived in the yard. I called them in before the Committee and asked them if they had ever used their lorries to seize hay at Fintown. They assured the Committee that they did not.

Later that night Jimmie O'Donnell came to our house, and told me it was Packie's lorry that removed the hay. I nearly collapsed. I ran to the Post Office and 'phoned to Packie in Letterkenny telling him to come home immediately.

Three hours later Sally, Jim and I were sitting at the fire, when in steps Packie saying, 'What is wrong, father?' I said, 'Packie is it true that you acted the bailiff and seized Mrs. McShane's, of Fintown hay?' Packie said, 'Father, who told you that wild story, I never had any dealings with a woman of that name, neither do I know her.' I told him then the story which Jimmie O'Donnell had told to me. He ran out to the car, took his bag, opened it and took out a letter and read as follows:- 'Send your lorry up early as I have some hay to remove and as the distance is long I could not possibly remove it by cart.' He then said, 'Father, I never dreamt but the hay was his own, and I asked the lorry-driver Charlie McGee, to oblige Houston and remove the hay for him, that is all I know about it.' I said, 'Come on.' We went down to Charlie McGee's house, and questioned him about the removal of the hay, he said he also thought it was Houston's hay. Charlie's father who is now dead was in a worse state than I, we there and then decided to get the hay back to Mrs. McShane. The following morning we went off early, James McGee, Charlie McGee, Jimmie O'Donnell, Packie and I, we went on the lorry, when we arrived at Houston's I jumped out of the lorry with my gun, and asked Charlie to show me the hay which he had removed. He did so. The lads had forks with them, the hay was across the street from Houston's door, I ordered the lads to put the hay on the lorry. They did so. Then Houston came to the door, I had the gun ready but he did not come out, we left the hay back in Mrs. McShane's garden. I gave Mrs. McShane a few shillings for any hay which we may have lost in the shifting. That night nearly all the Rosses people had heard of the hay being left back to Mrs. McShane.

The day of the following meeting, James Durnion came to the door, knocked and asked if I was in. I went to the door and caught his hand and kissed him. It was one of the happiest moments of my life. I held his hand until he sat down. He said, 'Gentlemen may I come back?' All said, 'You are most welcome.' James then said, 'I am very sorry that I did not make a thorough investigation before I brought unjust charges against our President. I should have known him better, yes I guess I should. However, when thinking it over I am damn well glad that I told the rumour I heard, if our President had not heard it, it might have done a damn lot of harm, but I guess gentlemen it has done a damn lot of good, it has shown the Rosses and the world the stuff that is in our leader.' He came over and caught my hand, I can still feel that squeeze.

All the characters in the foregoing story are alive with the exception of James Durnion, James McGee, and Mrs. Logue and I might add that the only fictitious name in my story is Crudger.

Later on I was informed on very good authority that Houston was a very honest shopkeeper and that he did not add gombeen interest to his account. This debt was a just one and he got a decree in the court of Justice against Mrs. McShane.

My son Packie got married to Mary Campbell of Burtonport on the 7 September 1938. Sally insisted on them living in the Cope house with us. On the morning of the 13 June 1939, Sally called me into Mary's room and showed me a baby. I asked if it was a boy or a girl. Sally said, 'A girl.' I knelt down and said three Hail Marys for the Blessed Virgin Mary to thank God for sending us a wee girl. When I got up, I kissed the mother and said, 'Mary it is good of you to give us another wee Annie.' Well, needless to say, she was christened 'Annie' and is called 'Wee Annie the Cope' ever since.

I asked permission from my committee to have another business run to America and to bring a range of hosiery samples with me. My son Jim, was helping me in the store, and I was not afraid to leave. My committee agreed to let me go, so I prepared to sail on the *Transylvania* on 19 August 1939. Well damn but, I could not tell you whether Sally or Mary cried the most the morning I left. I was very vexed leaving. I thought when leaving wee Annie, that I was leaving the nicest child in the world. At the last moment, I was between two minds whether I should go or not. I think I would have stayed only I might be called a coward, as rumours of war were in the air.

My cousin, Neil O'Donnell, was travelling by the same boat. He is a wealthy man, and was home for a holiday. He had his own car with him and he had a first class return ticket; he wanted me to travel with him. He said, 'Paddy, I would advise you to travel first class. I tell you here and now, it is worth it. My man, you are manager of one of the biggest concerns in this country and you are going out to the States with your knitwear. You must put it over big, if you want results.' I said, 'I am paying my own passage and I could not afford first or second class. I'll be more comfortable in the steerage.' Finally, I agreed to go second class and my cousin travelled second with me.

When we reached Moville, Neil handed me *The Derry Journal* saying, 'Paddy my boy, you are early figuring in the Press,' pointing out the following in the Journal:-

> *Tomorrow the Copeman sails away o'er*
> *the ocean wild and wide;*
> *Tomorrow he goes to see the friends he*
> *has on the other side.*

*From San Francisco to New York, from*
*New Orleans to St. Paul,*
*They'll come to meet him at the boat,*
*this man from Donegal.*

*God grant him peace and weather fair*
*on his journey o'er the foam;*
*God send him safely back again to the*
*Co-Op in Templecrone.*
*God grant him health and strength*
*galore, and years to life's short span*
*For Dungloe off the map would go*
*without the famed Copeman.*

*Enjoy yourself while still abroad in*
*the mighty USA.*
*'Tis ten long years since last you took a*
*well-earned holiday;*
*And so we wish you peace and joy. Now could*
*we wish you more*
*Except to wish you safely back to the lovely*
*Rosses Shore!*

P.A. Ward

The ship was a grand one. Seamus McManus, the Donegal writer who has been living in the States since his boyhood, wrote to Captain Bone–captain of the *Transylvania*- telling him that the author of My Story (Paddy the Cope) was sailing on his ship. Well, on Sunday 20th one of the stewards handed me a note at 11.30 a.m. It read, 'Dear Mr. Gallagher, I would be very glad to see you in my quarters at about 12.15 p.m. (Sgd.) David Bone.' I went. Well, you talk about the height of hospitality, boy there's where it was–in Captain Bone's quarters. After that, some of the passengers began to notice me. No one was more pleased than Neil O'Donnell, to see the Copeman was invited to the Captain's state room. On Thursday 24th, the captain again sent for me. I had lunch with him in his quarters. He introduced me to the chief steward and gave me a copy of *Twenty Years a-Growing*. The captain wrote some books. He had no copies and I cannot remember their names.

The story soon went round that I was an author, and Neil and I had a grand time. In the end I began to get tired signing my name on all kinds of books and papers for the ladies that were travelling with us.

On Saturday, August 26, the ship landed at Boston. We were not allowed ashore. The chief steward came to me with reporters from the *Boston Globe, Herald*, and *Post* asking for an interview. They had their photographers with them. Damn but it is a funny thing I do not remember now what they asked me or what I said to them. A few days previous the pound went wallop, you could not get a dollar for it. I could only think of the coming war and the effect it might have on our Society.

I had intended, when I would land in New York, to go to my sister Margery in Rockaway. Neil wanted me to go to Bayonne with him but I had my mind made up. I got a kind of feeling as we were approaching the harbour that big Eddie, my brother-in-law, might be there. I had a zip shirt and cap on. All the other passengers were dressed up in white shirts, white or black hats. I had no white shirt; I never liked them. Neither had I a hat. I intended to buy an American hat when I would land. I was on deck hoping that Eddie might be on the stage. Heavens! I saw him towering over all the others. I shouted 'Eddie' three times before he saw me. Then the big hand shot up in the air. I turned away crying with joy; when I recovered, I looked again at him. He pointed to his wife, my sister Bridget, standing in front of him; with her were my sisters, Mary and Margery; Eddie and Bridget came from Ohio; Mary from Homestead, Pittsburgh, and Margery from Rockaway, my cousins from Elizabeth, Bayonne and Wilksburgh, and Sally's sister Mary. I fear to mention my second cousins and relations, as I would likely leave many of them out. When I got off the gangway, Eddie put one of his big hands round my neck and kissed me; with the other he reached me a glass bottle of whiskey saying, 'Paddy, you must be tired, drink that before you meet the bunch.' I took the bottle and had not time to put it on my head when my sisters and all my friends were around me and kissing me. I got the bottle into my pocket; thanks be to God, I have it here in my desk, waiting on the day that Eddie and I will drink it when he comes home. I hope we will split it out in Cleendra. I can only describe the scene by telling you that we all cried first and laughed afterwards. I had to get into a queue to get into the baggage department to claim my cases. While in the queue, Bridget came along with a young man and said, 'This is Mr. Gallagher, my brother that you are looking for.' He said, 'I am a press reporter, I would like if you would tell me why you are here and what the Co-Operative Movement means, and about your book.' I need not tell you that I told him damn all. How could I with all my friends waiting to hear from their nearest and dearest at home.

There were nine motor cars loaded with my relatives. All went to my sister Margery's (Mrs. Trainor) house at Rockaway. It was a very warm day. Two rooms, with sliding doors between, were not big enough for all. Mrs. Cannon suggested to go to the beach until lunch would be ready, and come back in relays. This was agreed to. Bridget took a look at me and said, 'No, Paddy cannot go out dressed like that. Wait until I come back.' Off she went, and in ten minutes she was back and asked me to come into the bedroom. She asked me if I had an extra pair of pants in my case. I said that I had. She opened the case and in about five minutes she had three or four little loops on my pants. She opened the parcel she brought in and slipped a belt through the loops; then she handed me a white shirt and hat saying, 'Put these on Paddy. You would be laughed at if you were seen out like that.' She left the room. I did as I was told, and as soon as I appeared she took me back to the room and said, 'For heavens sake, take off that waistcoat. Surely you are not cold.' I obeyed. Then we all went down to the beach and I heard Bridget say to Mrs. Cannon, 'Doesn't he look swell now?' We all got lunch, through time. I was with the first lot. I was never among so many friends at home at one time.

The following day I went to Elizabeth, to see my cousins and friends. There was one I think I would rather see than my own sisters, and that was Maggie Tully, my uncle Tully's wife. Oh! Such a grand woman, the mother of such grand children. A few years previous, her daughter, Mrs. O'Donnell (Lizzie), came home to Ireland for her and took her to Elizabeth. No child ever got or is getting as good care as Maggie is getting from her daughter, Lizzie, and her husband John. Well, when I met her, she put her arms around my neck, kissed and kissed me, and cried with joy. Yes! And I cried too. She must be about eighty years of age. I hope and pray I will see her again before God calls either of us. God! Is it any wonder I was glad to see her when I remembered how thirty-three years previous she befriended me, when Smith the policeman was searching through Cleendra hoping he would get someone to swear information against me so that he could get me arrested.

The next day I went back to my sisters in Rockaway. Mary and Bridget were still there. Margery said, 'Paddy we got the surprise of our lives when Mrs. Butler came running downstairs yesterday telling us that the Radio people were looking for your address.' Of course I thought Bridget made up the story to have a laugh at me. I said, 'Don't be codding, I am not as green as I look.' Margery called Mrs. Butler in and introduced me. Mrs. Butler assured me it was no codding, that she was listening in when she heard Terry Long saying, 'I would feel obliged to any person that would put me in touch or give the address of Paddy Gallagher of Donegal, who landed from the *Transylvania* at New York last Sunday. We would like to meet Mr. Gallagher in the studio.' She added, 'I took the liberty of sending him your address. I hope you are not displeased.' Mr. Long is very pleased and we all heard him today say as a token of gratitude to the Cork Lady (Mrs. Butler came from Cork) that sent him Mr. Gallagher's address, he would play the *Bells of Shandon*, and 'Mr. Gallagher, I bet he did play them.' Bridget said, 'Mrs. Butler, do you think it is the police that are after him? Poor devil, he is always in trouble.' The following morning Johnnie Curran and another chap called at Maghery's, as we were getting up. Mr. Curran said, 'Mr. Gallagher, we are anxious that you make an appointment to speak over the radio. Tell us something about Ireland.' I refused, as I considered that I would make a mess of it. I might take the risk of doing a bit of bleathering at home but heavens, what would the Cleendra people say if they heard that Paddy Pat Bawn was speaking into a Radio in New York? Bridget said, 'Mr. Curran, fix him up, he has plenty to say when he is talking to us.' He must go. He will never see half of his friends and they will be delighted to hear him talk – just because he is a brother of mine – not much to himself.' Well, she sat down and she laughed just the same as if she was in Cleendra. Mary and Margery then began to force me, but even if they were not there, it would be damn hard to refuse. Curran had such a wonderful way with him, and I finally agreed.

I had a range of hosiery samples with me. I intended to call after a few days' rest, on the New York house with whom we were doing business, but on Sunday, 3 September 1939, war was declared. I therefore decided not to show any samples but made up my mind to return home the following week. There was no sailing so I remained in the States for almost nine weeks. Well boys, such a grand time I had. There were two receptions for me in Bayonne, two in New York, two in Elizabeth, one in Homestead, one in Chicago and one in Wilksburgh. I was invited to others which I could not attend. I would like to mention the names of all that invited me to their homes but there were as many as would fill a book. Oh! such friendship. Everywhere that there was a big night for me, Bridget was sure to be there, coming all the way from Ohio, and I had to make a wee speech each time. At one of the receptions, organised by the Donegal Association in Bayonne, Father McDevitt, presided. At the luncheon, Bridget and I were at his table and also Captain T. Gallagher, whose parents come from the Diamond, within a mile from Cleendra. The Captain said to Bridget, 'Mrs. O'Donnell, you sure are proud of your brother, he is a grand man. I was delighted to hear him speak, he put over swell.' She began to laugh and said, 'Him bedamnt, sure I made him. I had to put a shirt on him when he landed.' She roared with laughter, and all who heard her did enjoy the joke.

Oh, I must tell you this. When I had the time, I made up my mind to visit Chicago. I especially wanted to see Captain Hugh O'Donnell's daughter Norah, of Aranmore – a distant relation of mine. It was her mother that set a fire to a tar barrel in Aranmore Island, the night I came out of gaol. I left New York on Monday night and arrived in Chicago at 5 p.m. on Tuesday, dead tired. I went to an hotel, paid my railway fare and hotel bill for the first and last time while in the States. Any other place I went, before I could get to the booking office I was presented with a ticket by some of my friends, and I slept every night in some friend's house. The reason I went to the Chicago Hotel was that I was so tired I thought I would be no comfort to anybody. I had a good rest and next morning I called Norah. I need not here describe the welcome. She had two other sisters and two other brothers in Chicago. All of them wanted me to spend a week with each of them, but I had arranged previously to leave Chicago on Saturday morning as I had to attend a reception meeting that was arranged for me in Homestead near Pittsburgh. I had to disappoint my many Chicago friends and I stayed for the other three nights with Nora.

On Friday morning, after visiting some friends accompanied by Hugh O'Donnell (Norah's uncle), we passed a house. Hugh said, 'There is a Mrs. Duffy living in there, she came originally from Rutland Island. Did you know her?' I said, 'No.' He said, 'Her maiden name was Ward.' Hugh walked on. I opened the gate going in when Hugh said, 'Paddy, sure you said you did not know her.' (Rutland is only ten miles from Cleendra.) I said, 'Damn but Hugh sure she is a neighbour.' I went up to the door, rang the bell, and a lovely young girl came to the door. I asked if Mrs. Duffy was in. She said, 'Mamma, there is a gentleman waiting to see you.' Mrs. Duffy came downstairs. I said, 'Are you Mrs. Duffy?' She answered 'Yes.' I then said, 'I came from Ireland a few weeks ago. I am Paddy Gallagher from Cleendra.' She asked, 'Where is Cleendra? I never heard of it.' I told her that Cleendra was in the Parish of Templecrone, that I was known as 'Paddy the Cope'. In an instant she had her arms round my neck, crying with joy, saying, 'You will stay with me for at least a fortnight.' I told her I was leaving on Saturday morning and that I was staying with Nora for the few nights. That Friday night, there was a party for me in my friend's house – big Bill Connolly's Hotel. Next morning a convoy of six motors came with me to the station. I was fully determined not to shed any tears as all were laughing and joking. Within five minutes before the train came, I began to shake hands with my friends. Mrs. Duffy and her children were there with their car. I bade them goodbye first. Norah was the last. She put her arms around my neck and began to cry. Not one, young or old that came with me to the station but cried. I had no relations there nearer than fourth cousins. Need I tell any more about friendship?

On my way back I stayed in Homestead with my sister Mary. Bridget and Eddie were in from Ohio. The house was packed. Next morning my cousin, Father Doogan was in from Mount Pleasant with his car. Bridget and I went out with him; on our way we passed the convent where our sister Maggie (Sister Kieran) died. He brought us to the poor soul's grave. I cried my fill. It was the only sad hour I had in America. Well, we stayed that night with Father Doogan. After Mass, at the breakfast next morning, Father Doogan said 'Paddy, I offered up the Holy Mass this morning for your safe return home.' It is only a Roman Catholic that can imagine the courage, happiness and joy those few words gave me.

I was invited to a Testimonial Dinner given by the Knights of Columbanus to the Rev. Joseph Dolan, Chaplain of their Council on his twentieth anniversary as chaplain. The dinner was held in the Victory Memorial Hall Building, 13th Street Avenue, Bayonne, New Jersey. Among some of the people to whom I was introduced were the popular Mayor of Bayonne, Mr. James J. Donovan, Mr. Patrick Gallagher, Captain of the Bayonne Police and the Hon. John F. O'Neill, Supreme Director. Well, well, my sisters and all my friends were delighted when they heard that I was invited to such a distinguished party. I was delighted myself to be asked for this reason, that ten days previously, my niece Mary Kelly, was operated on in a Rockaway Hospital. After the operation she required a blood transfusion. All that were in my sister's house, including myself, rushed to the hospital. None of us had the type of blood required. Mick O'Donnell 'phoned the Knights, telling them the type of blood required; they immediately sent a young man who gave a blood transfusion.

I was informed that for the very type of blood required that each council has at least six volunteers. I thought they were as good as if they were a co-operative society. It brought back to my mind February 1937, when my son, Jim, was in the Belfast Mater Hospital. There came one of the worst snow storms for many years, the roads were all blocked and the farmers could not get their milk into the city. Sally was crying about Jim. Packie left Dungloe with a dozen bottles of milk in his car for the hospital. When he got as far as Limavady in County Derry, he got stuck in the snow. Next morning he got the train and got into Belfast late that night. He rushed to the hospital, met a kindly porter at the door who let him in. The first thing Packie did was to reach Jim one of the bottles of milk. Jim said, 'Packie why did you bring milk for me? Thank goodness we have plenty of milk. The Belfast Co-Operative Society gets 4,000 gallons by boat daily since the roads got snowed up, and the hospitals are the first to be supplied.' Now if there never was another co-operative story to tell, this wee one should attract the humane man and woman to the co-operative movement.

On 18 October 1939, I did go to New York, met Johnny Curran who introduced me to that famous artist, Terry Long, who put me sitting in front of the microphone, saying: 'Now Paddy, fire away.' I made a wee speech. When I had finished I was sure I made a hell of a mess of it, but Terry and Johnny said I put it over swell. My sisters and all my friends were listening in and were pleased, if I made mistakes. Not even Bridget said I did. The Americans are very charitable.

On 18 October 1939, the eve of my departure for home I decided to go to confession – it being the last night, I told my sisters, the three of them were there. I decided to go into New York, into that little Church–St. Joseph's behind Gimbel's where I met Miss McCauley ten years previous.

Bridget said, 'Damn but, Paddy, I'll be with you, I would not like anything to happen you on the last day. It is not safe to let you travel alone.' She then laughed that hearty laugh of hers. Off we went.

I went into the confessional box, knelt down before one of the Fathers, blessed myself and said, 'Bless me Father for I have sinned' and said the Confiteor that I learned at my mother's knee, and said, 'Father I am sailing for my home in Ireland in the morning, I want to be free from sin.' He asked me if I wanted him to help me; I said, 'I do Father.' I then, with his help, told all my story.

After he gave me absolution he said, 'God bless you, pray for me.' Well, I hope that there are lots of people in the world as happy as I was at that moment, but I do not think anyone could be happier.

When we returned to Rockaway to my sister's, Bridget called my other two sisters into the room told them that nothing could happen to Paddy, no German would dare touch the s.s. President Harding. She was right. When we came back to Rockaway the house was packed and there was no sleep for us that night. My friends from Ohio, Pittsburgh, Wilksburgh, Philadelphia, Elizabeth, Bayonne, New Jersey, Brookyln and New York were there. We motored to New York on the 23rd. I do not know how many cars were with us.

I got aboard the s.s *President Harding*. All my friends were crying. For some reason the ship did not sail for two hours after the gangway was lifted. I was walking up and down the deck and all my friends on the quay waving and shouting goodbye. As it was raining, I appealed to them several times to go home, but none would go away. I heard many of the porters say, 'Who is that Paddy guy that they are all talking about?' In the end, Heavens, I plucked up courage and made a wee speech from the ship. I do not now remember what I said, but I do remember that no one moved or spoke while I was speaking. We sailed two hours late and no exciting incident happened.

We arrived safely in Cobh on the morning of November 2. I rushed to the Post Office, wired to Sally as follows:- 'Landed in Cobh now, will be home tomorrow.' No one at home knew that I was coming as I knew they would not rest content if they thought I was on the ocean. I would have left America content had I seen one man and that man was Mr. Henry L. Wallace, American Vice-President. His father honoured Dungloe by paying it a visit in 1913. I hope I'll not miss the pleasure of seeing that great statesman next time, if only at a distance. I was not the least afraid. I'll not describe the welcome that was for me. My Committee and members were all around me. God, such a welcome.

I was so much impressed with the American people and the possibility of doing business that I wrote a letter to Mr. Kenny of *The Connacht Tribune* on October 24. The following is a copy:-

"God helps those who help themselves."

Dear Kenny,

I often heard it said that God helps those who help themselves. Then in God's name, let us Irish buy two ocean going ships that will carry our people and merchandise across the Atlantic.

Why should we go with our hat in our hand to any foreign nations or company, begging them to supply us with shipping facilities? I suggest that the Dublin, Cork and Galway Chambers of Commerce meet and appoint one or two members each to meet quickly, that they invite a half-dozen trustworthy Irishmen to meet them and that they take the necessary steps to promote a company; the ships to call at Dublin, Cork, Galway and Donegal. I feel there is plenty of business waiting.

I have been in the States eight weeks recently. I had the pleasure of meeting members of the Irish Chamber of Commerce, which had been recently registered. Mr. Hugh Mullen, president, told me that it is the considered opinion of the members that the chamber will be of great help to Irish Industry, if Irishmen do their bit. Other countries have Chambers of Commerce in New York for a number of years. I suggest all Irish manufacturers should become members. The fee is only twenty-five dollars. The address is 307, West 14th Street, New York. Mr. Hugh Mullen, president; Matthew Finnegan, first vice president; Collins Healy, second vice president; Thomas Connolly, treasurer; A. C. Quirk, secretary.

If we had our own ships our people would not be stranded in Cobh or New York, begging to get to their homes.

In writing this letter I feel confident that Donegal will subscribe liberally.

Yours sincerely,
Paddy Gallagher,
(The Copeman).

It appeared in the next issue of *The Connacht Tribune* and was copied in some of the American papers.

We were buying herrings and curing them for over twenty years. In 1940 there was a good demand in Britain for fresh herrings, and we decided to send a consignment to the Scottish Co-Operative Wholesale Society in Aberdeen. They arrived in bad condition. The Co-Operative Manager, Mr. Davinson, wrote to us a very human letter. He said it was a pity that we did not kipper those good herrings. I called a special meeting of my Committee and read Mr. Davinson's letter. After a long discussion it was unanimously agreed that I go to Aberdeen to see how herrings should be kippered.

Off I went and damn but, as I was in a hurry, when I reached Belfast what the hell do you think I did? I hopped into an aeroplane and while you would be saying Jack Robinson, I was flying through the air. I began to think that if my father was alive and with me the grand story he would tell my mother and the Cleendra folk when he got home again. It is a pity he was not with me. Before I stopped thinking about my father, the 'plane was crawling along the ground in Scotland.

When I reached Glasgow I went to see a friend of mine – Thomas Lucis, North Frederick Street. I went to his office, the windows were boarded up and the buildings on the opposite side were levelled to the ground. That was my first sight of war- destruction. God, but I hated the men that perpetrated such dastardly crime on innocent people.

I then went on to the Kenilworth Hotel and passed that once grand warehouse – Arthur's, which was flattened out. I had a horrible feeling, if I had the strength and power and could get hold of the men that did such destruction they would never do it again.

I reached Aberdeen on 3 December, 1940, met Mr. Davinson, his assistant-manager and office staff. They were every bit as friendly for me as my own Cleendra people, the only difference was the accent. They showed me everything about kippering. Lord! But they were friendly. I left Aberdeen on December 4, reached Manchester on the 5th, stayed in the Victoria Hotel, sold some gloves in Manchester. Ten days afterwards the Victoria Hotel was flattened out. Ah, but I was sorry. I reached London about 11 p.m. on the 6th. The train stopped often on the way and all lights were put out. It was a wearisome journey.

When I signed at the office of the Charing Cross Hotel, I went to the lounge. There were many people sitting there. I ordered a 'quick one' and then I heard an unearthly sound. I thought that weird sound would never stop. When the waiter handed me the glass I threw its contents into me before I asked the price. I then asked him what that wild sound was. He said, 'That is the siren, sir.' I said, 'I thought that when the siren went all would run to the air-raid shelters.' He answered, 'Sometimes they all run, sir, and sometimes no one moves. If one gets up they all get up, but we have no cowards here tonight.' I had another quick one and felt quite happy. When I went off to bed I heard the sirens again and then the anti-aircraft guns. I pulled the bedclothes over my head and was soon fast asleep. I do not know what the others did. Next day, the sixth, I went to the East Side to meet Mr. Norman Kither, 43 Fore Street, off Milton Street. Outside the co-operative people, I never met a more friendly man. We are selling woollen gloves to him and his father for the past twenty years. He was glad to see me. I saw some sad sights from the time I left Charing Cross until I reached Kither's. After he gave me the usual big order he took me out for lunch where he arranged for some of the biggest glove buyers in London to meet me.

At the lunch I expressed my sincere sorrow for what the Londoners suffered, but no one present showed any sign of fear. I could hear all of them say, 'We will get the blighter yet.' God, but I admired their pluck. Mr. Kither's young brother was then in the firing line. Mr. Kither thought that he would not be called up as he was the head of the firm and about forty years of age.

When I got home my Committee and all my friends were, I think, more glad for me than when I came home from America. The following night we had a special Committee meeting. I was asked many questions. When I produced Kither's order, and explained the destruction I saw in London one of them said, 'Paddy, did you promise to deliver that order? It is dangerous, sure that firm might be burned out, aye, and God save us, everyone in the firm might be killed and our money might be lost.' I said, 'It is for the Committee to decide. All might be lost but the Kithers were very good people and always gave us plenty of orders. It is hard to refuse them now.' Heavens, to my delight every member of the Committee agreed to give the Kithers all the goods they ordered and what they might order for the duration. Their place was bombed out over a year ago. Their office is now, 43 George Street, Croydon. What makes me write the foregoing is, that I had got the following letter from the firm on the 22 September, 1942:-

Dear Mr. Gallagher,

You will be surprised to hear that Mr. Kither is now in the army–he was called up about a month ago. We are carrying on here as usual and trust that we may look to you for your continued support.

Yours sincerely,
D. Clarke.

When I read the letter I went into the kitchen and read it for Sally. She blessed herself and said some prayers. Then she said, 'I hope God will protect him and his brother.' I went back to the office. Sally followed me and handed me an Agnus Dei, saying, 'Send the holy relic to Mr. Kither. It will save him I hope, although he is a Protestant and may not believe as we Catholics believe. We will pray and ask the Blessed Virgin to ask God to protect Norman and his brother.' Damn but, whether you believe me or not, I never felt as proud of Sally in all my life.

I wrote to the firm on the September 22, and enclosed a note for Norman saying:-

'I am sending you a small holy relic and I would ask you as a personal favour to sew it in the garment which you are wearing while on duty and we will pray to God to protect you.

Yours sincerely,
P. Gallagher.'

Mr. Kither's father, mother and his beautiful sister, Miss J. Kither, visited us in Dungloe about fourteen years earlier. Sally was crazy for them. Norman visited us a few years ago. Mr. Kither senior died some years ago. Some of our girls are now working on a big order for the firm.

At the special meeting after my return I got permission from my Committee to erect a kippering store at Burtonport. In six weeks, we were kippering herrings and sending them to the Co-Operative Society, Aberdeen.

The herrings do not remain long in the one place – five or six weeks, and then swim away to some other place, as the Rosses coast is very exposed to the wind nearly always blowing hard across the Atlantic. The Rosses small boats could not follow the herrings around the coast so after five weeks our kippering house was a White Elephant on our hands and I was very sorry for the expense which was incurred.

I was very worried and one night I was in one of the 'locals' with some of the fishermen. One of the lads said, 'Paddy, did you stop the kippering?' He knowing damn well that we could not get any herring to kipper. I began to get annoyed. Charlie Sharkey said to me, 'Paddy, do not heed him. Go on, my bully man, buy a good boat that will keep your kippering house going, and give employment to twenty or thirty people, the same as you have done in the past six weeks. I hear the MB. *Prevail* is for sale.' Well, I came home and slept on it. Next morning I got our Secretary, Leo Brennan, to write to the owner of the MB. *Prevail* to ask him if his boat was for sale. He replied by return of post that it was.

I got Leo to call a special meeting of the Committee for Friday.

I told them about the talk in the local, and they unanimously agreed to give me a free hand to purchase the MB *Prevail*. On 15 February, 1941, I purchased her. We got her fitted up with a fleet of herring and trawler nets and gave the skippering of her to Big Micky Gallagher, conditions being that we supplied all gear, did repairs etc., and that from the gross takings the oil and crew's food be deducted, the remainder then divided fifty/fifty between the crew and the Society. The venture was an immediate success, so much so that we bought another boat MB *Celina* on Friday 16 May 1941, and another MB *Naomh Eine* on 5 September 1942. The first two have 44 h.p. motors and the last a 64 h.p. The first night that the *Naomh Eine* shot her nets at Downings the catch realized £84 although herrings were not plentiful that night; it was the end of the season at Downings. The average earnings of the crews up to 14 October, 1942, was £8.3.4d per week, after being fed. Boys! It is a great pleasure for me in my old days to be the manger of a Co-operative Society that has made and is making so many happy homes.

I am delighted with this venture; I hope God will spare me until I see the Cope loading an aeroplane with kippered herrings for America and London.

About 12 February, 1944, we were not getting sufficient oil to keep our boats fishing. The little drop we were getting, God forgive me, we were stealing it from the boats for our engine to keep the factory, bakery and mill going, which were giving employment to eighty-five per cent more people. I hope the end justified the means. I was worried about the crews, such good men anxious to get to the fishing grounds, knowing that the fish were there, and that they could not catch them, their boats and gear ready but no oil. I and the crews had a little chat, and we decided that Big Mick and his crew should slip around to Ardglass, Northern Ireland, where we heard there was lashings of oil. We got the necessary permit from the British Fishery Department and on 12 February, 1944, Big Mick and his crew sailed away, but met with no success. We were on the 'phone to them every day, and we were very disappointed when they were not catching any fish. After two weeks, I hooked off for Ardglass and met Mick and the crew. They were downhearted. Mick said it was soft ground, not what they were accustomed to. I asked them if they had any trouble with the Customs. He said that they landed on Sunday morning and went to Mass. When they came to their boat there was a crowd of people on the pier including the police and customs officers. Many questions were asked. Mick did not tell me all, but he said 'Damn but Paddy, I thought at first we were going to be arrested, but it boiled down to this, that the only offence we committed, was not having our flag up, and I had it in my pocket all the time, when I should have had it on the mast, but Paddy, the Police and Customs Officers were very nice and all the people around were nice to us.'

I met a lot of fishermen there. I met Samuel Palmer, skipper of MB *Eventide*. He had just landed a nice catch of fish. I congratulated him on his success, asked him into the pub for a drink. In we went. After we had one, Samuel said, 'I am sorry Mr. Gallagher, your boat had no luck since she came to Ardglass. Our ground is different to yours, and I think they are going a bit fast. I would like to tell them, but I do not know them and they may resent my advice.' I said, 'I know, Samuel, that they would be glad for your advice.' We had another one and then I said, 'Samuel would you mind taking our skipper, Big Mick, and our driver John Cannon out in your boat tomorrow and let them see your method?' Samuel said, 'I'll be delighted!' The pub was not twenty yards from the harbour. I went down to the harbour and took Big Mick up and introduced him to Samuel. Samuel said, 'If you and your men are at my boat at 6.30 tomorrow morning, you can come along with me.' Boys! If you saw the smile on Big Mick's face. Mick said, 'What are you drinking?' Samuel said, 'No more drink, we have to be fit in the morning and off early.' I was glad the glass of whiskey was four shillings. It was only two shillings in Donegal the most northern county in Ireland.

I went to Joe Mulhern's hotel. Next day was Friday, and when I met Mick that night, he could only talk about the kindness of Samuel Palmer and his crew. They do not fish in Ardglass on Saturday. On Monday morning our boat went out at 6.30 along with the rest of the fishing fleet. I wanted to go out with them but Big Mick would not let me. He said, 'Paddy it is not a good day, and there will be big rolls in the sea, between here and the Isle of Man, and Paddy you are not as young as you think you are.' What could I do then, but stay ashore. It was an anxious day for me. About 6 p.m. some of the boats began to come into the harbour, some with eight, ten, twelve and fourteen boxes of fish and one with thirty boxes. Then someone said, 'Here's the Donegal boat.' I thought my heart would jump out of my mouth. Someone asked, 'How much have you?' Mick said, 'About twenty boxes.' He had twenty-five boxes -£42, thus making £5.5.od. for each of the crew and £21 for the Cope, and ever since they have exceeded these figures. Well, well, I cannot describe my happiness, you would need to be inside me to know how I felt.

I was in a great run of luck. I was introduced to that Scottish expert fisherman, Mr. Alec Thomson, (18 Argyle Street, Lowsiamouth, Morayshire) in Joe Mulhern's. Boys, he is the great man. What he does not know about fishing no one else does, except his brother who was decorated in England by the King last year. Alec gets great pleasure in advising and helping every fisherman he meets. We were so pleased with our fishing venture that we erected this year a cold storage here in Dungloe, where we have plenty of water power and now if there is a strong wind blowing and the sea raging mountains high, we still have fresh fish for our people. Talking about fishing, it is a grand sport when you can fill the bag or the boat. It is nice to see the live fish jumping on the deck, but the nicest sign of all is the ringing of a ball of herrings and bailing them into the ship. When dumped on the deck they wag their tails and squeal on their passage down to the hold. It is as nice a thrill as the taking down of two grouse with the left and two with the right.

# CHAPTER EIGHTEEN

## *Diplomatic Incident*

We received on 15 March, 1943, the following letter:

> (Cooperatieve Superfosfaatfabriek)
> Vlaardingen,
> Holland.
> 11 December 1942.

Templecrone Co-Op Agr. Soc. Ltd.,
Dungloe (Co. Donegal).
Irish Free State.

Dear Sirs,

Now that the year's end is again approaching, we wish, like last year, to send a sign of life to our pre-war friends and to inquire how they have got on in the meantime.

We express the hope that you have reason to be satisfied about your business dealings in the year now almost elapsed and that in your personal life too everything has gone well.

On the occasion of the coming festive season we send you our most cordial greetings and we add our best wishes for all of you for the year of 1943. That this year be a more fortunate one than its predecessors and bring us peace again, is a wish we feel sure of all humanity.

Yours truly,
Eerste Nederlandsche
Co-Operatieve Kunstmesteabriek Director

I replied as follows:-

Templecrone Co-Operative Agricultural Society Ltd.
Dungloe,
Co. Donegal,
Eire.
16 March, 1943.

MS. Co-Operative Superfosfaatfabriek,
Holland.

Dear Sirs,

Your letter of the 11th Dec. 1942, was just received here on the 15th March, 1943. It was a long time on the way but the writer can assure you that your letter gave myself, and the staff great pleasure. It was very nice of you to write and I hope the day is not far away when we will be able to get some of your manures again. We never handled any Super-phosphate that gave our members so much satisfaction. As you know we are a neutral state. Would it be at all possible to get a cargo of manures from you this year provided we can arrange for shipment? It would be a great blessing to us and to our country if we could get even a small cargo.

We sincerely hope that you and your people will come through this unfortunate war successfully.

I am sending this letter by airmail and if you think it would be possible to supply manures we would feel greatly obliged if you would reply by airmail.

It was the writer who had the pleasure of calling at your works in Holland.

Yours faithfully,
P. Gallagher.


I did not think I was committing any offence, that the Germans would take control of one of the best co-operative factories in the world.

I take it for granted that my letter never reached those good people as I had a note from the United Kingdom Trade Commissioner, Dublin, dated 30 April, 1943, asking me to call at their office first time I would be in Dublin. I called shortly afterwards and was told that the substance of my letter was an effort to trade with enemy occupied country.

It was only then I realised that I should not have solicited any business, as it left our Society open to be put on the black list so that we could not get any goods from the British Isles or send them any. I was, if I may use the term, tried by gentlemen who made it a pleasure to sit before them. It was like being in England sitting amongst the English gentlemen I met in London and Manchester. The verdict was – 'Don't do it again, Mr. Gallagher. We are sorry for causing you so much trouble. How are you all up in Donegal?' And then a warm shake hands as I took my leave.

# CHAPTER NINETEEN

## *Fire in the Bakery*

On Saturday, 27 January, 1945, I had a conference with our bakers concerning our fuel position. We had not been getting any coke for a considerable time and I feared our turf would not last until June when the new season's would be ready. We decided that we should stoke the fires at night with turf mould which we usually dumped in the tide.

It was Owenie Boyle's turn to put on the fires on that Sunday night. As he was not long in our employment, I told him to call for me and that I would direct him how to stoke the fires with turf mould. He called for me at eleven o'clock on Sunday night – January 28. We both went into the bakery where there was turf and mould in front of the ovens.

I directed Owenie as to how to stoke the ovens, and I then told him to stoke the boiler. He did so, and in a few moments there came a blast down the lum, and sparks flew all over the bakery, but they died out. We waited for five or ten minutes, and nothing further happened. I felt content and went back to the house where I continued writing a new chapter for *My Story*.

We had a few weeks of the hardest frost that I ever remember. The street was packed with people young and old – sleighing. At 11.40 someone came to the door shouting:- 'Paddy there is smoke coming from the bakery.' I ran to the bakery, but I could not see any fire–only smoke. All was in darkness. I got out–I do not know how, but when I recovered there was plenty of light. The flames were going to the heavens. The clergy and guards were directing the people to get water from the river, 285 yards from the Cope, and they formed two human chains–one taking the empty buckets, and the other passing the full buckets from one to the other. I then came to the conclusion that the bakery, shop and dwelling house were gone, and called to the helpers to bring the water to the Wholesale. I said, 'If we can save those six wooden pillars we will save the Wholesale, and the town.' The helpers came rushing with water, sand and cement, and they saved the Wholesale and the town. When I felt confident that the Wholesale was saved, I went to the street, and saw nothing of the shop and the rooms of the dwelling-house that were over the shop but the debris which was smouldering on the ground floor.

Until that moment I had forgotten about Sally and my grandchildren Annie, Sallie and John, and when I remembered, I shouted and roared 'Sally and the children are burned.' Packie, my son,  got hold of me and said, 'Father! Mother and the children are safe and sound down in Anna's.' Sally was in her sick bed before the fire started. Wee Annie, wee Sallie and John were sleeping in a room over the shop. They were rescued in good time.

When Sally was taken downstairs, she went to look for me, but could not find me. She went into the yard shouting:- 'Where is Paddy?' She was then told that I was working in the Wholesale, and she then went with the children to Anna's. Mary and Packie went early in the evening to

Burtonport to visit Mary's mother who was ill, and on their return home when near Dungloe, they saw the Cope on fire. No one can describe what they felt, as their three children were sound asleep when they left home.

I had many letters of sympathy from our friends in America. They saw a report of the Cope fire in the first issue of *The Irish World*, which was printed after the fire. The report was headed:- 'Paddy the Cope's Co-Operative Stores at Dungloe, Co. Donegal, Gutted by Fire.' My sister Bridget sent me the report and she wrote:- 'I feel sorry from the very bottom of my heart for you in your old age, that this should happen. On the other hand I am glad it happened while you are alive, for I can see you build a bigger and better Cope.'

We were all surprised that we should get so much sympathy. The following appeared in *The Irish Press*:- 'Peadar O'Donnell said last night – So long as Paddy himself has survived the fire, his restless body and restless brain will soon catch up with the disaster.'

The following is a copy of a letter I had from Mrs. Eileen Phelan (Anna's daughter):-

7, Lomand Ave.,
Fairview,
Dublin.

Dear Paddy,

I want to tell you how sorry I was to read and hear about the Cope Fire. You must be heartbroken over the disaster after spending your life getting it up to such a high standard to see it all gone in flames within a few hours. I cannot imagine what Dungloe must look like without the Cope in the Main Street. I always remember it there, and some of my happiest days were spent in running up and down to and from the Cope for every little and big thing we wanted at home.

The Cope was a household word in every family in the Rosses and anything which couldn't be got in the Cope wasn't worth looking for anywhere else.

You must have thought it hard to see it all go without warning, but Paddy it was not only you who suffered but the whole Rosses. I'm sure people did not know where to turn to, being so used to say 'Run up to the Cope and get me this or get me that.' Anyone I met here from Donegal could not talk of anything but the Cope fire. To Donegal people here, it was even a bigger blow than to those living in the county, as we didn't or couldn't believe it was true.

Thank God there was no one hurt and that you and all the family were saved. If anything had happened to you, I think we would all pass out. Thank God again you were spared and with your ability the Cope will be on its feet again in no time – a bigger and better Cope premises – if such could be the case – in the same place as it has always been since I remember it.

With every best wishes for your success,

I remain,
Yours sincerely,
Eileen Phelan.

On Monday, January 29 , I was standing on the street, looking up at the room window over the shop where wee Annie, Sallie and John were sleeping when the fire started.

I was crying with joy that the children were safe, and I was delighted that we were able to give our customers their rations, through the window of our dwelling house, when a small boy, named O'Donnell, from Brockagh gave my jacket a pull, and said, 'Paddy, my mother told me to ask you if her money was burned. She told me to tell you that if it was burned, not to be vexed because she did not care as long as you were not burned.' I was surely touched by that poor woman's tribute.

We have £28,000 of local money on deposit in our Society, not one penny was asked for or withdrawn after the burning.

I am sure that I would never have had the pluck to tell that it was I who burned the Cope, only when the insurance assessor arrived on the scene, and stood on top of the ovens, he asked me who had been last in the bakery on Sunday night. I said, 'Owenie Boyle and I.' He then asked me what time we were there, and I said, 'Ten minutes after eleven o'clock.' His next question was – 'When did the fire start?' I said 11.50 p.m. he then said, 'It was malicious.' The wee bit of gas that was left in me exploded, and I said, - 'That bedamned. It was I who burned it.' He then asked me – 'Why?' I explained. My son Jim, and Leo our secretary, blamed me for telling that it was I who burned the Cope; they were sure we would not get any insurance. I got a bit annoyed and said, 'How dare he say that it was the town people that burned it, after every one of them helping to extinguish the fire. To hell with the insurance!' By my admission we did not lose one penny, the insurance people (The Hibernian Insurance Company, Dublin) paid us every penny that we were entitled to, and did not dispute one item.

We got piles of telegrams, letters of sympathy and offers of help, from everywhere including, Glasgow, Manchester and London.

The following, composed and inserted by one of our storemen, (P. Ward) appeared in *The Derry Journal* on February 9:-

*SURSUM CORDA, PADDY.*

*When a man's life-work comes tumbling*
    *down in a pitiless hour or two.*
*And that which took sweat and years to*
    *build is shattered before his view.*
*If his dream is spoilt, his ambition wrecked,*
    *won't his spirit be rent in twain.*
*And we all agree he's a superman if he*
    *arises again.*

*Will he ever rise? Will he ever rise? But*
    *who will say him dare?*
*None. For though the flames burned all, his*
    *spirit still is there.*
*That same great spirit of by-gone days, that*
    *beat harder blows than this.*
*And gave to the Rosses' workers all, a ha-*
    *ven of social bliss.*

*We pray that that hand so tender, yet firm,*
    *guide us for years to come.*
*(May the Recording Angel treat him well*
    *when Gabriel sounds his drum).*
*Oh! That long the great God may leave you*

*here is the people's earnest hope.*
*For poor indeed would our lot be, if we*
*hadn't Paddy the Cope.*

On Wednesday, 21 November 1945, we had a glut of herrings at Burtonport owing to the scarcity of shipping space. My son, Jim, wired the Scottish Co-Operative Wholesale Society, telling them about the glut. They wired back stating:- "SHIP TO AYR. WE WILL TAKE ALL.' We immediately commenced to load our wee boat the MB *Naomh Eine*, 60 h.p., although she was aground. Then someone inquired if we had a chart. We had none. We sent two men in a small boat to Jack Boyle, skipper of the Aranmore lifeboat, to see if he had a chart, but unfortunately, he had mislaid his, and it could not be found. The boat floated about 4.30 p.m. in very deep water. Big Mick and the crew, five in all, were ready to sail, but we had no chart or Custom papers. There was no custom offices or custom officer nearer than Letterkenny. Big Mick never skippered a boat further than five or six miles off the coast. There was a big crowd on the pier, photographers were waiting to take snaps. We were in a hell of a fix. Early in the day we made good provision for the crew, plenty of food–meat, bacon, and boiled ham, a bottle of Power's Whiskey and six half-pints of Scotch Whiskey which I got from Mrs. Mulhern that morning–every drop of Scotch Whiskey she had in the house. I gave Mick the Irish Flag and got him to nail it to the mast. Well, when we heard there was no chart, and no hopes of getting the custom papers, we were about to unload the boat again, when Jim said, 'Father, I hate like hell to see you unloading, the weather is so good, you should go.' I went abroad and said to Mick, 'Will you go if I go with you.' Heavens! If you saw the smile on that big pleasant face. All the crew was abroad. I called Jim aboard and told him we were going. He bade us good luck and goodbye, and then went ashore and threw us the rope.

Off we went. All went well, until next morning when outside Portrush we ran into a thick fog. When we got out of it we lost sight of land. On we went hoping every minute to pick up the Scottish coast. Night came on, still no land in sight. Friday morning we say a boat fishing for clams; we went alongside. It was the *Erica* B.A. 20. I said to the skipper, 'we are for Ayr we lost our chart, will you give us one of your men to take us to Ayr?' He said, 'I'll do that, mon.' We pulled alongside and a man named William Andrew came aboard; he said he would take us to Ayr. I drew the cork (the first time since we left) out of the bottle of Irish whiskey and offered him a glass, but he said, 'I do not touch it, ma mon,' I then gave it to one of the crew. I did not like to take the risk of being caught with a bottle of Irish Whiskey in our possession in Scotland.

We landed in Ayr at 11.40 a.m. on Friday. I tried to get ashore to wire home that we had landed safely, but no one would be allowed ashore, not even William Andrew, until the Customs examined us. After about an hour, (I thought it was ten hours), a Custom officer came aboard, asked me if we had any dutiable goods to declare. I showed him the six half-pints of Scottish whiskey. Then after he had examined the wee boat, he said, 'You may go ashore now, if you wish.' I said, 'You are welcome to a drink, and to one of the bottles.' He shook his head and went ashore. I tell you I made a race for the Post Office and wired Sally that I was safe and sound. I then went back to the boat.

The Co-Operative people had seven or eight lorries waiting there for about twelve hours and had a cargo of salt on the pier for us to take back with us.

When I went aboard, John Cannon had the dinner ready, plenty of soup, potatoes and the best of beef. I opened one of the bottles and we finished it. We then commenced to unload the herrings. We had them all out before 6 p.m. Next morning we commenced to load the salt.

The Custom people sent word for the Skipper and me to call at the office. We went. One man asked me where we got the herrings. I told him. He then asked for the ship's papers. I said – 'Sally has them.' He asked, 'Who is Sally?' I said, 'She is my wife. I had on a light overcoat and just as we were about to leave home, Sally made me change into a heavier one, and I forgot to change the papers from the pockets, also the chart, and that is what kept us a day late.' I shall never forget those boys; they were gentlemen.

We sailed from Ayr at 12.45 p.m. on Saturday morning and arrived in Burtonport at 1.15 p.m. Sunday. The pier was packed, and we did get a cheer. Such a welcome. We were very lucky, as the weather broke on Monday. If we were on the sea, our wee boat and all of us would be drowned.

The press gave me all the praise – I, that did nothing, and not a word about Big Mick and his crew, or the Scottish Co-Operative people who saved our fish from being dumped and their men who sat patiently in their lorries for twelve hours waiting for us.

We had a large catch of herring landed in Burtonport during the week ending 17 August, 1946. We were very short of barrels, as none were being made in Ireland, and

Going to Scotland with a cargo of herring. Forefront: Skipper Big Mick, Paddy the Cope and Jim the Cope.

Opening the new store on 3rd April, 1946. At front: Rev. T. Molloy, D.D. At back from left to right: Mr. Lecky, Secretary of the Scottish Co-Operative Society Ltd., Glasgow, Mr. Simon Murphy, Manager of the Campile Co-Operative Society Ltd., Mr. Beaty, President of the Scottish Co-Operative Society Ltd., Glasgow, and Paddy the Cope.

the British who have supplied us with herring and mackerel barrels for the past twenty years would not allow any to be exported to Eire,- no blame to them, as they had not supplies for themselves. We did not want to see the fish dumped back into the sea, so we piled them on the cement floor of our shed and salted them. We got a cooper, MacBride, from Downings, and we went out and cut trees, sawed them into staves and then dried them on the kiln where we used to dry our oats, and our barrels were as good as any we ever handled. A short time afterwards we got another cooper from Downings who was, like MacBride, home on holidays from Britain, and now all our herrings are lifted from the cement floor and safely packed in our own barrels ready for export. We are making thirty-two barrels a day, and we hope, in a short time, to double and again treble our output and hope within a year that our Society will make all the barrels required in Eire.

# CHAPTER TWENTY

## *Rebirth*

On 3 April, 1946, we opened our rebuilt store. The following are accounts which appeared in *The Derry Journal* on Friday April 5, and Monday, April 7:

*Derry Journal*, Friday 5<sup>th</sup>

### LIKE A PHOENIX FROM ITS ASHES.
*Paddy the Cope turns ruin into Triumph.*
*Great New Co-operative Building Opened in Dungloe.*

A BIG DAY FOR THE ROSSES.

The gloomy memory of the almost disastrous Dungloe fire, of fourteen months ago, which, at its height, seemed almost certain the ruin of the life work of Paddy the Cope, has just given place to one of gladness and pride, and great expectations for the future, writes our Special Reporter.

From the Ashes that littered the frost-bound streets of the Rosses capital on that night of the closely-averted calamity, an ornate building has arisen, surpassing far in structural lay-out commodiousness and modern appointments, the premises consumed in the flames.

Wednesday was the joyous occasion of the opening of the new emporium which, fresh from the hands of the tradesmen and decorators, revealed itself as a splendid addition to the many fine buildings in this thriving, irrepressibly go-ahead community. It was a big day for Dungloe, it was in a very special sense a big day for Mr. Gallagher, to whose courage, industry and enterprise it is a worthy monument. Present at the formal opening were the President and Secretary of the Scottish Co-operative Wholesale Society, one of the biggest concerns of its kind in Great Britain. They flew from Glasgow specially to attend the event.

When I visited the spaciously brilliantly-illuminated stores on Wednesday forenoon, workmen were busy applying the finishing touches to the arrangement of stocks and general tidying-up. The activity was intense and not a moment was wasted. The happy culmination of many anxious months of planning and construction was at hand. The new premises, bigger far than the old, carried a huge stock. Everyone of the scores upon scores of shelves, every type of goods, had its generous quota. An elaborate central-heating plant will soon be functioning in all departments. In for a minute and out again, to attend to some business matter, the beaming countenance of Paddy himself told of the complete satisfaction he must have felt.

BANDS IN BIG PROCESSION:

Close on three o'clock the distant sound of music brings Paddy to the street to accord a warm greeting to the first of the bands to reach the town. At the head of a big procession was carried a banner inscribed:- *Long live Paddy the Cope*. The bands taking part were the Derrydruel Pipe Band, the Meenacross Pipe Band, and the Maghery Flute Band. In turn they paraded the street discoursing national and martial airs.

BLESSING AND OPENING.

By three o'clock a large crowd had assembled. The esteemed parish priest, Rev. T. Molloy, D.PH. wearing a surplice and soutane arrives, and there is an impressive and hushed interlude whilst he prays the blessing of the Church on the new stores. The doors are then thrown open to the public who quickly fill it to overflowing capacity. Members of the staff sing: "Bless this House" as the procession moves to the Co-Operative yard where a public meting is held. A public meeting was held subsequently, and a report of it will appear in our next issue.

*Derry Journal*, Monday 7<sup>th</sup>

CO-OPERATIVE IDEA A SOUND ONE

.

*Very Rev. Dr. Molloy's Tribute to Paddy the Cope.*

The idea of co-operation was a sound one, and there was no reason why it should not be widely spread, said the Rev. Dr. Molloy, P.P., speaking at a public meeting which followed the formal opening of the new co-operative stores at Dungloe.

Dr. Molloy, who presided, recalled the tragic night of the burning, and said that it was only through the loyal co-operation of all the townspeople that the premises escaped complete destruction. That magnificent new building would stand as a permanent record of the industry and thrift of the people. The idea of co-operation was a sound one, and there was no reason why it should not be widely spread. The very last shadow of feeling in the town against the movement was wiped out on the night of the burning. (Hear, Hear). They were proud of the new Co-Op and proud of Paddy who has such a big part in its creation. (Applause).

### BEST STAFF IN THE WORLD.

Mr. Gallagher, who was received with loud applause related several stories of the many vicissitudes through which his enterprises passed down the years. He said he got all the publicity for any successes they ever achieved, but all the credit was due to his loyal and efficient workers, "the best staff in the world".

Having thanked all for their presence and good wishes he concluded: It was well worth living to see this day, and I am very proud.

### GREETINGS FROM SCOTLAND

The next speaker was Mr. Neil Beaton, President of the Scottish Co-Operative Wholesale Society, whose trading returns last year amounted to £40,000,000. He said he brought greetings on this great occasion from 1,160,000 Scottish householders.

He wanted to congratulate the members, staff and committee of that Society on its outstanding success. He had had the opportunity of going through their most recent balance-sheet, and he could assure them it was a credit to every member. (Applause).

They had done exceedingly well, and he was glad to learn that the opposition of the early days of the movement had melted away.

This splendid idea had made great headway in Great Britain, where they had over 9,000,000 members. In the International Co-Operative Movement they had over 20,000,000 members. He had just returned from Denmark and Sweden, where the movement also flourished. At a meeting in Denmark forty countries pledged themselves to work on behalf of this great movement. The first movement attacked in the European countries overrun by Hitler in recent years was the Co-Operative Movement.

Pleading for greater support for the Co-Operative Movement, Mr. Beaton said he saw in that the solution for the ills of the world today. In conclusion he paid high tribute to the energy and splendid business genius of Mr. Gallagher whom he warmly congratulated on this auspicious event.

### Wexford Felicitations

Mr. Simon Murphy, chairman and manager of the Shelbourne Co-Operative Society (Wexford) conveyed felicitations, as did Mr. P. O'Donnell, solicitor and Mr. Philip McCauley, vice-chairman of the Templecrone Society.

Mr. Robert Leckie, secretary of the Scottish Society, said Mr. Gallagher had spent his years in an effort to get the people to do something to help themselves.

A hearty vote of thanks was passed to Dr. Molloy for presiding. Apologies for absence and expressing best wishes, were received from the Co-Operative Wholesale Society, Ltd., Manchester, Mr. James A. Flanagan, (former editor-in-chief, Co-Operative Press, Ltd.), the Irish Agricultural Organisation Society, Ltd., and Mr. Frank Hugh O'Donnell, Dublin.

Sure I do not need to say any more. It was a happy day for me, and I think the happiest moment of my life when Mr. Robert Leckie, secretary of the Scottish Co-Operative Wholesale Society, Ltd., caught my arm and said, 'See, Paddy,' pointing to the Maghery Band's banner on which was inscribed '*Long live Paddy the Cope.*'

# CHAPTER TWENTY-ONE

## *Trip to Scotland*

A cousin of mine, the Rev. Father Flavin O'Donnell, a Major Chaplain in the USA army, arrived here in Dungloe, on 21 June 1946, and gave Sally, Mary, the family, and me great pleasure when he stayed in our house for the few days he was here. He had only ten days' leave, from the time he left Italy, until his return there again.

I had a telegram from the Scottish Co-Operative Wholesale Society at 6 p.m. on Saturday June 22, to say that a meeting of the Central Committee of the International Co-Operative Association was taking place the following week. I promised Mr. Beaton and Mr. Leckie when they were here on April 3 that I would be with them whenever the meeting took place. I was in a hell of a fix. If Father O'Donnell had two or three weeks' holidays, I would have asked him to come along, but he had such a short stay that if he came with me he would not be able to meet half of his friends here. When I told him of the invitation he said, 'Paddy you must go, do not mind me, Jim will take me around to see my friends.'

He was so very interesting, telling us of his war experiences. He was three years in Italy and previous to that he was in North Africa. He would take a tear out of a rock, telling about the hundreds of little children congregated in hospitals, no fathers, no mothers, and very little to eat. He preached a grand sermon here on Sunday the 23rd, asking the people, to give freely any penny they could spare for the suffering children of Europe. The collection was a great success that Sunday.

I made up my mind to bring him to Dublin, and if possible to get him introduced to Mr. de Valera. We left Dungloe on Sunday night for Sligo, left Sligo the following morning and arrived in Dublin at 1 p.m. on Monday. I got in touch with Miss Kathleen O'Connell, Mr. de Valera's secretary, immediately, and she arranged for an appointment on Tuesday at 3.30 p.m. Father O'Donnell said to me then, 'Paddy, now that you got that interview fixed up you must go to Glasgow to see your friends. I agreed, and went to the booking office to book a ticket, I was asked for a passport and visa. After a good deal of enquiries I was advised to go to the Eire Minister of External Affairs, and get fixed up there. I had some difficulty, as I had no letter of recommendation from the Dungloe Guards. I then had to go to the British Passport Office, get into a queue for about two hours. Finally I reached the office and got fixed up there. At 2 p.m. I got a train for Belfast and got into another queue there at 5.30 p.m.; got my ticket and sailing ticket at 8.05p.m. There was no berth available. We sailed about 9.10 p.m. and landed in Glasgow on Wednesday morning June 26 at seven. I went to the Kenilworth Hotel and got a wash up, and opened my bag for a collar. I had neither collar nor tie in it. Sally did not think that I was going to Scotland, so she did not pack any. I had breakfast and waited until ten o'clock for the shops to open. I turned into Argyll St., went into a shop and asked for two collars and a tie. A very nice girl attended me. I made my selection and she said – '5/11, and three coupons please.' I said, 'Miss, I am sorry I have no coupons, I came from Ireland this morning and forgot my collars and tie, do please give them to me I will pay you whatever you charge,' she said, 'I am sorry, but I dare not.' I tried a few other houses with the same result.

I then went to the SCWS Ltd., premises in Morrison St., and asked for the Secretary or Chairman and was told they were not in. I then told them who I was, and I could see a little flutter, but I thought everyone was looking at my neck without a collar or tie. Then the assistant secretary came in and took me to his office, and one of the directors came in. I may be wrong but I am sure he had another peep at my neck. I said. 'Sir, I am sorry I have no collar or tie, when I was leaving home, my wife did not think I was going to Scotland, so she did not pack them; I tried many shops in Argyll Street, this morning looking for collars and a tie, but I was unable to get any as I had no coupons.' I got fixed up then, and I was happy for a little while, as all the others had collars and ties on, but in a short time I became uncomfortable and I said a wee one on the man who invented collars. I hope God will forgive me for that wee one.

About noon Mr. Beaton, the chairman of the SCWS Ltd., arrived. Well, I then felt at home. He said, 'Paddy we are going now to our hotel at the Bridge of Allen, the cars are outside.' There were two Rolls Royces at the door. I popped in beside the chairman. We passed through Denny where I worked in the pit about fifty years ago. As I was passing the house I had lodged in I asked the driver to stop the car. He did but when I looked, to my sorrow I saw it was a derelict house. I told Mr. Beaton that was the house in which my father waited for me when I came in from the pit. Off we went through famous Stirling, on to the Bridge of Allen, into the Society's Hotel. Off again to Aberfeldy where the Society owns a good part of that beautiful village, back to Allen Bridge Hotel then. I was then introduced to delegates from the following countries:- AUSTRALIA, BELGIUM, DENMARK, FINLAND, FRANCE, GREAT-BRITAIN, HOLLAND, ICELAND, POLAND, SWEDEN AND SWITZERLAND. Mr. Beaton came along with a fine big man, who must at least have been 6ft. 4ins. or 6ft. 6ins. tall, and built in proportion. Mr. Beaton said, 'Paddy I wish to introduce you to our chairman, Lord Rusholme.' Lord Rusholme caught my hand and said, 'Paddy I am delighted to meet you,' and other nice things. On Thursday we all went to Glasgow where we were the guests of the SCWS Ltd., in their grand restaurant the Ca'Doro. If ever you are in Glasgow, go to it and you will be amazed.

Lord Rusholme called the meeting to order. Then a fine young man got up and spoke for a considerable time. I did not know a damn word he was saying. When he sat down Lord Rusholme called on Mr. Leckie, secretary of the SCWS Ltd. Mr. Leckie got up. You would never be tired listening to him, proposing the toast of the International Co-Operative Association. When he sat down amidst applause the young man got up again and I did not know a word he said. When he sat down Lord Rusholme called on Miss Polly, of the Alliance. She responded to the toast. Oh! She was the girl that could speak. She was the best lady speaker that I ever listened to. She got great applause when she sat down. Then the young man got up again, this time I understood three words which he said, when he said, 'Paddy the Cope' then he sat down. Lord Rusholme got up and called on Paddy the Cope to address the meeting. Well I can never describe the feeling I had at this moment; if Lord Rusholme was not such a fine, big, charming man I certainly would have refused. I took a chance. As soon as I got to my feet, I got a grand reception. That finished the speech making that night. When no others were called I came to the conclusion that I had made such a hash of it, that it destroyed the remainder of the night. Someone took me by the hand – I don't know who it was – but I was taken in to the centre of the floor; a glass with plenty in it was put into my hand, and all the guests made three or four circles around me and sang, 'For he is a jolly good fellow.' When we sat down again I went to Mr. Beaton, and said, 'you must have got fun out of my speech, I made a hash of it,' He took me by the hand and said, 'Paddy, it was a pleasure to hear you speak.' I am sure I got nearly a hundred handshakes of congratulations. When I went to bed I began to recall the events of the evening. I was then convinced that I did not make any serious mistakes. I began to talk to myself. I must have said many things, but one thing I remember I did say to myself was:- 'I wonder if I am still Paddy Pat Bawn.' I have seen a copy of *The Co-Operative News* dated July 6, with photographs of the speakers etc. One heading in letters ¾in. - ½in. was as follows:-

### 'PADDY THE COPE CHARMS DELEGATES FROM OVERSEAS'

The Scottish Co-Operative newspaper had a heading:-

'CHEER THE MAN FROM DUNGLOE.'

and another heading was:-

'PADDY THE COPE, LOOKING AS FRESH AS A
DAISY, HIS BRIGHT EYES TWINKLING WITH
LIFE AND GOOD HUMOUR, DELIGHTED THE ICA
DELEGATES WHEN HE ATTENDED A DINNER IN
THE FINE CA'DORA RESTAURANT OF THE  SCWS
LAST WEEK.'

Another report:-

LAST WEEK MR. PATRICK GALLACHER
OF COUNTY DONEGAL, AS IRISH  AS THE
SHAMROCK, AND FULL OF IRISH WIT, CAME
TO TOWN AND WALKED SLAP BANG INTO THE
ICA CELEBRITIES.

Is it any wonder that from lapse of memory now in my old
age, I sometimes wonder if I am still Paddy Pat Bawn?

# CHAPTER TWENTY-TWO

## *Co-Ops are Best*

The British Co-Operatives are proud and justly so, of that Society which is known as the Rochdale Pioneers, which was started at 31 Toad Lane, Rochdale, England in 1844; but they were not really pioneers.

LENNOXTOWN FRIENDLY VICTUALLING SOCIETY.

The above Society was established in 1812, and is still flourishing. It is the oldest active Co-Operative Society in the world. Situated at the foot of the Campsie Falls, Lennoxtown, Stirlingshire, it is about eleven miles from Glasgow and has a population of 2,500.

William Thompson, a rich Irishman, who lived at Clonkeen, Co. Cork, was so interested in co-operation, that at his death in 1780, he bequeathed all his wealth for the organisation of a co-operative community, but unfortunately his trustees did not carry out his wishes. Had they done so, what a difference it would have made to our forefathers. The gombeen parasites that sprang up in 1846 and '47, the years of the Famine, would have been snowed under and would not have got rich as they did on the poor and needy.

346

I was thinking the other night, judging from the stories which I heard my grandmother tell, it must have been before 1780 that the Cleendra people bought the big pot, for scouring flannel. All had equal shares in it. It was certainly a co-operative effort. It is a pity that they did not make a charge for every web that was scoured, and then divide the profits at the end of the year. That might have led to other activities; but what am I talking about? Sure when St. Peter was fishing in Galilee, and caught a great multitude of fishes in Lake Gennesareth, he called St. James and St. John and filled their boats. That was a real co-operative effort. If St. Peter was a capitalist he would cut his nets and let what he did not want for himself go to the bottom of the sea. The capitalist would have gloated at the scarcity which would enable him to enrich himself, not giving a damn if his neighbours would die of hunger. That is what the English and Scottish fishing boat owners do, they dump the fish into the sea, rather than give cheap food to starving people. I challenge anyone to deny this. I do not know what other countries do, but if the fishing ships are controlled by Capitalists, I take it for granted that they would do likewise. I heard that the Chilian capitalists burn the coffee if there is a surplus. Aye, and I have heard that the American capitalists often burned wheat to keep the price high. I cannot believe this story it is a horrible one. Is it therefore any wonder that such brilliant men as Father Tom Finlay SJ and his successor, Father Coyne, devoted so much of their time to the Co-Operative Movement, which is doing so much for the good of the people?

I hope the day is near at hand when the clergy of all denominations will throw in their lot with the co-operative movement. Some of them have done great work. It was priests by co-operative means that brought prosperity to the fishermen of Nova Scotia. They lead very important sections of the Co-Operative Movement in Belgium, France, Italy and Holland. Some of the American and Canadian bishops have spoken in support of the Co-Operative Movement. Of course, the Jesuits are out on their own.

The Jesuits invented the use of gas for lighting purposes. It was a Jesuit, Father Dunn, who founded the first gas company at Preston, England, in 1815. Long before Benjamin Franklin, a French Jesuit – Deacon Nallet – discovered that storms are no more than discharges of atmospheric electricity. Father Angela Secchia SJ is one of the greatest astronomers of our time. He built the first Meteorograph. (An instrument to mark the meteorological variations of the weather).

Father Magnenon was the inventor of the microscope. It was the famous Jesuit, Father Lana, who in 1887, invented a method of enabling the blind to read.

If the business of the world was run by co-operative societies there would not be the terrible slaughter that is going on in the world for the past four years, not only killing the fighting men, but the blind, the lame, women and children, sane and insane. If all were organised in co-operative societies there would be no motive for wars as the co-operative's motive would be to help all the people of the world.

Can anyone imagine what such a body could do for humanity? Think of all the scientists in the world sitting at a co-operative conference studying what is best for the human race, instead of acting today in their individual capacity in the interests of individuals inventing weapons to destroy the other fellow.

# CHAPTER TWENTY-THREE

## *AE and deValera*

One day I received a letter from Chicago from Mr. Daniel McGrath, the then Irish Consul, with a cutting from a Chicago newspaper enclosed. I do not now remember what paper it was, but it was a report of a lecture by AE; and in the course of the lecture he mentioned me. For many years he mentioned me in his lectures, but in the Chicago lecture he said, 'I hope Paddy the Cope will leave his story behind him before he passes away.'

Daniel wrote: 'Paddy, do write your story, you have a grand one to tell.' Well, before I closed the Cope that evening, I stuck a copy book in my pocket, and when I went home I commenced to write. I did not stop until I had finished the copy book. Sally did not get saying the Rosary that night until it was very late. Every now and again when I was on my knees, I could only think of the grand story I had written. Sally said, 'Paddy, you are working too hard, why not get Jim or Leo to do the writing for you. You will kill yourself. You went through the two decades of the Rosary tonight.' I never remember you missing a word before.'

I did not sleep much that night. After breakfast next morning, I handed Sally the old copy and said, 'Read that, won't it make a grand story?' At dinner time when I sat at the end of the table, Sally stood at the other end, her hand behind her back. She began laughing; she laughed and laughed. I got afraid she would break her sides. I said, 'Stop! What are you laughing at?' She then took around her hand with the copy in it and said, 'Paddy, this is surely a grand story! For goodness sake burn it. Do not let the boys see it. There is neither head or tail to it. I can hardly make out a word of it.' I snapped it from her and put it in my pocket. That evening when the store was closed, I came into the house and opened the copy. I got the first line all right and damn but, I could not make head or tail of any of the rest. I threw the bloody old copy in the fire. Sally seemed to enjoy the scene and this annoyed me.

When I heard of AE's death I felt very sorry. I recalled his visit to Dungloe in 1903, to organise the Co-Operative Bank which laid the foundation of our Society.

I remembered my visit to him at his request in his office at Plunkett House, Merrion Square, Dublin. It was the queerest room I ever entered; all kinds of queer pictures painted on the walls. After he gave me a warm shake hands, he pulled a chair near the fire, spread out his big fat hands, bowed to me to be seated. When I sat down, he pulled his chair in front of the fire and began to ask me how the Society was doing, how many people had we employed, what we intended to do to give more employment, and so on. He then sat back in his chair until it rested on its two hind legs – popped his two feet up under the mantelpiece – and he commenced to talk. I wish to goodness I could remember what he said. Oh! the flow of interesting language that came freely from his great lips, through his big, long, brown whiskers; one would like to listen for ever and ever to AE.

Again I remembered the note Daniel McGrath sent me from Chicago. I felt ashamed of myself that I did not write something that some other one would read, and send to AE before God called him.

A short time afterwards, I was going to London looking for orders for our workers. On my way through Dublin, as I was passing Woolworth's, I went in for a bite to eat and eyed some scrap books on the counter. I bought three of them. That night I made another attempt, and made up my mind that whatever I wrote I would be able to read it myself.

When my story was published Mr. Norman Kither of London sent me a letter congratulating me and enclosing a copy of *The Bystander* with my photo in it and the following review:

'There are dull writers, but there are no dull subjects – not even the Co-Operative. It was one of the entrancing anomalies of Irish life that AE ran *The Irish Homestead* and gave to egg marketing the eloquent sanction of the Irish kings and the Indian Mystics. One might have doubted the desirability of the influence of the doctrine of reincarnation, as preached by the theosophists of Rathmines, on the Irish breakfast egg, but doubt was unjustified. The more remote the belief, the more practical and pragmatic the energy it stimulated; the benefits the Irish Co-Operative Movement gave to the Irish peasant may be seen in Mr. Pat Bawn's – Paddy the Cope. (Cape; 10/6.)'

'But before the piece of economic uplift throws a gloom on the reader's mind, especially on English readers satiated with the success stories of other people, let me say at once that *Paddy the Cope* is one of the freshest, liveliest, warmest and most entrancing autobiographies imaginable. It is in the class of *Twenty Years a-Growing*, the loveliest of all Irish autobiographies. Paddy Pat Bawn or Paddy the Cope, as they call him in Donegal, is more than a kailyard character; he is a gorgeous, unaffected, pre-industrial human being, who though not conventionally lettered, manages to get himself down on paper, and to talk straight out of the page until you are with him in everything he does.

'The child of poor Donegal peasants, he grew up to be the shy, uncouth boy who used to stand barefoot at the Irish hiring fairs waiting to run doggedly home behind the trotting horse of his new master. Later he went on the old cattle boats to Glasgow, and tramped the Scottish roads till he found a job. These boys with their Oliver Twist appetites, were shrewd, if helpless judges of the temperaments of farmers. There was one lodging-house keeper who kept control of the butter allowance by putting a hair from his head across it; he used also catch a fly and put it under the lid of the sugar-bowl. If the fly was not there later, he knew someone had been at the sugar.

'In due time Paddy Pat Bawn married and returned to Donegal, and it was when in his twenties he began to put into practice what he had seen of Co-Operative ideas in Scotland. A man with an affecting beard (AE) had come to Donegal to pour out beautiful words on the subject, while the peasants listened suspiciously; but soon Paddy got them started, and then the row began. The result was boycotts by the shops, bribery of the police, campaigns with the gombeen men which were more like guerrilla warfare than commercial competition, flights to the mountain side, hints of smuggling – a kind of race meeting, excitement with dirty work mixed in, touched at every point by farce. A man not cut as Mr. Bawn is, straight and laughing out of Nature, would have made this merely picturesque and arty; under him the book takes on the easy ripeness of a picaresque novel. There is no city knowingness on him at all, none of the townee dread of appearing foolish or admitting a mistake. He takes one vividly, simply and at once to an intimacy with his affairs and his people, a grace which has vanished from the English life entirely.

'Whether you judge by the unaffected Paddy the Cope, or by the sophisticated, esoteric, and over-civilised side of the Irish talent, there is no doubt in my mind that the Irish writers, with certain Americans, are the only living writers who know how to use the English language. They preserve what the English have lost: the resonance, the full-bodied power and rotundity of our tongue. The only stylists we have and the only satirists of style – are Irish.' - V.S. Pritchett.

I stuck both in my pocket. After dinner I got up, put Mr. Kither's letter and *The Bystander* on the table and said to Sally, 'Maybe you will be able to read that.' I walked out nearly bursting with the laughing. I got my own back at her. She ordered the next day a dozen copies of *The Bystander*.

I put down the letters as plain as I could, so that some good scholar could read what I put down and fix the spelling. So, as you can see, I started where I was born. It was so simple, just telling a story. One thing followed the other. I am ever so grateful to my friends who drew my mind back to things I forgot in my first attempt.

I would like to put on record that Templecrone Co-Operative Society never asked for any favour from any British or Irish Government, never wronged man, woman or child, never oppressed any of our debtors, issued only two processes since it was started in 1906, and settled both of them. I am indeed pleased that I am still its president and manager,

| | | | |
|---|---|---|---|
| Our Sales turnover last financial year ending 30 September 1945, was | £154,440 | 0 | 0 |
| Paid Interest on Share Capital | £87 | 14 | 0 |
| Dividends on Members' Purchases at 2/- in the £ | £3,755 | 16 | 11 |
| Interest on Deposits | £605 | 13 | 1 |
| Wages | £10,985 | 4 | 8 |
| Our Investments exceeded our deposits by | £16,917 | 12 | 3 |

One of the most pleasant days of my life was in October 1944 when our Auditor shook my hand and said 'Paddy, your investments exceed your deposits.' I went down to Anna's and told her. She was as glad as I was, and would not let me pay for what I ordered.

The Rosses people considered it an honour that Paddy Pat Bawn was elected to preside at Mr. de Valera's meeting in Dungloe, on 29 June 1937. I would be a hundred times more pleased if my father, John Gillespie, and Johnnie Brown were alive and present at the meeting. James Durnin was confined to bed. Lord! but he would be glad to have the pleasure of shaking hands with his fellow countryman, that great Christian statesmen, soldier and scholar who was sentenced to death, reprieved on account of his American citizenship after the general amnesty in 1917. Again in May 1918, he was arrested at Ennis, Co. Clare, when making a speech and imprisoned in Lincoln gaol. He sent a postcard to a friend on which was drawn a drunken man trying to fit a key into a lock saying, 'I can't get out.' The friend put it away thinking de Valera was going mad. Later came another postcard showing a smaller key. In each case the drawing was an exact representation of the key to the prison yard. A key was made, and smuggled in. Then one day in February 1919, with the help of Michael Collins, and Sean Milroy, de Valera slipped out. He reached Manchester and went straight to Ennis, and started to make a speech. The first words he said were:-

'As I was saying when I was interrupted here …'

In 1916, when in Boland's Mills, he surrendered at the request of his superior officers, he kept shouting, 'Shoot me if you like, let my men alone.' Oh! such a man. Long may he live.

He again visited Dungloe on 11 June 1943, and I presided at his meeting. Aye! damn but he paid Sally and me a great honour by drinking a cup of tea with us in the Cope house.

He appointed me a member of the Commission on Vocational Organisation which sat under the chairmanship of one of the ablest men in Europe – Dr. Brown, Bishop of Galway. Damn but sometimes he leaned back while others spoke, until his chair rested on its two hind legs, just like AE. I think if de Valera, instead of appointing a Commission of twenty-five just asked Dr. Brown and that other genius, Father Coyne, SJ, President of the Irish

Mr. de Valera in Dungloe, 1944. (Paddy the Cope on his left.)

Members of the Vocational Commission: The Chairman, His Lordship, Most Rev. Dr. Patrick Brown, Bishop of Galway, is seated in the centre of the front row. The author is second from left in the middle row.

Agricultural Co-Operative Society, to produce a scheme on vocational organisation, and the future planning of our country, he would have a satisfactory scheme in three months' time, instead of waiting for three or four years.

I think I feel a little proud that I am still president and manager of the Society that was started with fourteen half-crowns – £1. 15s. (less than eight dollars) when the fight was at its height.

The men and women that came to me on the quiet with their sixpences, their shillings and an 'odd fiver', saying 'Take that Paddy, it might help you,' none of them lost a penny; it was returned twenty times over. When I was ill in 1932, and not much hopes of my recovery, when the crisis was over, Sally said, 'Paddy, you could not die, sure the factory girls were in the chapel every night praying and lighting candles for your recovery, and do you know ---, she went up one night on the quiet, and lit a candle for you.'

The person is a Protestant. It is a pleasure to be manager of a Society, in which never a week passes, but some of the workers' wages are higher than their manager's. I never had to pay a penny Income Tax, until I began to get royalties on my book. So do you wonder if I feel proud that I was born in Cleendra, in the heart of the Rosses, Co. Donegal; the country that gave birth to Saint Columcille, to that great warrior, Red Hugh O'Donnell? My grandfather's (Shean Og) mother, Maire Beag, was one of the O'Donnells of Innisall. They were near relations of Red Hugh's, and of one of the ablest generals that ever led a British Army, General Montgomery.

Finally, I wish to thank from my heart, the many readers who wrote to me such nice letters in praise of the first edition of *My Story* and also the Irish and British and American newspapers which gave it such prominent reviews.

*Yours sincerely,*

PADDY GALLAGHER,
(Paddy Pat Bawn)
now Paddy the Cope.